THE ESSENTIAL GUIDE TO GENERIC DRUGS

THE
ESSENTIAL GUIDE
TO
GENERIC DRUGS

M. LAURENCE LIEBERMAN, R.PH.

1817

HARPER & ROW, PUBLISHERS, New York
Cambridge, Philadelphia, San Francisco, London
Mexico City, São Paulo, Singapore, Sydney

FIRST EDITION

Designer: C. Linda Dingler

Library of Congress Cataloging-in-Publication Data

Lieberman, M. Laurence.
  The essential guide to generic drugs.

  Bibliography: p.
  1. Drugs—Generic substitution. 2. Drugs—Prescribing. 3. Drugs—Marketing. I. Title. [DNLM: 1. Drug Industry—popular works. 2. Drugs—popular works. 3. Therapeutic Equivalency—popular works.
QV 38 L716e]
RS55.2.L53   1986   615'.1   85-45210
ISBN 0-06-181535-7   86 87 88 89 90 10 9 8 7 6 5 4 3 2 1
ISBN 0-06-096040-X (pbk.)   86 87 88 89 90 10 9 8 7 6 5 4 3 2 1

CONTENTS

ACKNOWLEDGMENTS

I would like to thank the many individuals, pharmaceutical manufacturers, government agencies, and industry and professional organizations who provided information useful to the development of this book.

My special thanks goes to my wife, Barbara, who was so understanding of the demands on my time while writing this book; to my parents, Ira and Tonie Lieberman; to Leonard and Phyllis Melser, my wonderful parents-in-law; to Allen and Ruth Melser, especially Allen for his legal advice; to my brother, Peter Lieberman; to Harry and Cindi Steinmetz, who have been so inspirational and such dear friends; to Rob and Beth Clarfeld, who have given so much support and understanding; to Murray Gallahou, who embodies the true spirit and compassion of the pharmacy profession.

Barbara Lowenstein, my agent, guided me in focusing the presentation of this material to Harper & Row, and my sincere thanks extend to her as well.

Special thanks go to my editor at Harper & Row, Carol Cohen, and assistant editor Gail Gavert for their uncompromising attention to detail and their unbounded enthusiasm for this book.

THE ESSENTIAL GUIDE
TO GENERIC DRUGS

Note to Readers

The information provided in this book is intended to help you through the misconceptions and confusion that surround the subject of drug manufacture and to provide a coherent, rational and safe strategy for getting the most for your prescription dollar. This book is not intended as a substitute for the advice of your doctor or pharmacist, but rather to educate you about what questions to raise with your doctor and pharmacist. The discussion of indications and side-effects is necessarily brief; you should consult your doctor or pharmacist for more complete and individual information, and naturally, any questions on symptoms or medication should be addressed to your doctor.

The author holds no interest in any company that manufactures or distributes drugs.

INTRODUCTION

Generic drugs are touted as good for doctors, good for pharmacists, good for insurance companies, and good for the government. But are they good for you?

As a pharmacist, I repeatedly see confusion on the faces of patients confronted with a choice at the prescription counter. Should they fill their doctor's prescription with a brand-name drug or with its generic alternative? More often than not the decision is made either without their knowledge or with their consent but solely on the basis of price.

With more than six hundred companies manufacturing generic drugs, their quality, price, and availability vary widely. How does this bewildering array of drug products affect you? Just in terms of price, you may needlessly pay more than necessary for a brand-name drug that offers no additional advantage. Or you may save money on a generically filled prescription that proves to be no bargain at all.

Large research-oriented pharmaceutical houses have disparaged their generic competitors as detrimental to overall public health interests. Meanwhile, parties interested in containing health care costs have sung their praises.

This book's purpose is to show that no blanket judgments are valid. Each product must be examined on an individual basis. A drug's value is judged by many factors. The best choice for short-term drug therapy may not be ideal for long-term use.

Crucial to the choice between brand and generic is the doctor who writes your prescription. Massive advertising and sales campaigns are waged by big brand-name companies to influence doctors' writing habits. Countering this is pressure on them to hold the line on medical expenses. Many feel that one way to do this is to prescribe lower-cost generic substitutes. But the plain fact is that many physicians are as much in the dark about generic drugs as is the average patient. Often doctors are not even aware of existing generic substitutes.

A MASSIVE, GROWING INDUSTRY

Drugs are the fourth most profitable industry in the United States. With 80 to 90 percent of all health problems managed through the use of drugs, over 1.5 billion new prescriptions are written annually, representing a yearly sales volume of $17.3 billion in 1984. Of this total, generic drugs were dispensed only 20 percent of the time.

According to the American Association of Retired Persons (AARP), generically filled prescriptions can save an average of 50 percent over the cost of a brand-name drug when purchased in quantities of 100. Some generics can save in excess of 80 percent!

Currently about one-third of all new prescriptions have the potential to be filled generically. This will soon change dramatically. While 15 of the 50 biggest selling prescription drugs are available today in generic form, the patents on 24 more will run out by the year 1990. Thirty-eight of the 50 will be eligible for generic substitution. Translated into dollars, the currently estimated $3.5 billion generic drug business could grow to $5 billion annually by decade's end. And that prediction is not counting the entry onto the generic market of some 150 drugs whose patents have already expired and whose imminent availability is virtually assured with the passage of the Drug Price Competition and Patent Term Restoration Act of 1984. These products, now sold by brand name, account for $4 billion in yearly sales.

Drugs commonly prescribed for chronic conditions affecting the aging offer numerous opportunities for generic substitution. Elderly Americans currently account for 11 percent of the population and consume 25 percent of all prescription medication. By the year 2025, it has been predicted, older adults will account for at least 23 percent of the population. This, coupled with increases in third-party payment of drug costs and promotion of generics by the nation's drugstore chains, could see generic products accounting for 25 percent of all prescriptions by 1990. Some projections predict consumer savings of up to $1 billion over the next twelve years.

A NEED FOR INFORMATION

In an AARP survey of Americans over age forty-five, only 42 percent of respondents who were aware of generic drugs said they try to buy and use them. Three-fourths of these same people admitted that they don't ask their physicians to prescribe or their pharmacists to dispense them. A CBS/Broadcasting Group survey showed that nearly three-fourths of all prescription drug users in the United States feel they don't receive enough information about the drugs they take.

That is what this book is all about. *The Essential Guide to Generic Drugs* is intended to help you see your way through the misconceptions and confusion that surround the subject of drug manufacture, and to provide you with a coherent, rational, and safe strategy for getting the most for your prescription dollar.

Essential to any understanding of the use of generic drugs is a review of factors and issues affecting the pharmaceutical industry in general. That is the reason for the discussions contained in chapters 1 through 5, and I urge you to read through them attentively.

In THE GUIDE TO GENERIC DRUGS you will find an alphabetical listing of drugs by generic name, cross-referenced by brand name. You can quickly look up any product for which a generic alternative exists. Each drug is discussed with regard to its use, when to avoid using it, major or most frequent side effects, how much money can be saved through generic use, and when it is safe to do so.

A listing of manufacturers of generics approved by the Food and Drug Administration (FDA) is provided for each drug. The products in this listing are considered bioequivalent—of equal therapeutic value—and interchangeable, providing an invaluable method for double checking the status of any generic you receive at the prescription counter.

You don't have to be confused every time you have a prescription filled. *The Essential Guide to Generic Drugs* will arm you with the right questions to ask your doctor and pharmacist to make sure you get the best health value for your money.

ONE

MANUFACTURING AND MARKETING DRUGS

WHAT IS A GENERIC DRUG?

In order to understand the distinction between generic and brand-name drugs, as well as the differences that exist among all drugs, it will help to review briefly how pharmaceuticals are manufactured and marketed.

The distinction between generic and brand-name drugs is, simply stated, the difference between the original formulation of a new drug and copies of that drug subsequently manufactured by those other than the originating company.

United States patent law grants the innovator of a new drug up to fourteen years of exclusive marketing rights. During that time, plus its development period, the drug and its manufacturing techniques are protected from competition.

Every drug developed is given two names: its official designation, also known as its generic name, and its trademarked title, known as the brand name. The U.S. Adopted Names Council determines the generic name, following certain rules of nomenclature that help medical professionals identify it. A drug's brand name is invented by the particular pharmaceutical house holding the drug patent. This name is usually easier to remember and shorter than the generic name. It is this name that is promoted and advertised to the medical profession.

During the terms of the applicable patent, the brand-name formulation of the drug is the only version available. However, once the patent expires, the door is opened to other manufacturers to formulate copies. These may then be sold in competition with the original brand-name product, but not under the brand name. The fact that they are essentially the same medication is evident in their having the same generic designation as the innovator formulation.

WHAT IS A BRANDED GENERIC?

You might believe that all generic drugs issue from small "copycat" companies. In truth, 80 percent of the generic drug trade is in the hands of the major pharmaceutical houses or their subsidiaries. In the trade their products are termed *branded generics*, although they are generally not so identified to the public. The giant drug firms, which seek to discredit generic drugs through political lobbying and advertising, dominate the generic drug industry at the same time.

It is estimated that branded generics have been most responsible for the threefold increase in the generic drug market during the 1970s. This may be due in large part to pharmacists' long-established faith in the reputation of the pharmaceutical giants, starting a trend in generic dispensing even before that became a popular consumer and political issue.

The brand-name manufacturers have also long alleged an advantage over small firms by promoting the fact that they cover pharmacists with free product-liability insurance. In reality, most generic drug manufacturers, big or small, carry this type of protection. And pharmacists generally carry their own liability insurance as well, which protects them in the course of performing their professional duties, among which is generic drug selection. So although the pharmaceutical giants have argued an advantage here, raising the specter of potential legal problems, evidence does not support their claim. However, the generic substitution laws have yet to be fully tested in court actions.

Branded generics may at times be a real bargain. Some are the very same products that are sold as brand-name pharmaceuticals at a higher price. That means there can be no doubt of their bioequivalence in comparison to the original drug. The difficulty facing the medical community and the public is that it is so difficult to know when branded generics are identical to the brand-name drug.

COST OF NEW DRUG DEVELOPMENT

It now takes an average of $94 million to bring a new drug product out on the market. Research and development costs take up a substantial percentage of these funds, but millions also go into paying for compliance with complex regulatory procedures mandated by the FDA in order to obtain approval for public use. And not included in that figure are the other millions that go into marketing campaigns to publicize the drug and its treatment benefits, including educating the medical profession about the availability and use of the new product.

The intensive research and development programs that are so vital to establishing the product lines of the research-oriented drug companies are not a major factor for companies that concentrate on production of generic drugs. By the time they step into the picture, the drug has already been developed and proved. Its therapeutic value has been established in the medical community. The generic manufacturer basically has only to set up a production line, win FDA approval for its formulation—as opposed to having to win approval for the drug itself, with all the laboratory and clinical experimentation that requires—and then distribute its generic version to a market already primed to accept the drug. The cost advantage? The difference between the approximately $100,000 it takes to ready a generic for FDA approval and the $94 million the originating company has had to spend to put the original formulation on the market. In fact, the research and development investment for just eight or nine new drugs equals the yearly sales for the entire nonbranded generic industry.

Bolar Pharmaceutical, one of the nation's largest strictly generic houses, has annual sales of less than one-tenth of most brand-name manufacturers. And Bolar is one of the biggest. Except for a handful of companies, most other generic firms are minute by comparison.

Zenith Laboratories, another of the leading nonbranded generic manufacturers, spent roughly $1.5 million on all research and development in 1984. That is less than one-sixtieth the cost of readying just one new brand-name drug for sale in the U.S. market.

The initial investment needed to start up the average generic lab is insignificant by comparison with capital investments standard for innovating pharmaceutical houses. The entire start-up bankroll for a generic lab may even be less than the amount a larger generic firm like Zenith spends to prepare just one drug for marketing. The major pharmaceutical houses argue that this low level of capitalization means inadequate resources to assure first-rate quality-control programs for generic products. Additionally, they maintain that loss of market shares to generic manufacturers offering drugs at substantially lower costs undercuts profitability, making it increasingly difficult to sustain the enormous research and development programs necessary to put newer, better drug therapies on the market. In both cases, it is alleged, the public comes out the loser.

IMPORTANCE OF DRUG PRODUCT FORMULATION

The development of a drug dosage form involves many manufacturing processes and techniques that determine a drug's ultimate quality and level of performance in the human body. I've listed the more common drug dosage forms here. Each form has its own manufacturing requirements; each is susceptible to a variety of problems in the manufacturing process.

aerosols	inhalations	solutions
capsules	injections	spirits
creams	jellies	suppositories
elixirs	lotions	suspensions
emulsions	ointments	syrups
extracts	pastes	tablets
gels	powders	tinctures

With so many potential vehicles in which to place an active ingredient, drug formulation is an industry in itself, requiring highly skilled scientists.

The myriad components and processes that go into the manufacture of a finished drug product create a situation in which a drug's ultimate effectiveness may have less to do with the active ingredient than with the skill used in its production. If proper attention is not given to this exacting art, the drug may turn out to be generically equivalent—that is, it will have the same amount of active ingredient as the originator drug—but therapeutically nonequivalent—that is, it will not act in an identical fashion to the brand-name product once it has entered the patient's body.

When one considers that there can be more than thirty separate factors influencing the outcome of the finished drug product, it is easy to see why the issue of generic bioequivalence is so complex. (When we speak of a drug being bioequivalent, we mean that it acts the same as the originating product in the patient's body.) When the mathematical permutations of these thirty-plus variables are examined in light of their delicate interrelationships, this makes for truly dizzying possibilities.

For example, in a compressed tablet, the most common form of drug taken, the formulator must blend an active ingredient with several inactive ones. These "inert" substances are needed for disintegration (the breaking apart of the tablet once it reaches the stomach or intestine); binding (holding the tablet together until it is ready to do its work); flavoring (especially in the case of chewable tablets); lubrication (to help the powder move through the machinery during manufacture); coloring (to help with product identification and esthetics); and diluents (needed to bring some tablets up to a workable size if the amount of active ingredient is too small).

Add to this the state of purity and quality of the ingredients, which can vary as to crystal or particle size and degree of water content. The condition and calibration of the machinery used to mix the powders and compress the tablets are also critical factors.

All these variables can become even more critical when dealing with a tablet containing an active ingredient in a fraction of a milligram dose, as in the drug reserpine, used to treat high blood pressure. The minute dose of active ingredient incorporated in each tablet—one-tenth of 1 milligram (0.1 mg.)—necessitates the addition of 1499 parts of "inert" material to bring the tablet mass up to a workable weight. If just one small miscalculation has been made in the manufacturing process, such as incomplete mixing, or if there is any unanticipated reaction between the many so-called inactive ingredients used, the tablet will not reliably deliver up its intended dose to the human body. In the case of reserpine, the FDA acknowledges the difficulties of production by refusing to certify any maker's brand of the drug as bioequivalent.

Other dosage forms commonly encountered—capsules, ointments, syrups, and so on—likewise have their idiosyncrasies in the production process, but their manufacture is generally not as complex as tableting. How the drug works can be affected just the same.

To cite just one other example, it has been well documented that corticosteroid activity in cortisone creams and ointments (used as antiitch or antiinflammatory medication) can be affected by the base used to blend with the active ingredient. This vehicle can either enhance or limit the extent to which the drug exerts its intended effect. A drug manufacturer will occasionally come out with the same active ingredient in a new cream or ointment base and properly rate it a more potent product, even though the active drug is present in exactly the same concentration as the original.

Role of "Inactive" Ingredients

As illustrated by the example just given, the inactive ingredients are what truly determine whether a product will be bioequivalent. The active ingredient can usually be weighed or otherwise quantified to assure an acceptable dose available in each tablet, capsule, suppository, and so on. But there are numerous supposedly inert components comprising a dosage form that are never mentioned on the label. They are considered a trade secret. It is these fillers, binders, coloring agents, lubricants, preservatives, drying agents, flavors, disintegrants, coatings, and wetting agents that are the real determiners of how available to the body the active ingredient will be.

In addition to the individual actions of any one of these "inactive" ingredients, interactions between two or more of them are possible, further complicating the formulation process. Interaction possibilities also make it difficult to predict the outcome of any changes made in one or more of these variables.

Dicalcium phosphate had a history of use as a filler for antibiotic capsules, most notably tetracycline. Then researchers discovered that it formed a chemical bond with the active ingredient, severely inhibiting absorption into the blood. This gave rise to the further revelation that certain foods containing calcium and other similarly acting substances could seriously decrease tetracycline's effectiveness if taken at the same time. That is why doctors and pharmacists now caution patients against ingesting milk products, antacids, or iron preparations when taking this drug.

In a reverse situation, dicalcium phosphate had, unknown to formulators, been depressing the bioavailability of phenytoin capsules. (Phenytoin is used to control epileptic seizures.) When the manufacturer replaced this supposedly inert filler with another diluent, lactose, the effect was to increase the capsule's bioavailability—the amount of medication released into the blood—to such an extent that blood levels of the drug reached toxic levels.

In some cases a drug that is inert for some people can affect others adversely. Lactose is one such ingredient. Lactose intolerance is a characteristic of many people of other than northern European extraction. Although most common among Orientals, it is often encountered in the U.S. population as well. Digestive upset is a typical symptom. New York pediatrician Dr. Jeffrey L. Brown has filed suit against the Food and Drug Administration to require that lactose be listed in drug labeling whenever it is used as a filler ingredient. Ralph Nader's Health Research Group is trying to force the FDA to require drug labeling to indicate *all* ingredients used in drug products.

The main opposition to this movement, the brand-name drug industry, contends that the disclosure of inert ingredients would constitute divulging trade secrets. Considerable research and development go into working out the mix of those ingredients. The brand-name companies do not wish to devote millions of dollars to formulating a delivery system for a new medication only to be forced into publishing the information, making it available to any generic manufacturer desirous of copying their techniques.

Some changes, however, have been made. The Proprietary Association, representing 90 to 95 percent of all manufacturers of nonprescription drugs sold in the United States, has issued guidelines for its members encouraging them to list inactive ingredients on package labeling, effective late in 1985. But there is a catch to this seemingly benevolent gesture. Under their proposal, any ingredient considered a trade secret need not be disclosed in the package labeling as long as the listing of inactive substances mentions "other ingredients." Following the lead of the Proprietary Association, the Pharmaceutical Manufacturers Association (PMA), representing the major research-oriented pharmaceutical houses of the prescription drug industry, and the Generic Pharmaceutical Industry Association (GPIA) have unveiled a similar policy of voluntary disclosure of inactive ingredients.

This is really a halfway measure on the part of the drug industry, a strategy of self-policing designed to head off stricter federally imposed regulations. I anticipate stricter disclosure regulations in the very near future.

The Mechanical Factors

Modern drug manufacturing is an almost totally automated process, as it must be in order to yield products consistent enough to comply with regulatory standards. The major pharmaceutical houses spend enormous sums to maintain, modernize, and guarantee that their equipment keeps pace with state-of-the-art production methods. Major drug manufacturers usually have a separate quality control program solely for the purpose of machinery maintenance. This includes the examination of all parts. Often the equipment used for the inspection program is itself sophisticated and expensive.

The generic firms, which may have only a fraction of the sales volume of the larger companies, are not always in a position to plow money back into a continuous modernization program. While all generic companies do not use second-hand equipment, the manufacturing equipment they purchase is often used machinery that a major pharmaceutical house has replaced. While such machinery is always retooled, the quality of manufacture can nevertheless be affected. And the smaller firms typically cannot afford equivalent quality control measures to ensure optimum operation at all times.

One further key to maintaining manufacturing equipment at peak operating efficiency is the keeping of logs indicating everything done with or to a piece of machinery. To best reequip a machine with new parts, a record of past performance is essential. When equipment is purchased second-hand, these records are not likely to follow along. Consequently the new owner may be operating in the dark, unable to anticipate problems that could arise.

Another major area of concern with all drug manufacturing equipment is contamination. All gaskets and sealing rings must be in perfect condition to avoid possible adulteration by machinery lubricants. Normal wear and tear can result in other impurities, such as metal filings finding their way into the finished products. Nonmetallic contaminants—hair, fibers, rubber, wood, paint chips, paper—can also turn up if equipment is in less than perfect working order.

As part of their quality control programs, large drug companies employ sophisticated detection methods to eliminate impurities from the production process. These include magnetic and electronic separation, X-ray techniques, and solution filtration. So in addition to starting out with new equipment, other expensive procedures give the bigger pharmaceutical houses an edge in guarding against the distribution of adulterated drug products. The chance of inferior or adulterated drugs passing onto the market increases if the most modern methods of monitoring production are not part of a manufacturer's quality control plan.

The use of reconditioned equipment also raises the specter of manufacturing by obsolete methods, and this, too, can affect product quality.

Used drug manufacturing equipment, while not precluding the production of quality drug products, does put the formulator at a disadvantage. If the manufacturer had the resources to devote to a top-quality machine maintenance program, it would probably not have to resort to second-hand apparatus in the first place.

EFFECTS OF COMPETITION

With 80 percent of the $3.5 billion spent on generic drugs in 1984 going to brand-name companies, that leaves only $700 million in sales for the strictly generic manufacturers. There are some 600 of those. With this kind of competition for a relatively small market share, generic firms necessarily find themselves working to keep drug costs down, lest their products lose the price edge that makes them attractive to the public.

But many generic houses also rely on specific marketing strategies in order to remain profitable. Zenith Laboratories concentrates on manufacturing only products with a market sales value of at least $10 million that are thought to be popular for drug therapy in the foreseeable future. Another generic drug manufacturer, Mylan Pharmaceuticals, has taken aim at less competitive drug products in the $5 million to $10 million range. By also concentrating on drugs used to treat chronic (long-term) diseases, Mylan hopes to provide itself a steadier, long-term market. At the same time, the company has pursued contracts with brand-name pharmaceutical houses to manufacture drugs, especially antibiotics, to be redistributed by the giants as branded generics.

It is obvious that generic drug houses like Zenith and Mylan, once considered unsophisticated, opportunistic small-time operations, now rely increasingly on well-considered strategies to secure and maintain a share of the burgeoning generic drug industry.

Adding to the ever-changing dynamics of an industry with more companies than drug products, many generic firms are filing new applications with the Food and Drug Administration for approval to produce and market drugs similar or related to products they now manufacture. Using this as a way to expand their sales, a company that is marketing a relatively new generic high-blood-pressure medication, for example, may decide to expand into other proven antihypertensive agents whose patents have also expired.

Brand-name manufacturers maintain that generic producers haven't the resources to ensure a consistent-quality product. And it's true that the smaller manufacturers are sometimes at a technological disadvantage when compared to the big companies. But there is little truth to the allegation that generic substitution undercuts the profit margins of research-oriented producers and thereby limits the amount of money that can be allocated to develop new drugs. The branded generics' dominant position in the overall generic market means that competition remains primarily among the major pharmaceutical houses—without much if any adverse affect on profits.

In 1983, the average investment in research and development by the major brand-name drug producers (expressed as a percentage of sales) was 6.7 percent. By comparison, the aerospace industry averaged 4.6 percent; the electronics industry came in at 4.1 percent; semiconductors were 8.3 percent; information processing for software averaged 7.4 percent; peripherals, 6.9 percent; computer hardware, 7.2 percent. Far from being an endangered species, the research-oriented pharmaceutical industry is spending right alongside what are considered leading-edge industries, which also extensively rely on research and development investment to maintain their markets. In fact, it has been estimated that about fifty *significant* new drugs (those representing a real advance for medicine) have been marketed in the past ten years. And five times as many are presently under development.

Looking at the health of the drug industry from the perspective of profits as a percentage of sales, the larger research-oriented pharmaceutical houses averaged 10.7 percent in 1983. By comparison, the aerospace field averaged 3.6 percent; electronics, 3.7 percent; semiconductors, 0.68 percent; information processing for software, 9.3 percent; for peripherals, 6.1 percent; and computer hardware, 9.4 percent. These statistics, based on data published in *Business Week* magazine (July 9, 1984, pp. 64–78), show the major brand pharmaceutical corporations leading all other high technology fields in profitability. In reality, the stimulus the big companies claim they are creating for the generic manufacturers in the form of new drug products to be exploited ensures their own profits in the generic aftermarket.

And it's not as if product development swallowed up every extra dollar earned. Many research-oriented pharmaceutical houses spend up to twice as much on advertising and promotion as they allocate to research and development. Considerable resources are dedicated to "educating" prescribers to the superiority of their brand-name products, with an eye toward fighting off the competition from generic alternatives once a patent expires.

This strategy has paid off exceedingly well for Hoechst-Roussel Pharmaceuticals, maker of Lasix, a potent diuretic with annual sales in excess of $100 million. The company still controls 94 percent of the market after several years of generic competition. Boehringer Ingelheim's Persantine, used to relieve anginal chest pain, has managed to hold on to 85 percent of its business, posting yearly sales of $80 million.

Some manufacturers are not always so successful. Ives Laboratory's drug Isordil, also used to treat anginal chest pain, has lost over 50 percent of its market position since generics became available.

Actually it may not be generic competition at all that the major producers need fear. The real threat comes from other major houses that respond to a newly patented chemical entity by devising and marketing "me too" drugs, usually nothing more than molecule manipulations designed to move in on the new ground broken by the innovator. This happened when Hoffmann-La Roche first marketed Valium. The company's innovation of an antianxiety drug with a wide margin of safety soon gave rise to numerous imitators whose effect was more to dilute Hoffmann-La Roche's market than to provide any real therapeutic advantage over Valium. The same is true of Inderal, the beta blocker that revolutionized the treatment of hypertension and certain heart disease.

But this sword cuts two ways. To counter loss of revenues to "me too" drugs, the innovators can play a similar game. They can effectively extend their drug patents by performing their own molecule manipulations. By altering a minor characteristic of the active ingredient or formulating a new dosage vehicle—making changes in the composition of the inert ingredients—the original licensee can "pyramid" a new patent on top of the old. By doing this, and with a new advertising and promotional blitz, the innovator firm can transfer much of the goodwill and prescription-writing habits built up over the years to the new product. The Generic Pharmaceutical Industry Association claims that by doing this, it is possible for the top-selling brand-name prescription products to enjoy an average of eighteen and a half years free from competition.

TWO

ASSURING QUALITY OF DRUGS

Generally neither the raw materials nor the basic production processes represent the major cost of the final drug product. The hidden expense is quality control, the real key to turning out products of consistently high standards. About 17 percent of the drug industry's manufacturing staff are engaged in quality assurance. These personnel must be well educated and experienced; many have advanced academic degrees.

If it were simply a matter of available resources, one might draw the conclusion that brand-name drugs or branded generics are always the consumer's best bet. But it isn't only a matter of resources. It's also a matter of maintaining standards that are enforced through the agency of the Food and Drug Administration. And the requirements to meet those standards are as much a matter of concern to the smaller generic houses as they are to the pharmaceutical giants.

To get an idea of what is involved in ensuring adherence to standards of quality, let's review what the FDA requires of drug products.

HOW DRUGS ARE TESTED

All the FDA's drug product standards are established by this country's official compendia of pharmaceuticals, the *United States Pharmacopeia* and the *National Formulary,* which have recently been combined into one volume, designated the USP/NF. The criteria for proving that a product meets official standards vary according to the type of drug involved. These criteria are set forth in the USP/NF and are based on performance in the requisite series of tests that apply to the particular drug.

Disintegration Tests

These determine whether a tablet or capsule will come apart when it reaches the stomach. Each drug formulation has certain specified times within which this must occur. It is an important test because it ensures that the tablet or capsule will not pass through the gastrointestinal tract intact, which would render it useless.

On the other hand, just because a tablet or capsule disintegrates as it should is no guarantee that it will be utilized by the body in its intended manner. Dissolution tests provide a more reliable gauge here.

Dissolution Tests

These evaluate whether a drug actually dissolves in the intestine after passing through the stomach, thereby allowing absorption into the bloodstream, which is necessary if the drug is to exert its intended effect. There is a correlation between the results of a dissolution test and the amount of a drug's active ingredient that reaches the bloodstream (bioavailability). Dissolution tests are probably the best method, apart from costly clinical studies such as those performed by the brand-name innovator, to predict how well a generic drug will compare to the original brand-name formulation.

There is a catch, however. A meaningful dissolution rate for each drug has not yet been determined. Since every chemical has different molecular and therapeutic characteristics, it is necessary to devise separate test procedures and standards for every drug. In fact, these procedures and standards have been established for only a few drugs. The USP/NF introduced dissolution standards for only six drugs in their 1970 revised compendium and have not added many more since that time. They have been more involved in developing better equipment and procedures to assure accurate testing than with individual test standards for each drug.

Weight Variation and Content Uniformity Tests

These tests are designed to ensure that certain dosage forms such as tablets, capsules, and some less frequently encountered formulations have a nearly uniform content, that is, a consistently even distribution of the active ingredient within each dose. This is determined in one of two ways: by physical measurement (direct weighing of sample batches) and chemical assay (used for dosage forms containing 50 milligrams or less of active ingredient).

USP/NF standards permit weight variation among uncoated tablets (weight variation testing does not apply to coated tablets) according to the average weight of a twenty-tablet sample batch. Some tablets can vary by up to 10 percent; as many as two can differ by as much as 20 percent. Capsules subject to weight variation testing are permitted to have up to 10 percent of the sample group deviate from the average weight by up to 25 percent.

A content uniformity test is used for tablets with less than 50 milligrams of active ingredient. Out of a ten-tablet sample, each is required to be within 85 to 115 percent of labeled potency, with one tablet allowed to vary by as much as from 75 percent to 125 percent. The requirement for capsules is essentially the same.

Many of these percentage fluctuations are based on the average weight of the samples used. If, for example, another manufacturer tests a batch of its own version of a generic drug and its average weight per tablet is different, it is calculating percentage deviation on a new base figure. This introduces the possibility of a wide disparity among generics from different manufacturers, or even among varying lots from the same maker. This wide latitude seems particularly disturbing when considering drugs in which there is only a small difference between a therapeutic dose and a toxic one.

Stability Studies

These determine how long a drug retains its potency.

Unfortunately, it is difficult if not impossible to know ahead of time exactly how long a drug will retain its labeled strength once it is handled, packaged, and eventually stored on the shelf. When the Food and Drug Administration receives an application from a drug manufacturer seeking to market a generic, the firm must promise to adhere to certain product stability testing guidelines. Approval of the application, however, is not dependent on the results of these studies, since they may take several years to complete.

FDA policy is to require accelerated stability studies—that is, tests that simulate in a brief time the cumulative effects that factors like temperature and humidity would normally exert over a more extended period of time. Accelerated studies are not universally accepted as reliable.

Most tablets and capsules when first marketed are automatically assigned a two-year expiration date by the FDA. This means that a drug could be on the market for up to two years before long-term stability studies reveal any formulation problem. In this way, it is possible for a subpotent product to be dispensed to a patient despite what appears to be a perfectly valid expiration date.

Bioavailability Studies

Bioavailability studies are the most effective means of determining how well a drug performs in the human body when compared to a recognized standard—in the case of generics, the original brand-name drug.

When submitting an application to the FDA for approval to market a generic drug, a requirement to duplicate the costly methods proving the safety and effectiveness of the prototype brand-name drug is waived. Instead, the generic manufacturer may be asked to supply data proving that its version has a nearly identical effect in the human body. This can be accomplished by two methods: a blood level study, which is expensive, difficult, and time-consuming, demonstrating the drug level achieved in the blood over various elapsed times; and urinalysis, based on the theory that if a substance shows up in the urine, it must have come from the blood. Urinalysis is a much simpler, cheaper method and is more often utilized when bioavailability/bioequivalence data is required.

The only startling revelation regarding this type of testing is that the FDA does not consistently require it for all drugs. Since the USP/NF, which sets the guidelines the FDA follows, requires no animal or clinical (human) tests for bioavailability, the agency insists on it only for drugs already known to pose a problem.

This list of tests that must be run in order to assure quality in a finished drug product is not complete. Bacterial contamination, for example, is also considered, and where necessary, preservatives must be effectively incorporated into a final product in adequate concentrations and in uniform dispersion to protect the user from infection from microorganisms.

In addition to tests on finished products, there are also the many quality control checks that must be run during production. We've seen something of the complexities these can involve in our brief look at manufacturing considerations.

In a recent development, Hoffmann–La Roche maker of the brand name Valium (an anti-anxiety drug), has suggested a new type of bioequivalence testing. In response to imminent generic competition following the expiration of its patent and loss of exclusive marketing rights, they claim that computer-analyzed EEG measurements have shown differences between Valium and its generic competitors. Whether or not this method of targetsite testing in the brain is a meaningful tool or just a ploy to fend off a loss of market share remains to be seen.

A saying in the pharmaceutical industry sums up the vital role of quality assurance: The actual tablet or capsule swallowed by the patient is never the one tested. Good quality control assures that the drug is fully as potent, effective, and free of impurities as the ten, twenty, or one hundred samples actually tested out of a batch of up to five million.

STANDARDS AGAINST WHICH GENERICS ARE MEASURED

How is the "standard" against which a generic is compared arrived at? Most generics must attempt to duplicate the absorption rate of the originator's brand-name product (the level of active ingredient that reaches the blood at various calculated time intervals). This absorption data is plotted on a graph that measures the blood or urine levels of the drug against time. Then the resultant "bioavailability curve" obtained for the generic is superimposed over the information available for the original drug. The differences or similarities are supposed to be immediately apparent.

Once generics become available, any deviation, either above or below the "standard," is looked upon as unreliable. Too high a blood level of a given drug can often be as undesirable, and in some cases even more dangerous, than a subpotent formulation.

I have had patients complain that switching from one brand-name diuretic to the same drug under a different brand name (in this case, Hydro-DIURIL and Esidrix, both trade names for hydrochlorothiazide) resulted in a different therapeutic response. So it is not only the strictly generic manufacturer who can encounter problems in exactly duplicating a drug. Big brand-name pharmaceutical houses can find it troublesome, too.

Theoretically any drug manufacturer, large or small, can originate a drug dosage form that subsequently becomes a standard for generic duplication. However, the research and development costs that must be invested to put a new drug on the market effectively squeeze out all but the major pharmaceutical houses. High prices on drugs still under patent protection not only reflect a temporary monopoly on their production, they also reflect the enormous commitment of time, money, and highly trained personnel to devise a successful formulation in the first place and then to assure that it is uniformly manufactured under strict methods of quality control. By the time generic manufacturers enter the picture, the drug is pretty much a proved entity, and the cost of putting a generic version into production is vastly lower.

FDA STANDARDS

As part of the government's assurance to the public that any drug product meets legal requirements, a great deal of emphasis is placed on the Food and Drug Administration's Current Good Manufacturing Practice code. Adherence to the code's guidelines is supposed to ensure high quality in all drugs manufactured in the United States. Areas covered by the FDA code include the site of manufacture (buildings, equipment, etc.), records, production procedures, personnel, drug testing, packaging, and labeling. FDA inspections are supposed to occur every two years.

But are the standards really strict enough, and is enforcement rigorous enough to guarantee compliance on an industry-wide basis?

In 1971 the FDA conducted 4,710 routine inspections and 1,649 follow-up inspections for previous violations. Seventy-five percent of the reinspections showed that *no* corrective action had been taken to correct indicated violations. In trying to elicit more recent inspection data, I found the FDA totally uncooperative. I was shuffled from department to department, with each claiming total ignorance of the information I sought. Even the agency division responsible for overseeing manufacturing practices refused to divulge information on inspection findings. This can only lead to the suspicion that very little improvement has occurred with the passage of time.

However, we can get some sense of the state of things by comparing the FDA's inspections with another government-run inspection program—that of the Department of Defense, which conducts its own investigations to determine which drug manufacturers are capable of fulfilling the military's needs for quality pharmaceuticals.

The Defense Department's system of inspection is generally considered more thorough and comprehensive than that of the Food and Drug Administration. One reason for this may be that all military inspectors are graduate pharmacists specially trained in all aspects of the evaluation of drug manufacture.

A key difference between the two programs is in the scope of the inspections. The FDA has a responsibility to monitor all drug manufacturers. The military examines only firms wishing to bid for armed forces contract awards.

That examination is more rigorous than the FDA's review procedure. It includes an analysis of a firm's overall organizational structure, checking to make sure that a company's personnel requirements are adequate for delivery of a quality product in the necessary quantity. The efficiency of a plant's layout, its maintenance, and even its sanitation program are evaluated as well. The military wants in particular to see an "objective and effective" quality control system functioning.

As a result of the military's rigorous standards, the ten years between 1962 and 1972 saw 45 percent of *all* plants inspected fail to meet minimum requirements, and about one-half of all drug product samples requested prior to contract award were rejected upon assay.

In all fairness to the FDA, I must point out that it operates on a much more limited budget than does the Defense Department, preventing it from maintaining the required frequencies of inspection. The FDA's standards of analysis are, of necessity, very broad. The military justifies its inspection program by observing that not all manufacturers who are FDA-licensed can be depended on to supply a quality drug product consistently.

WHAT DRUG RECALL PATTERNS REVEAL

It is very difficult to get a true picture of the overall reliability of generics versus brand-name drugs on the basis of drug recall data, since the drug companies tend to interpret raw product recall data to their own advantage. The Food and Drug Administration maintains that branded and generic drug manufacturers have similar track records for drug recalls, but the question of whether quality control significantly differs between them remains without a clear answer.

A 1978 study by Eli Lilly & Company used the FDA's own recall data to show that research-intensive firms (then totaling twenty-three manufacturers spending more than $10 million each annually on research and development) had fewer recalls and court actions initiated against them than did firms engaged in little or no research and development. ". . . Firms not spending great amounts on research have at least seven times more FDA-initiated court actions against them, and one and a half times more FDA drug product problem reports than those of the twenty-three firms in the research-intensive category."

The FDA itself pointed out major flaws in the Lilly study, including recalls having nothing to do with the quality of drug products. The FDA issued its own eighty-page report, stating that the topic was too complicated for clearcut conclusions to be drawn. For one thing, the recall rates for the most frequently substituted generic drugs were very low.

Duquesne University pharmaceutics professor Lawrence H. Block subsequently defended the Lilly study. Block, funded by a grant from Hoffmann-La Roche Laboratories (another pharmaceutical giant), offered his own research statistics on bioequivalence and drug recall data. He claimed that the small generic companies, controlling but 15 percent of the market, were responsible for almost 80 percent of FDA citations and 96 percent of court actions.

Officially, the issue remains unresolved. The FDA has yet to respond to Professor Block's critique of its stand. But one thing is clear in all this: Numbers don't tell the whole story. Statistics can be manipulated to prove any point. It is important to examine the nature of each drug recall. Some research-intensive pharmaceutical houses have occasionally recalled a product in order to issue a new, improved formulation. Although this counts in the statistics, it is not a recall due to a defect in the manufacturing process.

One must also consider the size of the company involved. Six recalls in a year's time is statistically more significant to a small firm than the same number attributed to a pharmaceutical giant with a thousand times greater sales volume. On the other hand, in terms of effect on the public, the sales volume differential may be more significant.

In an attempt to shed some light on the recall controversy, I have compiled the FDA's own drug recall notices for 1983, as published in the *Federal Register*. This information covers both prescription and over-the-counter drug products.

The adjusted statistics show 77 percent of all recalls traceable to small manufacturers.* The big firms accounted for 23 percent of the recalls. Labeling problems were responsible for 44 percent of recalls for small companies. For brand-name pharmaceutical houses, that figure was 32 percent.

Formulation problems were behind 64 percent of all recalls for big houses; the corresponding figure for generic firms was 52 percent. As a percentage of total recalls, formulation problems with products from the big houses accounted for 14.7 percent, while those of small companies were 40 percent. But again, this does not take into account the exact nature of recalls—some products will have put the public at more risk than others; the actual numbers involved in each specific instance vary widely; there is no indication of the ratio of prescription to nonprescription formulations included.

WHY PRICE IS NO INDICATION OF QUALITY

Many consumers assume that a more expensive drug has to be better, and that the lower the price of a generic drug, the poorer the quality. But too many variables affect drug pricing for this to be true.

The generic drug manufacturer Zenith Laboratories was the first to market a generic version of the brand-name drug Flagyl, which is used to treat trichomonal and amoebic infections. Zenith started selling the drug at about half the cost of the brand-name product. Their head start on the other generic manufacturers gave them an eight-month exclusive on a generic version of Flagyl. But then other firms were able to market their versions. The result was a lowering of Zenith's price by about half again in order to maintain its competitiveness.

Does this mean that Zenith lowered its product quality, too? Of course not. It was a simple matter of the dynamics of the marketplace in

---

* In 1983 the FDA announced the removal of all camphorated oil products from the market. This recall, needed to protect the public from a compound that had been determined to be potentially hazardous, was published in the *Federal Register* and included in raw reliability data. My adjusted statistics do not include recalls of camphorated oil products, which did not reflect any fault or error attributable to a specific manufacturer.

operation. Some generic drugs have seen price reductions of as much as 75 percent.

Price alone is a poor indication of drug quality, and price reductions should not be viewed as an automatic sign that quality is being sacrificed in the manufacture of a drug. A manufacturer must produce a drug in the exact manner described to the Food and Drug Administration in its application for approval. If a company wanted to cut corners in the production process in order to maintain a desired profit level, it would first have to win approval for those changes from the FDA.

Moreover, price differentials do not only depend on varying production costs. A generic drug's method of distribution also affects its price.

Intuitively, one would reason that a manufacturer's generic product, one step removed from the pharmacist-retailer by an intermediary (a drug distributor), would usually be more expensive than a product the pharmacist buys directly from the producer. However, the reverse is more generally true.

All drug prices for products sold in the United States are listed in publications such as the *Red Book* and the *Blue Book*, product reference manuals that are made available to pharmacists. In checking these published prices, I discovered some interesting facts. Often the manufacturers' average wholesale price (AWP) to the pharmacist ranges anywhere from 7 percent to more than 50 percent higher than those quoted by distributors for the exact same product. Does the lower price from the distributor reflect a product inferior to that available directly from the manufacturer? Impossible. It's the same product.

Pharmacists often use *Red Book* or *Blue Book* AWP costs as a basis for pricing prescriptions even though they may purchase the drug for less. This means they may be passing on higher costs without the consumer benefiting from any increase in quality. In the nonbranded generic drug market, it would seem that supply and demand has more influence on prices than any reflection of product quality. With respect to branded generic drugs, which tend to be more expensive—although still cheaper than the original prototype—the companies' marketing strategies commonly aim at reinforcing a brand-name bias—specifically, that a brand name means greater reliability. The picture that emerges is of two different generic drug markets existing side by side, each directing its efforts toward separate aims—one toward competitive pricing, the other fostering an image of quality.

When it comes to the distribution of nonbranded generics, the emphasis today is on price. Distributors, who do not usually manufacture their own generic products but buy in bulk from the producer and then repackage them under their own label, tend to go with whichever supplier offers the lowest price. This makes it difficult for a given pharmacy using a particular distributor to consistently purchase a generic drug originating from the same manufacturer. While an alternate manufacturer's product may also meet FDA specifications, appearing on the FDA's *approved prescription drug products* list and thus theoretically being interchangeable, there are several categories of drugs (and patients) for which bioequivalency among generic manufacturers cannot be guaranteed.

Consumers may do themselves a disservice by comparison shopping among pharmacies for the lowest possible price, since not all pharmacies use the same suppliers. With the hundreds of buying sources available to the pharmacist, there is a good chance you'll be unable to find the same generic brand in a different store. What you do find may not be wholly bioequivalent.

BIOEQUIVALENCE—THE ESSENTIAL DETERMINANT

The point in seeking out generic alternatives to brand-name drugs is to get the *same* medication at substantial savings. While the issue of savings is important, the overriding concern should always be to get a product that effectively treats the medical condition for which it has been prescribed. That concern is at times too little emphasized in the rush to save a buck. It serves you little to economize on a drug if the formulation you purchase doesn't deliver its active ingredient in a manner comparable to that of the brand-name original, that is, isn't bioequivalent.

It is often very difficult to assess when a drug actually is not bioequivalent. Every patient is unique, and people react differently to the same drugs. Older people, children, and persons suffering from various diseases can have profoundly altered responses to drugs. This can be more meaningful, in many cases, than any variation among brand-name and generic products.

The issue can often be more clearly stated as one of control rather than of quality assurance. When a doctor starts a patient on a drug regimen, he or she will usually initiate therapy at a dosage normal for the individual's age, body weight, and/or other relevant factors. Dosage levels are then adjusted either upward or downward, depending on evident lack of benefit or the appearance of side effects. The doctor's efforts are directed at establishing a therapeutic balance, and those efforts—often based on past successes—can be thwarted if a new drug formulation is used that is not truly bioequivalent.

A doctor failing to see a clinical response to a drug may wrongly assume that the drug agent is inappropriate, never suspecting a bioequivalence problem. Rather than increase the dose or try another manufacturer's formulation of the same drug, he or she will commonly initiate a different and perhaps more hazardous choice of drug therapy. (After all, the initial drug selected by the physician should be the one presenting the fewest side effects.) A patient may needlessly be exposed to increased risks because a drug's bioequivalence problem was not recognized in the first place.

The problem may as readily arise in a change to a brand name from a generic as from a brand name to a generic. The important consideration is to stick with the product initiated if there's any question of bioequivalence in another formulation. With many drugs, the implications of switching manufacturers are not that profound, but in cases where bioequivalence is essential—as in some drugs that follow—consistency is vital.

Examples of drugs for which concern is warranted for even small differences in bioequivalence are warfarin, an anticoagulant for the blood; digoxin, a heart pill that improves cardiac efficiency; various hormone replacements, such as estrogens, thyroid, and cortisones; and many other agents used to treat serious diseases such as heart arrhythmias, asthma, and epilepsy. A number of antidepressant drugs are claimed to pose bioequivalence problems when it comes to generics, even though the FDA has approved generic versions for many of them. There are both patients and doctors who still maintain that differences in response are common when brands are switched.

The dynamics of a generic drug industry with more than six hundred competitors may make it difficult to locate the same generic manufacturer each time. Often generics are purchased by pharmacies on the basis of price, and given so many industry participants, the competitive positions of firms can change monthly or even weekly. Besides the trouble you may have ensuring bioequivalence from one prescription filling to the next, it is quite possible that the time and effort needed to locate the same generic manufacturer each time cancels out the potential savings over the brand-name drug.

THREE

REGULATING
THE DRUGS

PASSAGE OF THE DRUG ACTS

In certain cases a drug marketed without FDA approval and not certified as bioequivalent to the brand-name product by either state or federal authorities can nevertheless be dispensed to a patient in a perfectly legal fashion. Although the public commonly assumes that the Food and Drug Administration serves as a first line of defense against inferior quality in any drug preparation, FDA authority does not extend uniformly over all drugs.

Government regulation in the area of drugs dates from the passage of the Pure Food and Drug Act of 1906, enacted as a reaction to the public's concern over adulteration of the nation's food supply, influenced by Upton Sinclair's novel *The Jungle*. However, this act failed to provide for meaningful enforcement of standards set. It was not until 1937, after 107 people died as a result of taking an elixir of sulfanilamide containing diethylene glycol, a poisonous substance, that Congress passed an effective drug regulation law, the Federal Food, Drug and Cosmetic Act, signed into law by President Franklin D. Roosevelt in June 1938. The important provision of this law was that no drug could be sold in interstate commerce unless it was proved safe. The responsibility of overseeing this was given to the Food and Drug Administration.

In 1962, following the numerous publicized instances of terribly deformed children born to European mothers who had taken the drug thalidomide during pregnancy, the FDA was given expanded authority. The Drug Amendments of 1962, also known as the Kefauver-Harris Amendments, stipulated that henceforth all new drugs must demonstrate safety as well as effectiveness. Drug companies had to report all adverse drug reactions to the FDA and were required to furnish complete information to doctors detailing not only the benefits but also the risks in taking each drug product.

These requirements also applied retroactively to drugs marketed between 1938 and 1962, and that included generic copies of drugs originally put on the market in this time span.

Naturally a review of all the drug products that came on the market during these years was a monumental undertaking, and the FDA enlisted the aid of the National Academy of Sciences–National Research Council to accomplish that. This group examined all available literature for the drugs involved and classified them as (1) "effective," (2) "probably effective," (3) "possibly effective," or (4) "ineffective." This review, known as the Drug Efficacy Study Implementation (DESI), has formed the basis for FDA certification of 1938–1962 drug products.

The Kefauver-Harris Amendments tightened the review process for new drugs considerably. The stipulation was introduced that drug companies wishing to develop any new drug must obtain an Investigational New Drug Exemption before any clinical testing—that is, tests with human subjects—could begin. This pulled the FDA into all phases of drug development, beginning with a drug's inception, rather than simply acting as a reviewer of data submitted after the fact, as previously.

DRUGS EXEMPT FROM FDA BIOEQUIVALENCY STANDARDS

While the foregoing indicates a pattern of increasingly strict regulation, several jurisdictional loopholes exist, allowing production of certain prescription drugs and over-the-counter formulations with no official monitoring of performance standards.

Pre-1938 Drugs

Although we tend to think almost all the drugs used in medicine today date from the postwar period, in fact, a significant number were developed earlier. The Kefauver-Harris Amendments applied retroactively only to 1938. Drugs marketed before then were exempt from stringent FDA regulation. These have long been eligible for generic substitution, so generic versions can be manufactured without having to meet any bioequivalence standards. Neither do they have to follow the premarket clearance procedures required of other prescription drug products.

The drugs in the following list are among those that are exempt by virtue of having been developed before 1938:

- Acetaminophen (e.g., Tylenol, Datril, and Tempra)
- Amobarbital (e.g., Amytal)
- Aspirin (e.g., Bayer, Empirin)
- Atropine, used alone or in combination with numerous other products
- Chloral hydrate (e.g., Noctec)

- Codeine, used alone or in combination with numerous other products
- Colchicine, used alone or in combination with several other products
- Digoxin (e.g., Lanoxin)
- Ephedrine, marketed alone or in combination with numerous other products
- Epinephrine (e.g., Adrenalin), also used in combination with numerous other products
- Ergotamine (e.g., Gynergen), also used in combination with numerous other products
- Insulin, from various manufacturers and in various formulations
- Methenamine mandelate (e.g., Mandelimine)
- Nitroglycerin (e.g., Nitrostat, Lilly Nitroglycerin)
- Papaverine (e.g., Cerespan, Pavabid)
- Paregoric, marketed alone or in combination with several other products
- Phenazopyridine (e.g., Pyridium), also used in combination with several other products
- Phenobarbital (e.g., Luminal, Barbita, Solfoton), also used in combination with numerous other products
- Pilocarpine (e.g., Isopto Carpine, Pilocar, Adsorbocarpine, Almocarpine, Pilomiotin), also used in combination with several other products
- Testosterone (e.g., Oreton, Android, Metandren), also used in combination with several other products
- Thyroid (e.g., Armour Thyroid)

DESI Exemptions

Although the Kefauver-Harris Amendments stipulated controls retroactively for all drugs produced since 1938, a substantial number of these have also been exempted from strict regulatory control by court order.

The Drug Efficacy Study Implementation Program (DESI) undertook an evaluation of 3,443 prescription drugs first marketed during the period 1938–1962. With 94.8 percent (3,264) of these studies completed as of 1984, 70 percent (2,222) of the drugs were found to be effective and 30 percent (1,042) were evaluated as ineffective.

Among the products declared exempt from meeting the standards mandated by the 1962 law were a number evaluated as ineffective. Others found to be less than effective by the FDA are awaiting a decision on whether to remove them from the market, pending the outcome of additional evaluations. Meanwhile these products continue to be sold without FDA approval or bioequivalence evaluation data to use as guidance. The FDA takes no position on these drugs at present but concedes that "no substitutability is implied." According to Dr. Marvin Seife, director of the FDA's Division of Generic Drug Monographs, which oversees generic drug production, ". . . Manufacturers may market these products on their own responsibility pending the FDA's final determination of these products' effectiveness."

Recently the FDA ran a computer inventory of all drugs marketed in the United States. The printout revealed 5,129 drug products that have not received premarket FDA approval. About 1,800 are part of the DESI review, and 2,400 involve pre-1938 drugs. Under a uniform code, these drugs, plus the remaining 900-odd other products, would be considered in violation of federal food and drug laws.

In addition to the pre-1938 and DESI exemptions, any drug put on the market between 1938 and 1962 may be sold without first performing stability tests to determine its effective shelf life (expiration date).

COMPANIES POLICE THEMSELVES

Even for fully regulated drugs, the FDA's requirements for stability testing may be found somewhat lacking. A supplement attached to the transcript of a speech given by Dr. Seife states, "For most solid dosage forms (tablets and capsules), a 'tentative' two-year expiration date is assigned to the drug." If, over the first two years of marketing, a generic does not "meet the specifications which assure identity, strength, quality and purity, the FDA will be notified and the manufacturer will immediately withdraw the drug from the marketplace."

That means a generic drug can be *on* the market for up to two years before any problems with formulation turn up—two years during which subpotent or poor quality drug products may be substituted for brand-name drugs.

From the wording above—"the FDA will be notified"—it's clear that the initiative to report any deviation from FDA-approved specifications for a drug product rests primarily with the manufacturers. Unless a problem with a drug comes directly to the FDA's attention from a pharmacist, doctor, or unfavorable publicity due to some serious adverse patient reaction, the firms are left to police themselves.

According to Dr. Seife, "The holder of an Abbreviated New Drug Application (submitted for generic drugs) is also required to make certain reports to the FDA. These include reports of any problems that arise in relation to the drug itself—contamination, label mix-up, failure of potency or other deterioration—which may necessitate the lot being recalled from the market. Unusual or unusually severe reactions to the drug, or unusual frequency of a reaction, must also be reported to permit an FDA reevaluation of safety considerations."

The frightening part of this statement lies in the injunction to report "unusual or unusually severe reactions to the drug, or unusual frequency of a reaction." Why? Because the policy refers to a manufacturer already marketing a drug with FDA approval. The Abbreviated New Drug Application (ANDA) now used for all generics released for sale to the public does not usually require clinical studies to be performed first, as they must be for release of newly patented drugs. Generic houses market only drugs requiring ANDA approval and therefore have little expertise in evaluating "unusual" reactions. They do not generally employ professionals qualified to interpret relevant data, so they may not be competent to supply the FDA with the feedback necessary to assure the safety of patients using their products.

In another speech Dr. Seife complained about the lack of compliance by some generic drug firms in submitting additional data to the FDA in order to document the quality of their products. ". . . Firms continue to market products for which ANDAs were submitted a long time ago, but little effort has been made to get these applications to approval status." He warned, "If we ask for additional data, drug samples, or whatever to support a given application and hear nothing from you within a reasonable period of time, we will initiate a nonapproval letter to you, remove the application from our active file, and send it to the Federal Records Center. For this purpose, *a reasonable period of time is defined as being up to twelve months*" (my emphasis). That means an inferior drug product could legally be marketed for up to one year.

Is it realistic to assume that all generic manufacturers, especially small struggling companies attempting to carve out a market share in an effort to survive, will meticulously report all stability and bioequivalence problems to the FDA on a timely basis? Probably not. Even mammoth research-oriented pharmaceutical houses, which can easily afford setbacks in their marketing plans, have occasionally been accused of withholding vital information about adverse reactions to drugs they produce.

A case in point is the highly publicized story of the antiarthritic drug Oraflex. In 1983 the drug's maker, Eli Lilly, was accused in a report on national television (CBS, "60 Minutes") of failing to pass on to the FDA reports of liver failure, kidney complications, and even deaths experienced by patients taking the medication. Patients, their relatives, and doctors all testified to Lilly's unwillingness to acknowledge problems or act upon recommendations made even before the drug was placed on the U.S. market. An FDA investigation subsequently revealed that "Lilly failed to promptly report all deaths associated with the drug to the FDA, including 96 *known* deaths outside the United States."° Twenty-six of those deaths "were known to Lilly prior to the approval date of Oraflex." In fact, less than 50 percent of all adverse reaction reports submitted to Lilly were ever passed on to the FDA. The drug has been removed from the market.

If the major producers at times discount the public interest in their pursuit of profit, what can we expect from smaller, less cash-rich companies?

An elderly Ohio woman was being treated by her physician for hypertension and atherosclerotic disease (hardening of the arteries). Among several drugs prescribed was Lasix, a potent brand-name diuretic used to rid the body of excess fluid. Without her doctor's knowledge, the woman's pharmacist substituted a generic furosemide. The woman subsequently died, and her doctor, in a sworn affidavit, stated his belief that the pharmacist's generic substitution contributed to her death. (The pharmacist was later acquitted of any capable negligence in the case.)†

This unfortunate tragedy stemmed from a peculiar situation whereby several brands of furosemide were illegally marketed in the United States in 1979. Shortly thereafter, reports of the ineffectiveness of these generics prompted the FDA to seize the offending products, effectively removing them from distribution.

Pharmadyne Laboratories, Inc., one of the manufacturers whose products were seized, brought suit against the FDA, protesting the agency's seizure on the grounds that furosemide was not a new drug and thus not subject to premarket approval. The company's attorney argued that new generic products of older drug entities should be allowed to be marketed without preclearance by the FDA. (The FDA contended that furosemide was not a pre-1938 or DESI-exempt drug and was thus subject to approval before marketing.) He asserted that a company's adherence to the FDA's Good Manufacturing Practice Code would assure proper formulation and manufacture.

Fortunately the court did not accept this view. The court found that the FDA's Good Manufacturing Practice regulations were adequate only to assure general standards of manufacturing. They were never designed to deal with specific products or to address the issues of bioavailability, tablet uniformity, or intelligent product formulation. Further, since the law allowed up to six months between initial marketing and the listing of a drug with the FDA, if it were not for the preclearance requirement, the agency might be totally unaware of a product until it had been on the market for

° "Oraflex" on "60 Minutes," WCBS-TV. Transcript of broadcast, aired from New York: Sept. 11, 1983 and April 17, 1983.
† Shacknai, Jonah, & Squadron, William. "Liability for Substitution of Generic for Brand-Name Drug," *U.S. Pharmacist*, April 1983, pp. 8–11.

several months. Even once it came to the agency's attention, the process of review could well result in several more months of delay.

The trouble with the Pharmadyne generic had to do with the use of dicalcium phosphate as an inert filler in the tablet formulation. Dicalcium phosphate was incompatible with the active ingredient, causing a decrease in tablet dissolution and ultimately a subtherapeutic blood level of the drug.

As both the Oraflex and furosemide examples show, the tendency to rely on self-policing can at times expose the public to dangerous risks. Fortunately, although the Food and Drug Administration suffers restrictions both of jurisdiction and in its capacity for effective administration, its watchdog overseeing of the pharmaceuticals industry does largely protect the public against shoddy manufacture of drugs. Problems do arise now and then, some with tragic consequences for the persons involved, but fortunately the controls in place as a result of federal and state legislation protect the average citizen from danger as a result of poor formulation and manufacturing practices.

In some corners, the question now loudly asked is whether perhaps FDA regulation hasn't gotten out of control.

GETTING A NEW DRUG APPROVED

The 1962 Kefauver-Harris Amendments to the Food, Drug and Cosmetic Act inaugurated a mass of controls for new drugs. The requirement of proving a drug effective as well as safe necessitated a host of additional premarket tests; the need to win an Investigational New Drug Exemption before any clinical testing could begin complicated everything even more. The proliferation of red tape at every stage meant that the average time needed for a drug company to get marketing approval for a new drug went from between one to two years before 1962 to the almost ten years it takes today.

Estimates of the costs of marketing a new drug product vary greatly, but as of 1984, the most encountered average-cost figure was $94 million. A considerable part of this is attributable to the present bureaucratic maze.

The ten-year approval process also cuts into the time during which a drug innovator can enjoy patent protection. The clock starts running on a drug's patent even before clinical trials begin. With the seventeen-year exclusivity period in effect until 1984, that left only about seven years free from generic competition. With the passage of the Drug Price Competition and Patent Term Restoration Act of 1984, there was provision for an extension of up to five additional years of patent protection, and four extra years of exclusive marketing for any new "orphan drug." (We'll discuss those in a moment.) That has moderated some of the adverse effects of bureaucratic overseeing of research and development, but the cost of control remains high.

Before 1962 there were many more "new chemical entities," or NCEs (to use FDA terminology), being developed than after that year's amendments to the Food, Drug and Cosmetic Act. During the four years prior to 1961 an average of fifty-five NCEs per year were introduced. After 1962 the median fell to twenty-three for the next four years. Since 1968 there have never been more than twenty NCEs approved in any one year.

In 1961 the drug industry in the United States spent $245 million for research and development, with the average cost per drug estimated at between $1.2 million and $5 million. Contrast that with total industry expenditure of almost $3.5 billion in 1984, producing new drugs at the estimated average cost of $94 million.

What does the FDA itself add on to the expense of developing a new pharmaceutical in terms of regulatory compliance? One estimate places the increase in cost for going beyond just the necessary assurance of safety and effectiveness at 25 percent.[*] In other words, out of the estimated $94 million invested in each new drug, $23.5 million could be redirected to more productive use in developing new and better drug products or toward bringing the eventual market price for new pharmaceuticals down to more manageable proportions.

However, it appears that the biggest drop in new products entering the market has been among those rated as only modest therapeutic gains. The hurdles placed in the path of new drug development have probably not deterred major pharmaceutical breakthroughs. But the many less-than-revolutionary drugs prevented from entering medical practice would also have served an important function—the assurance of numerous alternatives for each new class of drug, thus fostering competition and preventing any one new product from establishing an absolute monopoly at whatever price the manufacturer desires. These "me too" products would also nourish a vigorous generic aftermarket, driving prices down in manufacturers' efforts to establish market shares.

The Question of Drug Lags

It has been noted that many new pharmaceuticals are available abroad, especially in Europe, much sooner than they can be marketed here. This has

---

[*] Hansen, Ronald W. "The relationship between regulation and R&D in the pharmaceutical industry: A review of literature and public policy proposals." The National Pharmaceutical Council. Proceedings of a Symposium and Workshop, "The Effectiveness of Medicines in Containing Health Care Costs: Impact of Innovation, Regulation and Quality." Washington, DC: National Pharmaceutical Council, 1982.

given rise to speculation about how many lives could have been saved versus the possible dangers to the public in speeding up New Drug Application procedures at the FDA.

To be fair, there is now special provision for new drugs the value of which is judged to be a significant improvement over existing treatments. The FDA has placed these select few on a "fast track," cutting down the red tape and other delays experienced by developers of most new pharmaceuticals. To give you just one indication of what's involved, companies must submit a New Drug Application to the FDA that includes all the raw testing data generated in the clinical research for the drug. That can amount to as much as 50 to 200 pages on each person who has participated in preliminary studies, and there may be as many as 3,000 subjects. The average New Drug Application is 100,000 pages long, and it usually takes about two years just to review that.

Many feel more is required than a "fast-track" review for the few drugs that are deemed potential breakthrough therapies. We in the United States should have a health care system second to none in sophistication, with the public granted access to all the newest drug therapies available anywhere.

Others take a more conservative approach. It is often very difficult to predict accurately whether a new drug has the potential to do harm. It can sometimes take up to twenty years, as in the classic case of diethylstilbestrol (DES), to detect damage that may be done. (DES, given to pregnant women in the 1960s to prevent possible miscarriage, is alleged to have caused vaginal and/or cervical cancer in some of the daughters born to them once the children reached the teen years. It was ultimately found to be worthless for preventing miscarriage in the first place.)

Anytime a new drug is marketed and subsequently shown to be hazardous, a great public furor is raised. We've already noted the case of Oraflex, the antiarthritic introduced by Eli Lilly & Company in May 1982.

To give another example, in May 1979 Smith, Kline & French Laboratories was granted FDA approval to market Selacryn, a drug that was supposed both to lower blood pressure and decrease uric acid levels. By January 1980 the FDA had received reports of 53 cases of liver or kidney damage and 10 deaths, all associated with this drug. There had allegedly been no indication of this problem potential in either animal studies or early human trials. By March 1980 the toll had risen to 363 cases of injury and 24 fatalities.

However, besides noting instances in which FDA regulations have not precluded public exposure to risk from a new drug, we should also note the instances in which the agency's tough standards have spared us potential tragedy. American women were fortunate to escape the horror of deformed children that followed use of the drug thalidomide by pregnant women in Europe. Other ill-fated drugs the FDA spared us from are Practolol, a heart drug used to control cardiac arrhythmias but found to cause eye and other tissue damage, and Clioquinol, also known as Enterovioform, an antidiarrheal found to cause paralysis and blindness in some people.

But it's not a simple balance to weigh. What about the deaths and suffering that could have been prevented if a drug had been available to the public sooner? Balance the twenty-four fatalities in the case of Selacryn against the estimated ten thousand lives that could have been saved if the beta-blocker Inderal (propranolol) had been available sooner to treat heart disease.

The problem is that the ten thousand lost victims remain faceless. They don't have the same impact on the public conscience as one unfortunate person who can be shown to viewers of the six o'clock news as having suffered the damaging effects of a new drug.

Testing Outside the United States

To circumvent the FDA's restrictive regulations and to save money, American drug firms have been going abroad for much of their initial new drug testing. Before 1966 almost no initial testing for domestic pharmaceuticals took place outside this country. By 1974 about half of all NCEs were developed that way. More recently it has been estimated that the last thirty years have seen the United States go from domestic research and development representing 60 percent of the world's expenditures to under 30 percent today.

In 1975 the FDA finally acknowledged the greatly expanded role of foreign drug testing by agreeing to accept and approve new drugs evaluated entirely according to the results of those studies, provided they were judged applicable to the U.S. population. Before 1975 the FDA did not consider any foreign testing data acceptable in support of a New Drug Application. Now the agency will accept such evidence, but it reserves the right to require tests to be repeated here.

Of course, the lower cost of foreign testing can work toward bringing down the average cost of developing new pharmaceuticals, hopefully to be reflected eventually in a lower price to the consumer. It may also be advantageous to have investigations of the same drug going on in different parts of the world, as that introduces a variety of perspectives in analyzing its uses.

But a more insidious issue lurks beneath the surface. For the last forty-five years U.S. pharmaceutical manufacturers have not been allowed to export new drugs developed here until the FDA has first approved them. So in order to compete in world markets, American firms have been forced to sidestep the FDA by developing and marketing new products abroad. FDA overregulation may in effect drive the drug testing industry abroad permanently.

The Plight of "Orphan Drugs"

One casualty created by the huge investments needed to bring a new drug to market today is a group of pharmaceuticals that have become known as *orphan drugs.* These are medications found to have value in the treatment of certain rare diseases but that, due to their limited profit potential, are difficult to justify economically. The giant pharmaceutical houses must concentrate their primary energies on new products that treat the most people in order to ensure adequate returns on their investment.

To cite just one comparative example, high blood pressure (hypertension) affects about 35 million Americans; Tourette syndrome, a rare disease characterized by involuntary muscle movements and uncontrollable vocalizing often including obscenities, affects "only" an estimated 100,000 sufferers.

Given the expense of developing a new drug and then winning FDA approval, relatively small populations suffering from less common conditions have been put at a disadvantage. Fortunately the FDA has recognized the problem here and in 1983 instituted an incentive program to help spur the development of orphan drugs. Special tax credits, faster FDA approval, and the opportunity to treat patients with the drug even while it is still in the investigatory stage have already had a positive effect. Recently a drug has been isolated that more effectively treats Tourette syndrome than any other mode of therapy—pimozide, developed by McNeil Laboratories and marketed under the trade name Orap. New treatments have also been developed for testicular cancer, kidney infections, dissolving gallstones without surgery, moderate hemophilia, and prevention of kidney stones. One orphan drug that has received particular attention is Cyclosporine, an immunosuppressant developed by Sandoz Pharmaceuticals, which has been instrumental in preventing organ transplant rejection.

In the long run these orphan drugs will add a new dimension to the generic drug market. Specialized pharmaceuticals, which are prohibitively expensive due to their limited market and corresponding inability to benefit from economies of scale in production, should eventually be within reach of all who need them at a much more reasonable cost.

New Streamlined Drug Approval Procedures

Among the innovations at the FDA that have been predicted to save an average of six months per application are:

- An abbreviated application format that would allow simultaneous review by different FDA departments, instead of the old method of passing around the entire New Drug Application to one division after another.
- A procedure for manufacturers to update applications while they are under review, assuring the FDA of the latest available data.
- The elimination of most individual patient testing records from the application. Although these reports would still be available to the agency, their removal from the NDA could decrease its bulk from an average of 100,000 pages to less than 30,000.
- New protocol for quickly resolving disputes.
- Closer attention to regulations requiring all fatal and life-threatening adverse reactions to be reported within fifteen days.
- FDA acceptance of foreign drug testing data performed according to U.S. standards as a sole basis for new drug approval.

And then there is the preferential review procedure for drugs seen as innovative breakthroughs offering a major advance in the state of medicine. These significant discoveries, put on a "fast track," have the potential for doing significantly more good than harm and justify their receiving priority approval.

Whether these new streamlined procedures really quicken the pace of drug innovation remains to be seen. There is certainly much room for improvement, given the average ten-plus years it now takes to introduce a new pharmaceutical. As always, it boils down to a tradeoff—some increased risk possible to the public versus more lives potentially saved. To the extent that improved therapies are made available sooner, safety in a broader sense would be promoted.

Can There Be Too Much Regulation?

Is it possible in the present overregulated drug testing environment for new wonder drugs to emerge at a healthy rate? Let's consider the answer by reflecting on two of the most revolutionary pharmaceutical advances that were registered within the last century: the introduction of aspirin in 1899 and of penicillin during World War II.

When aspirin was first introduced there were very few regulations regarding the marketing of medications to the public. The FDA did not exist; the sophistication necessary for today's clinical studies was practically nonexistent.

In 1982 the salicylate group of drugs, of which aspirin is the prototype, were implicated in causing a condition called Reye's syndrome. This potentially fatal disease may be linked to aspirin consumption in children under sixteen years of age. The symptoms of the syndrome range from nausea and vomiting, viral infection, and mild amnesia or disorientation to deep coma and death.

With several recently introduced new drugs used for their antiinflammatory effects and pain relief in a manner much like aspirin—Zomax and Oraflex are two examples—findings of severe adverse reactions in some people prompted their immediate removal from the market by the FDA. But because aspirin is such a mainstay of medicine, present in so many drug products, both over-the-counter and prescription, a recall was not considered.

If aspirin were a new drug being developed today, its link with Reye's syndrome or its propensity to provoke many allergic responses and stomach ulcers might have kept it from ever seeing the light of day under current FDA approval standards. Even if it weren't rejected outright by the agency, the inordinate delays it would encounter, with the resultant increase in the time and money needed to complete its development, might give us a drug with a current cost of perhaps as much as a dollar per tablet.

And penicillin? Given the extremely high percentage of individuals who are allergic to the drug, a case might be made for its being too hazardous if it were a new drug under development today. Considering the outrageously high prices of some of today's newer antibiotics, many of which are penicillin derivatives, it is doubtful the average citizen in the 1940s could have afforded this drug at a price comparable to what its introduction in the 1980s would cost. Keep in mind that 1943 was the era before the proliferation of Medicare, Medicaid, and other current comprehensive health insurance plans.

The fact that aspirin and penicillin—and hundreds of other drugs brought to market before the institution of today's stringent FDA regulations—are still in the mainstream of modern medical practice has lent the current generic market much of its vigor and competitiveness. If this is to continue into the future, we must not handicap ourselves with too rigorous an effort to prove that all new drug formulations are totally without risk to all segments of the population. A sense of balance between benefit and risk must be retained lest we prolong suffering in a large population out of fear that some few may suffer an unexpected adverse reaction to an agent promising relief to many.

WINNING APPROVAL FOR GENERIC DRUGS

In mid-1981 a U.S. court approved an FDA policy simplifying the requirements for getting generic versions of drugs that were originally marketed between 1938 and 1962 approved for sale to the public. Previously all manufacturers desiring to market their version of a generic drug had to file a

New Drug Application (NDA) with the Food and Drug Administration. Filing this application involved redoing all the work of the original drug patent holder. This included detailed pharmacologic and clinical studies designed to determine the drug's safety and effectiveness. These trials were time consuming, very expensive, and required large professional staffs of technicians and doctors. They constituted a considerable drain on a company's resources and obviously eliminated all but the best-financed drug companies from the generic drug market.

The new FDA policy provided for the generic equivalents of the 1938–1962 drugs to be marketed subject to the submission and approval of an Abbreviated New Drug Application (ANDA). It was now necessary only to furnish a description of the active ingredient and composition of the dosage form to be manufactured, give the name and address of the suppliers of all active ingredients, and promise to meet all appropriate quality specifications. In addition the applicant had to outline the procedures and equipment used to manufacture and package the product, promise to adhere to the FDA's Current Good Manufacturing Practices guidelines, provide acceptable labeling and package literature, and in some cases supply bioequivalency data—information to assure that the drug worked in an equivalent manner to the brand-name original when given to humans. (As a rule, the FDA does not carry out its own bioequivalency testing, relying rather on the information provided by the generic drug manufacturer as part of the ANDA.)

This revolutionary change profoundly affected the generic drug industry. By relieving generic houses of the responsibility of doing original research to determine safety, effectiveness, and therapeutic equivalency, the most prohibitive aspect of the drug approval process was swept away, opening the way for hundreds of small drug companies to enter the industry.

The Drug Price Competition and Patent Term Restoration Act of 1984 expanded the ANDA process to include drugs first marketed after 1962, creating a bonanza of further generic drug marketing opportunities. Now the FDA may apply the same shortcut approval process for drugs developed since 1962 whose patents have expired. The passage of this law will make between 125 and 150 additional drugs eligible for generic substitution under the ANDA process. The effect over the next few years will be a notable increase in the industry's sales volume, far beyond even the most optimistic forecasts made over the last several years.

Is the ANDA Approval Procedure Safe?

While the Abbreviated New Drug Application (ANDA) process has allowed many more generics to reach the market than would otherwise be possible, some have expressed concern that it is not wholly safe for the public. With only about thirty professional and supportive staff, the FDA's Division of Generic Drug Monographs is able to approve an average of three ANDAs every two working days, averaging roughly thirty-two approvals per month. For the most part, these application approvals consist of reviewing the data submitted by the applying drug company. The FDA does very little of its own chemical analysis or bioequivalency testing, reserving this for instances of known formulation problems or special situations as they arise.

In other words, the FDA really approves drugs after the fact. It approves a product if the paperwork looks to be in order and waits for any problems to develop *after* the drug has been made available to the public.

Given the budgetary and personnel limitations of the agency and the barrage of drug approvals it must contend with, another approach may not be feasible at present. But the procedures that are followed cannot help but affect the quality expectations for generic drugs approved for marketing in the United States today. The addition of the estimated 125 to 150 new drugs to the list of those eligible for ANDA approval as a result of the 1984 legislation will stimulate a host of new applications to process for approval—as many as 1500 new ANDAs as manufacturers seek to market their versions of these newly available products. Unless there are corresponding increases in the FDA's budget and staff, a more meaningful review process is almost certainly out of the question.

Critics of the ANDA approval procedures point to the fact that generics approved for release on the market have at times been found to behave differently from their brand-name prototypes. And they fear the risk of this happening will increase with the spate of new generic drug releases that can be expected over the next few years.

In 1966 Parke-Davis's antibiotic Chloromycetin went off patent, and other manufacturers were soon marketing less expensive generic substitutes. A California fish breeder who had been treating the water in his fishtanks with the brand-name product tried various generics as an economy measure. But when he emptied the capsules of the substitute into the water, he noticed that they behaved differently than Chloromycetin did. Instead of disappearing quickly into solution, he was left with a filmy residue floating at the top, which only gradually dissipated.

He informed Parke-Davis of this phenomenon. Company officials quickly organized studies to compare the bioavailability of various generics to their product. They found that blood levels of the drug ranged from only 23 to 61 percent of those obtained with Chloromycetin.

Confronted with Parke-Davis's evidence, the FDA sought other corroborating studies. One consultant found generics delivering only about half the peak blood levels obtained with the brand-name drug. This and other investigations convinced the FDA to order all generics not bioequivalent to Chloromycetin off the market.

Subsequent research pinpointed the problem as existing in the active ingredient's poor water solubility. It did not dissolve well in water, a prerequisite to adequate absorption in the gastrointestinal tract. The active ingredient's particle size exerted a significant effect on the drug's availability; the Chloromycetin formulation was characterized by a fineness not matched in the generic versions. Once this was understood, generic manufacturers were able to adjust the fineness of the active ingredient in their formulations to meet the necessary dissolution standards.

In the case of Dilantin, an antiepileptic manufactured by Parke-Davis, the brand-name formulation was found to release its active ingredient, phenytoin, more slowly than generic versions that appeared on the market. Patients previously stabilized on Dilantin capsules and subsequently switched to substitutes were sometimes showing toxic blood levels of phenytoin due to too-rapid absorption of the drug.

Phenytoin presents several bioavailability problems. For one, it has a low therapeutic index—that is, the difference between the effective treatment dose and a toxic one is very small. It is also poorly soluble in water, making formulation a difficult process requiring great care and planning to ensure proper dissolution and eventual absorption into the body at precise rates.

In September 1978 an FDA bulletin mentioned the agency's awareness of the problem and announced that new guidelines would be forthcoming for distinguishing between distinct forms of the medication. This ultimately led to the official recognition of two types of phenytoin capsules, which is still in effect today. Dilantin and recently one generic are the only products approved for once-a-day dosing and are appropriately labeled "extended." All other phenytoin capsules are labeled "prompt" and their directions for use call for multiple daily doses.

In the case of both Chloromycetin and Dilantin, the FDA had approved the generic substitutes that were put on the market. Fortunately the agency acted promptly to resolve the problems that became apparent, preventing potential problems for millions who were using the drugs. But the fact of occurrences like these, even though they are comparatively infrequent in terms of the scope of generic substitution, has some critics of the ANDA approval procedures worried. Reference is made in particular to FDA policies indicating a reliance on self-policing by producers and allowing a two-year period for an approved generic drug to prove its stability.

Those who support the FDA's simplified procedures point to the enormous benefit provided to the public through the availability of generic substitutes, with only a small percentage of these evidencing problems. The benefits far outweigh the element of risk, and to date the Food and Drug Administration has managed to resolve almost all problems that have become apparent before they endangered the public welfare. In addition, despite the relaxed rules newly in effect for marketing post-1962 generics, these drugs have good track records, having already had to measure up to tougher approval standards than those marketed before 1962. This bodes well for the safety of the new generation of generic drugs.

REQUIRING FDA APPROVAL STATUS ON THE DRUG LABEL

Congress is currently working on legislation that would help eliminate some of the confusion regarding a drug's FDA approval status. While some may question the adequacy of FDA approval standards, the fact that many drugs can be sold without FDA approval is far more worrying. And right now a consumer has little to go on when it comes to determining whether a drug at least has that approval.

The thrust of the proposed change in the law would be to require drug manufacturers to indicate on their labeling whether or not a product actually enjoys FDA approval. At present this is not necessary, so confusion exists. Pharmacists desiring to save their customers money by dispensing a cheaper generic alternative are often unsure of the status of many manufacturers' products. The use of a designation such as "FDA approved" would encourage pharmacists to substitute at a higher rate than is now possible, as it would mitigate their uncertainty relative to assuring dispensing of a medication meeting minimum bioavailability standards.

This new legislation would not eliminate some of the other problems touched on in this chapter, but it would be an important step in creating a simple means to aid pharmacists in quickly weeding out unapproved products. And that would be a significant stride toward consumer safety.

FOUR

INFLUENCING DRUG CHOICE

Price is only one factor in deciding what drug to buy. The more expensive brand-name product will not necessarily provide greater therapeutic benefit than a generic alternative. In some cases it's even possible that a patient stabilized on a generic drug will experience an adverse reaction when switched to the brand-name counterpart.

On the other hand, it's also true that certain brand-name pharmaceuticals have proved superior to their generic imitations. And patients stabilized on a brand-name product may be ill served by a switch to a generic formulation. The more expensive drug may at times be better. Shopping for a prescription drug simply on the basis of price comparisons can prove false economy.

All this might be a sufficient word of caution to the wise: Choose your prescription drugs carefully and with reference to more than just price—but that assumes that the consumer always has a free choice. Unfortunately that is not always the case. There's a great deal of pressure currently exerted to prompt consumers into opting for generic drugs whenever possible, and that pressure too often arises out of purely economic considerations. With pharmaceuticals accounting for up to 7 percent of the $387 billion spent in 1984 on health care in the United States, drugs are big business. And as in any big business area, priority interest is given to the bottom line.

THE INSURANCE INDUSTRY

Since insurance companies pay for more than 90 percent of the drugs taken by hospital patients and 14 percent of those prescribed outside the hospital setting, they naturally have a keen interest in encouraging public acceptance of generic drugs. With an average of one new prescription written for each day in the hospital, the typical patient uses eight different prescription drugs during a hospital stay.

But what do insurance companies consider as their primary objective: your health or their bottom line?

Insurance is a business like any other. There is always a concern for profits, and the industry depends on actuarial tables drawn up by experts to determine what premiums are necessary for continued profitability. Management is fully aware of the potential boost to earnings as a result of wider use of cheaper generic drugs. And management has been working out different ways to encourage such use.

Prescription Drug Plans

Many Americans are covered for prescription drugs under various insurance plans, often as part of a union health care package or of a package plan offered by major corporations to their employees. Some of these plans operate via agreements with various pharmacies that promise to fill a member's prescription upon presentation of a valid eligibility card. The pharmacy is then reimbursed by the drug plan on a monthly basis. The fee schedule varies from plan to plan and from state to state, but most operate by one of two methods:

1. Pharmacists receive their drug cost plus a fixed dispensing fee, which does not vary with the drug's acquisition cost.
2. Pharmacists are reimbursed on a sliding fee scale, reflecting the drug's acquisition cost.

Naturally the prescription drug plans would like to see their members use cheaper generic drugs. Pharmacists, on the other hand, are divided in their enthusiasm. Excessive preoccupation with price forces them to seek only the cheapest manufacturers of generics. In addition, many prescription plans will reimburse for generic drug acquisition costs based only on what *they* consider to be the cheapest generally available product. This has resulted in pharmacists' finding their professional judgment preempted by economic decisions arrived at by prescription plan administrators. These third-party-plan executives (prescription plans are referred to as third party plans—the patient is the first party; the pharmacy is the second party; and the third party pays for the prescription) dictate how much the pharmacist may charge for each prescription, in effect encroaching on the bounds of the latter's professionalism.

By dispensing a brand-name product, the pharmacist can often at least be assured that third-party reimbursement will cover actual drug costs, since acquisition costs for a brand-name product are uniformly established.

However, when drug costs get excessive, as is common especially with the newer brand-name products, the fixed fee reimbursement system makes it very difficult for the pharmacist to show a profit. For example, if a prescription plan allows a $3.50 dispensing fee to the pharmacist, this may be adequate to cover administrative and professional overhead if a drug's cost is below $10. But when procurement costs rise above that level—and they do for many brand-name drugs, frequently approaching $20 or more—where is the pharmacist's profit? He or she must invest $20 in the cost of the product; carry this inventory expense for at least one month until being reimbursed by the plan (and many plans hold up payment for extensive time periods due to bureaucratic errors); fill out various time-consuming forms requiring detailed information; process these forms, keeping records against which to check eventual payment; and spend valuable time communicating with the prescription plan in the event a payment is reduced or denied.

If you are a member of one of these plans and have ever been shuffled from pharmacy to pharmacy trying to get someone to fill your prescription, only to be told repeatedly that your medication is out of stock or that the item is not carried, examine the prescription carefully. It is probably written for an expensive drug in a large quantity of a hundred or more units, making it extremely unprofitable for the pharmacist to fill.

With generics, pharmacies need only invest a fraction of the money in inventory that is necessary for brand-name drugs, and fixed-fee reimbursement will be more nearly equitable based on the drug's acquisition cost. It is unlikely that you would ever be refused at the prescription counter with a generically written prescription.

Where prescription plans use a sliding scale fee system, the higher the drug cost, the higher the pharmacist's reimbursement. That is a more intelligent approach, allowing for the realities of the marketplace. With such a plan it is unlikely that you would ever be put in the position of having to seek out a pharmacy willing to do you the favor of filling your prescription. This fee arrangement is an equitable system, eminently fair to both patient and professional.

Some third-party insurers have come up with innovative methods for encouraging generic substitution. PCS (Pharmaceutical Card System), the nation's third largest claims processor, has a pilot program that offers the pharmacist a cash inducement of up to 25 percent of the difference between the cost of the brand and of the generic drug. The Michigan Blue Cross/Blue Shield prescription plan has adopted an incentive program that also benefits pharmacists who save the plan money through generic substitution.

A new twist, developed by a pharmacist advisory panel of the Eastern Ohio Pharmaceutical Association, would provide for possible cancellation of the patient copayment fee (many plans require partial patient payment for each prescription, similar to a deductible on your auto insurance policy). So in addition to a pharmacist incentive, the patient could also share in the generic savings.

Many different options are emerging. The dangers to be avoided are public exposure to substandard generics and the creation of a two-tiered health care system in which those covered by third-party payment plans receive second-class drug therapy.

THE GOVERNMENT'S MAC PLAN—TWO STANDARDS OF HEALTH CARE

In 1973 Secretary of Health, Education and Welfare Caspar Weinberger revealed a new government approach to containing prescription drug costs. Now known as the MAC program (for "maximum allowable cost"), it governs all federally funded health care programs—Medicaid among them—setting limits for reimbursement to the pharmacist for many prescription drugs, based on government estimates of their acquisition cost. However, the government's methods for establishing these prices have been both confusing and controversial. Unreasonably low reimbursement levels have been set for pharmacies, leading to the purchase of the cheapest possible generics in order to stay within the acquisition costs dictated.

Even in the case of brand-name drugs, certain products are reimbursed at levels based on buying very large quantities and dealing directly with the manufacturer. Unfortunately, a significant percentage of pharmacies are not able to purchase at this discount and so may lose up to 25 percent of their cost on a drug product by dispensing it under the MAC program.

Preoccupation with price has also made price the overriding factor in determining which drugs the government will pay for. The MAC reimbursement method, by dictating which manufacturers' products can be dispensed, removes the pharmacist's product selection expertise from the equation. Patients have no assurance of getting the best generic products available.

As with the insurance companies, the government may not be taking into account the eventual effect of therapeutic failures due to substandard drugs and/or the ultimate cost of extended health care. If a given generic does not perform properly, the physician may withdraw that drug, placing the patient on a new product. This would generate two separate prescriptions, which the government must pay for, when one intelligently chosen drug might have done the job immediately.

Add to this possibility that the patient will need to return to the doctor for rediagnosis, possibly be hospitalized, suffer additionally, and in some cases even die, and the original concept of the cheapest possible drug begins to lose some of its appeal.

The MAC program is in danger of creating two classes of patient, if it has not already done so: those who can pay, getting the full benefit of the pharmacist's expertise in selecting a quality drug based on determinants other than cost alone; and those who must submit to the choices made for them in Washington by bureaucrats with only one objective in mind— economy.

THE HOSPITAL DRUG FORMULARY SYSTEM

Economy can be served in the dispensing of prescription drugs without the result being that patients have no choice but to rely on the cheapest formulations available. One example of how this can be done is provided by the drug formulary system used by most hospitals, which is truly a marvel of efficiency. The hospital drug formulary system makes wide use of generic drugs and yet provides an economical way of consistently delivering quality drug products.

Individual formularies (drug lists that include medications stocked by the hospital pharmacy) are arrived at by a committee usually composed of doctors, pharmacists, and nurses. The committee, commonly called the Formulary and Therapeutics Committee, decides on appropriate drugs for various conditions with as little duplication as possible and with an eye to the lowest feasible prices. It may review the gamut of drug products on the market, selecting those the committee doctors have found most effective and that may be judged safest, according to either personal experience or published literature.

One reason for the overwhelming success of the hospital formulary system is that all members of the hospital care team have been responsible for its development and are in agreement as to its therapeutic aims. Rather than being imposed on physician and pharmacist, these guidelines are the result of everyone's input.

With regard to the actual drugs purchased by the hospital, the pharmacist is generally the professional responsible for product evaluation and procurement. In choosing a manufacturer of a generic product, he or she consults available literature, state laws where applicable, and the status of FDA certification of any prospective drug.

Since many hospitals purchase on a much larger scale than private pharmacies (not counting chains), competitive bidding is often used as a means of getting the lowest possible price. But this can have another, even more important implication. Since a generic drug is purchased in vast quantities from a single, low-bidding supplier, this ensures that once they are stabilized on a particular generic, patients are assured of a continued predictable response; there are unlikely to be substitutions midway through treatment. It doesn't matter so much which generic manufacturer is selected, so long as the same one's product is used each time the prescription is refilled.

Thus the hospital formulary system is ideal in achieving two very important goals: It promotes rational drug therapy by controlling the alternatives available; and it holds down drug costs, keeping inventory to a minimum by avoiding duplication and often purchasing by competitive bidding.

COMPETITIVE BIDDING

In an effort to obtain the lowest possible prices for drugs used in the military, the Veteran's Administration, state and local government programs, and most hospitals, purchases are usually determined by competitive bidding. Products must meet the quality standards set by the purchaser.

Competitive bidding naturally allows for economy of scale. There have at times been complaints that some municipalities are able to purchase at lower prices than others. New York has been singled out as receiving preferential treatment by bidders. But further investigation shows that prices are almost always determined by the quantities purchased. Because New York buys more than the next twenty cities combined, it comes as no surprise that it is able to purchase more cheaply.

The bidding procedure itself is often poorly understood and misinterpreted by many of those who are concerned with the generic drug issue. Nearly all institutions, be they hospitals, the armed forces , or local governments, require that all bids be solicited on a generic name basis, with reference made to certain minimum acceptable standards when specifications for each drug are published. These vary from institution to institution. They may be USP/NF standards or, as discussed in Assuring Quality of Drugs in the case of the Department of Defense, even more stringent.

In many cases, given the huge quantities being bid for, brand-name drugs can wind up being sold as cheaply as generics. And with the failure of many smaller firms to qualify as suppliers to the military, it is not surprising to find that a large percentage of the drugs purchased "generically" for the armed forces are actually brand-name products.

The generic industry often advertises that when the president or a senator gets sick and is treated at Walter Reed Army Hospital or Bethesda

Naval Hospital, he or she is given drugs that have been purchased generically. The argument, of course, is that if these are good enough for the president and other high public officials, they are certainly of sufficient quality for the general public. If the same quality checks were universally applied as the military uses, this would indeed be true of all generics. But in real life they aren't, and these public figures are more often than not in fact receiving brand-name medication.

FIVE

YOUR DOCTOR, YOUR PHARMACIST, AND YOUR PRESCRIPTION

When it comes to the selection of the medication you will use to treat or regulate a health condition, the decision must be made in consultation with both your doctor and your pharmacist. They are the professionals whose knowledge of drug therapy and drug behavior in the human body you must rely on; you do not have the necessary training to make treatment and dosage decisions. But you are an integral part of the health care equation, and you both can and should have some voice in deciding what drugs you use.

The key to playing an active, constructive role in your own treatment is to recognize that there are choices and to determine which are best for you, both therapeutically and economically. It means knowing what choices your doctor or pharmacist is committing you to in the selection of drugs and why. It means asking questions and making your preference known with respect to how a prescription is written and filled.

WRITING THE PRESCRIPTION

Almost two-thirds of all physician visits result in a prescription being written for the patient. It averages out to about 1.7 prescriptions per visit. But how much do doctors really know about the chemical entities they commit their patients to using?

Medical schools in the United States do not offer any formal course in pharmacology—the study of drugs and their uses—beyond the second year of training. This, unfortunately, is woefully inadequate to afford a complete understanding of drug products. The economics of drug prescribing is rarely, if ever, touched upon.

One reason may be that those who are responsible for teaching pharmacology are rarely involved in the actual practice of medicine. They are primarily academics with a thorough book knowledge of the subject but little if any experience in administering drugs to human subjects. They convey an abstract view of pharmacology, devoid of the practical realities of everyday medical practice, including the cost effectiveness of comparative drug therapies.

In clinical training, where most of a physician's real knowledge of drugs is learned, there is no in-depth study of how drugs are developed, how their chemical structures relate to their effectiveness as drug products, or how changes in their configuration can alter their performance. Most new drugs marketed today are "me too" products, nothing more than slight variations of drugs already on the market. An understanding of the chemical structure of drugs would be invaluable for immediately gauging the true worth of these more expensive versions of existing products. Physicians are rarely sufficiently trained to recognize that these products may have no inherent benefits over drugs that are already established in the marketplace.

Most of the emphasis in today's medical school curricula is placed on learning to diagnose. The prevailing attitude seems to be that once an accurate diagnosis has been made, the physician can learn about the course of drug treatment from various available reference sources.

Unfortunately, two of the most readily accessible sources of information, the *Physicians' Desk Reference* and drug company sales representatives, are biased in their presentation of data. Major drug companies wage expensive and extensive advertising campaigns directed toward "educating" the physician. But in relying on these research-oriented pharmaceutical giants with their sophisticated sales forces and literature, doctors get a one-sided presentation of the use and attributes of drug products. The truth is, many physicians take at face value the information they receive through sales reps and drug advertisements in their professional publications. It has been estimated that the drug industry spends about $3,000 per practicing physician in the United States for drug advertising and promotion. All this is aimed at a group that neither takes nor pays for the product.

The *Physicians' Desk Reference* is one of the most widely used sources of information for prescribers. It used to be written so as to highlight the favorable aspects of the drugs listed. This was because, to appear in this publication, a very high fee was charged to the drug company. In effect, each listing was an advertisement. However, the Food and Drug Administration stepped in to put a stop to this blatantly biased presentation of drug information, and the data now contained in the *PDR* is practically identical to the inserts included with each prescription drug package.

Because of the prohibitive cost connected with listings in the *PDR*, very few generic drug firms can afford to have their products appear. This in effect creates a situation in which most of the space is dominated by products manufactured by the large research-oriented pharmaceutical houses. When physicians refer to the *PDR* for drug information, they are being influenced in favor of the more expensive brand-name drugs, since this is all they generally see listed. The law does require the generic names to be given for each product, but the index emphasizes brand names, thus perpetuating the bias in favor of expensive proprietary products.

All advertising and promotion to the medical community uses brand names, with the result that prescribers become familiar primarily with names identified with particular drug manufacturers. (These names tend to be shorter and easier to remember than generic titles.) The result is that physicians get in the habit of prescribing by brand names. This advertising and promotion strategy has proved enormously successful in influencing the prescription-writing habits of generations of physicians. Introduction of a generic equivalent must overcome a virtually built-in resistance to change on the part of many doctors.

Adding to the influence of a brand-name bias is the reference material doctors are provided by drug companies. The major pharmaceutical houses regularly offer physicians research grants, consultation fees, fellowships, and/or personal favors. In some cases the effect can be to double a doctor's annual income. In each case the tendency is to prompt a positive reaction to the drug company and its products. When it comes to contemplating regulation of these industry practices, many doctors find themselves in an awkward position.

Besides all this, it is common for doctors to have a certain bias in favor of research-oriented pharmaceutical houses anyway. The groundwork for this is often laid in medical school—the big drug companies routinely provide money to the schools for research. Thus these companies are first introduced to the prospective doctor in a favorable light. This association is reinforced and continued by school faculty members who may be retained by these firms to evaluate products and otherwise act as consultants. (They may even be stockholders of these pharmaceutical houses.)

All these influences, coupled with even more direct approaches like giving away free medical instruments and doctor's bags to medical students, produce physicians who are favorably disposed to products from these companies. Doctors may tend to see generic drugs as a threat to the research and development money spent by the large pharmaceutical companies to develop new drugs in the future.

The conclusion of a report entitled "Physicians as Obstacles to Drug Product Selection by Community Pharmacists"[*] submitted to the National

* By John T. Cirn and Dennis K. Helling under a grant from the National Center for Health Services Research, July 1982.

Center for Health Services Research summarizes current prevalent attitudes in the medical profession.

There is clearly a need for much greater sophistication by physicians in their understanding of the structure, quality control processes, marketing practices, and research and development activities of the pharmaceutical industry. In response to interview questions on drug firms, nearly all the physicians in our sample indicated considerable confidence in the "big-name" labelers of brand-name products, but they were decidedly inarticulate in providing rational grounds for their assumptions about the trustworthiness of certain firms. Indeed, many physicians, after indicating their loyalties to brand-name firms, candidly admitted to the poverty of their factual basis. Prescribers' willingness to allow substitution may be in part a function of their assumptions about the manufacturing processes and other attributes of drug firms and about the propriety of the innovator firms earning large profits to support research and detailing. It is imperative, therefore, that physicians—both those in practice and those in training—receive exposure to: (a) valid criteria for the comparative evaluation of drug firms; (b) more factual information on how various brand-name and generic firms measure up according to these criteria; (c) the arguments in favor of alternative means by which our society can support pharmaceutical research and development and the dissemination of prescribing information; and (d) information on the price differentials among various brands of drug products. We can also add our voices to the growing clamor in favor of greater emphasis in medical schools and teaching hospitals on economic factors in clinical decision-making. . . .

Medical educational programs that make a point of referring to drugs by their generic names may turn out prescribers who find generic names easier to remember and use than physicians who have been schooled primarily in brand names, and this may lead to more generically written prescriptions of lower-cost equivalents.

The average physician office visit has been estimated to last fifteen minutes. In this time the doctor must listen to the patient's complaints, conduct an examination, attempt a diagnosis, define a course of treatment, write the patient a prescription, explain something about how the medication is to be used, and discuss possible side effects or precautions. If a discussion of generic substitution is added to all this—and many physicians are poorly equipped to explain generic substitution—it would put yet another burden on the already compressed sequence of events comprising the average office visit.

Why Prescribing by Generic Name Is Not Best

A doctor may prescribe a drug using one of two names—its brand name or its generic designation. If the brand name is chosen but the doctor indicates that a generic substitute is acceptable (the methods for accomplishing this are discussed for each state in Appendix A), the generic that the pharmacist dispenses must be certified as bioequivalent to the brand-name product.

If, on the other hand, the doctor writes the prescription generically, the bioequivalency issue has effectively been sidestepped. By calling for the drug by its generic name, no equivalence to the brand-name product is legally implied. For example, the state of New Jersey, in its rules and regulations governing the methods of drug substitution to be employed by the pharmacist, states that its list of bioequivalent generic drug products "does not apply to generically written prescriptions. Pharmacists may continue to use any manufacturer or distributor to fill a generically written prescription." Most states address this issue in a similar manner or do not deal with it at all, leaving the situation open to individual interpretation.

There is a large contingent of professionals, both in pharmacy and in medicine, who believes that prescribing solely by generic name would eliminate confusion and counteract the pharmaceutical giants' advertising and promotional efforts influencing doctors' judgment in prescribing effective drug therapy. This may be a dangerous trend, because it is then no longer necessary for the generic to be certified as bioequivalent to the brand-name original, a drug with generally known effectiveness.

When your doctor designates a drug only by its generic name, he or she is no longer holding up the brand-name product as a model for comparison. There is no implication that your doctor expects the generic's action to mimic in every way the bioavailability of the original. As long as the generic that is indicated is manufactured and made available to pharmacists in your state, it can be dispensed to you. If, for example, your doctor writes you a prescription for hydrochlorothiazide (a diuretic), that is a generic name. There is no implicit comparison to the brand-name counterparts HydroDIURIL, Esidrix, or Oretic.

Prescriptions written in a strictly generic manner will often excuse the pharmacist from the requirement of referring to a state formulary of acceptable or unacceptable generic substitutes for brand-name products. That is why you should be concerned if your doctor gives you a generically written prescription. Ask for a brand-name drug to be indicated on the prescription. Many physicians are probably not even aware of the implications of designating drugs by generic name only. Their true intention is almost certainly to prescribe a product that is up to the standards of brand-name performance they are familiar with.

As additional insurance, check the entry for the generic drug you receive against the list of FDA-Approved Bioequivalent Manufacturers in THE GUIDE TO GENERIC DRUGS.

GETTING ACQUAINTED WITH
WHAT YOUR PHARMACIST CAN DO

The pharmacist is perhaps one of the least understood of all the professionals working in today's health care system.

Before most drug dosage forms came premanufactured, pharmacists were compounders of medications, fashioning pills, capsules, suppositories, ointments, creams, and the like. Today, with most drugs dispensed in the same form in which they come to the pharmacist, the emphasis has shifted from actual formulation to drug education. Side effects, precautions, uses of drugs, and how they interact with food and other drugs has become a major area of study in today's pharmacy schools.

Furthermore, practicing their profession in a retail setting, pharmacists are also exposed to what few others in the medical community have the opportunity to learn—the economics of drug use. Pharmacists are in a position to counsel patients as to the options open to them for generic savings. They can advise when no savings will accrue or when it may even be dangerous to consider a generic alternative.

The combination of professional training as a drug expert and experience gained in the retail setting puts the pharmacist in a unique position to provide a crucial link between the patient and the physician.

Use your pharmacist's knowledge to save yourself time, protect your safety, and give you peace of mind. His or her professional expertise is valuable; don't make your choice of pharmacy strictly on the basis of price.

There are hidden savings in dealing with a druggist you know and trust. That person will know you and your family, your unique needs, possible drug allergies, and medical history. Many of these factors can have a bearing on your responses to the drugs you take, both prescription and over-the-counter. Drug interactions can occur from sources you may never have imagined. Food or other drugs taken at the same time can cause many unpleasant side effects. Your pharmacist can often anticipate these and bring them to your attention.

In the area of generic drug selection, pharmacists have the most knowledge of all health professionals. Their formal education includes two years of pharmacology, pharmaceutical analysis, several years in laboratory preparation of all drug dosage forms, pharmacognosy (the study of medicinal products of plant, animal, and mineral origin), physical chemistry, biochemistry, drug interactions, medicinal chemistry, and many other related courses teaching the processes of manufacturing and testing of pharmaceuticals. Not only does the pharmacist know how drugs operate in the body, but he or she understands how product quality can vary and whether a cheaper generic alternative really is a bargain.

Relying on one pharmacist also makes you a more important consideration, since the relationship you establish is often long-term. That is why you are sometimes well advised to deal with an independent pharmacy rather than with a drug chain outlet, even though chain pharmacies tend to charge slightly lower prices. If a store is owner-operated, you will most likely be dealing with the same pharmacist each time, as opposed to the customarily more transient personnel in a chain store. This is not to say that a chain store pharmacist is any less competent. It is simply a practical consideration in building rapport with a professional you can count on.

Whether you choose a chain or an independent setting, it is wise to have all your prescriptions filled in the same place. This provides you with a kind of clearinghouse where all your prescriptions from various sources—dentist, podiatrist, ophthalmologist, family physician, and so on—can be checked against each other, often by a patient profile system, to assure your safety. It is here that a potential disaster could be avoided by the pharmacist armed with complete information about you and your family.

One of the most frustrating aspects of pharmacy practice today is that with all the pharmacist's training, knowledge, and experience just begging to be used to the benefit of consumers/patients, most people remain unaware of the important service that is available to them. Once the prescriber has selected the proper drug to treat a patient's ailment, it is the pharmacist's counseling that can best ensure getting the best value for your money. Knowledge of the comparative values of brand-name versus generic drugs is a vital part of successful drug treatment. The pharmacist's service, well used, could greatly enhance the quality of medical care.

One reason for this unfortunate underutilization of pharmacists is that too many doctors regard a pharmacist as encroaching on their domain when the pharmacist consults with patients about drug treatment, dosage schedules, precautions, and side effects. Part of this is simple defensiveness; the pharmacist's advice may conflict with the physicians', showing them to be less than all-knowing. Often, when a pharmacist double-checks with a doctor about a questionable prescription strength, length of therapy, or proper use of the drug, the doctor proves unwilling to discuss the issue, to the possibly severe detriment of the most important person involved—the patient. Not all physicians react in this manner, but the behavior is sufficiently prevalent to rate comment.

In certain settings such as hospitals, pharmacists often make rounds with physicians, consulting with them to assure the best course of drug therapy for the patient. They provide on-the-spot information about the best dosage forms of a drug, optimal dosing schedules, any potential drug interactions, or the best alternative choices of drugs available. In the state of California there is at present a program allowing clinically trained pharmacists to prescribe medication and monitor their patients' progress. Although these pharmacists work with patients who have already been examined and diagnosed by a physician, the importance of this is that the pharmacist's qualifications are being recognized by the medical community. This may provide for an expanded role for pharmacists in the future.

A 1983 Gallup poll regarding public perception of honesty and ethics in twenty-five businesses and professions found that pharmacists came in as number two, second only to clergymen. This fact of public trust, together with pharmacists' education and experience in drug dispensing, makes them uniquely suited to counsel the consumer in choosing between brand-name and generic drug alternatives. But most state laws give physicians virtually total control over whether a generic substitute may be dispensed. This places the choice in the hands of someone who really has no expertise in the economics of drug therapy. You can help to correct this irrational state of affairs by attention to what you should know when dealing with both your doctor and pharmacist.

MAKING CHOICES

Before you grapple with the intricacies of selecting a generic drug alternative, you should be aware of the laws in your state. These vary from state to state and cover such areas as:

- which generic products are considered bioequivalent to their brand-name counterparts
- the protocol for your doctor or pharmacist to follow in selecting either a generic or brand-name product
- the degree of control you may exercise over the type of drug you receive
- whether you must be notified before substitution takes place
- how much of the generic savings your state requires to be passed along to you

Many aspects of your state's generic drug laws can have a subtle—some even a profound—effect on the degree of generic substitution taking place. (To fully understand these implications, see Appendix A, which reviews the laws peculiar to each state.)

When you are first considering how best to fill your prescription, you must determine whether a generic alternative exists. You can easily do this by consulting the listings in THE GUIDE TO GENERIC DRUGS. Once you are sure there is a generic substitute, read about it to get an idea of whether it is suitable to your needs and, if it is, about how much money you can expect to save with its use. Percentage savings are quoted, since specific dollar amounts change frequently. (The percentages given are averages.)

In many cases your pharmacist may stock branded generics. These, from the major pharmaceutical houses, will tend to be more expensive than those manufactured by the smaller generic companies, although they are less costly than the brand-name original formulation. As long as a non-branded generic also appears in either the FDA's drug equivalency list or on your state's drug formulary of acceptable products, there is legally no difference between it and a branded generic. In fact, in some cases branded generics are actually produced by a generic manufacturer for a major pharmaceutical house and then repackaged under the bigger company's name.

One excellent way to save money on any drug prescription, be it brand or generic, is to try a small quantity first, before investing in a large supply. This does not apply to antibiotics, since they must be taken for a minimum period of time in the quantity prescribed in order to be effective. It is also not practical to follow this strategy for medication supplied in fixed quantities, such as certain suppositories, vaginal creams, and nitro-glycerine products. But with most medications taken for the first time, it's a good idea to get a small quantity to start so that you can gauge your reactions to it and evaluate any side effects and its efficacy. Although you will pay more per tablet, ounce, gram, or whatever, depending on the drug, in the long run the savings will far exceed any premium paid in the beginning. It is very common for patients to pay for large quantities of a medicine only to learn too late that it is unsuitable for them. Under most state laws the pharmacist may not take back any unused medication once it leaves the pharmacy. This is good policy, since it ultimately protects the consumer, but it can be very hard on your pocketbook, especially considering the prices of some of the newer drug products on the market.

How to Talk to Your Doctor

As a rule, doctors are very receptive to their patients' needs and preferences. In fact, it would surprise most people to know that doctors are probably more responsive to a patient's preference for a generic drug substitute than to a pharmacist's professional judgment in dispensing one.

If you take the time to understand the applicable laws of your state as explained in Appendix A, you can have your physician write a prescription in such a way that your pharmacist, after consultation with you, can dispense either a brand or generic product. This is an intelligent approach, since your pharmacist is the one who can tell you how much money you stand to save and whether a generic alternative makes more sense than the brand-name product. He or she can take the time to explain the pros and cons, providing you information your doctor is just not in a position to have.

State your interest in the possibility of bioequivalent generic substitution to your doctor when he or she starts to write out a prescription for you. So you can investigate the relative merits of generic use, ask your physician to print the drug's name, strength, and quantity in *legible* handwriting on either the prescription form or a separate sheet of paper. (Doctors' penmanship is notoriously poor, often taxing even a pharmacist's decoding skills.) In the interest of safety, it is also desirable for your doctor to write no more than one drug on each prescription blank.

How to Talk to Your Pharmacist

At the prescription counter, ask for the price of the brand-name drug first. Then inquire about the generic price to see if an appreciable difference exists. In some cases, as with certain antibiotics, the savings may be only marginal, since competitive pressures do force brand-name prices down, too, at times.

If, after discussion with your pharmacist, a generic product is to be dispensed, double-check to see if the manufacturers name appears on the list of FDA-approved bioequivalent manufacturers given for the entry in THE GUIDE TO GENERIC DRUGS. *A word of caution:* many generic products are supplied to the pharmacist with both the name of the distributor and the name of the manufacturer; these two are often different. Make sure the pharmacist tells you the name of the manufacturer and does not inadvertently supply you with the distributor's name. This can be very misleading, since the distributor's name will not appear on any listing of acceptable manufacturers.

Regardless of the formulary system used in your state (the usual method of determining which generics are acceptable or unacceptable), if the maker of the drug you get does not appear in the FDA-approved bioequivalent manufacturers list, ask your pharmacist to show you where it is listed as an acceptable generic alternative.

Taking Your Medication

Up to now we've focused on the considerations that go into making sure you get an effective drug at an economical price when possible. But you're part of the final equation, too. Many patient-controlled factors—whether you follow the do's and don'ts you've been alerted to—can affect a drug's performance regardless of whether it is brand or generic. Among these are:

- Should you take a medication with or without food? Some drugs require an empty stomach to maximize their effectiveness in reaching the bloodstream; others must be taken with or after meals to minimize the potential for stomach upset.
- Should you consume alcohol? When taking some drugs you should not drink any alcoholic beverages. That's almost always clearly understood from the directions given for use, either by the physician or pharmacist or on the label, but you should be alert to the fact that some medicinal preparations, like cough syrup, have a substantial alcohol content, too.
- Should you complete the full course of treatment? Many patients have a tendency to stop taking a medication as soon as symptoms disappear. With antibiotics, the bacterial or viral agent of infection may not have been totally routed, and stopping the medication allows them to build up to levels at which the symptoms and illness return shortly thereafter. In order to work effectively, most antibiotics should be taken for anywhere from five to ten days, depending on the product and the condition being treated.
- Have you complied with your physician's instructions? One study recently showed that in the case of long-term illness, compliance with doctors' instructions averaged only 54 percent; other studies have revealed that from 25 to 59 percent of patients fail to comply with their doctor's instructions for taking any medication.

These important factors influencing the effectiveness of drug therapy are fully as significant as most differences among various generic and brand-name products.

WARNINGS

Elderly Patients

It has been well documented that the elderly at times react more dramatically to differences among various drug products than does the younger population. Much of this can be attributed to the normal processes of aging.

The liver, which is essential in metabolizing most drugs in the body, may become less efficient, often prolonging the effects of a medication. Kidneys can lose their ability to filter a substance out of the blood and into the urine as well as they once did, also resulting in enhanced drug blood levels. The inability of the digestive system to utilize the stomach's contents as completely as before can render absorption of many drugs and nutrients incomplete.

As a result of any of these changes, even minor deviations in a drug's bioavailability that might go undetected in a younger person can become meaningful when an elderly patient is involved.

Drug Interactions

In a health care system in which most doctors' visits result in a prescription being written, many individuals find themselves using two or more drugs simultaneously. This raises the specter of potential interactions between medications.

Although this possibility is considered by both your doctor and pharmacist, the use of generic substitutes could magnify the otherwise slight differences in a drug's performance by affecting its interrelationships with other substances being taken concurrently.

Check with your doctor or pharmacist to determine whether changing from brand to generic (or vice versa) could have any adverse effects on other drugs you are taking. Pay special attention if you are receiving any of the following drugs:

- warfarin (brand name Coumadin or Panwarfin), an oral anticoagulant
- digoxin (brand name Lanoxin), a heart pill that increases the efficiency of the cardiac muscle
- various antidepressants and antipsychotic agents
- oral antidiabetic drugs such as
  tolbutamide (brand name Orinase)
  chlorpropamide (brand name Diabinese)
  tolazamide (brand name Tolinase)
- phenytoin (brand name Dilantin), an antiepileptic drug
- various hormonal and steroid medications
- certain drugs used to control high blood pressure, including (but not limited to)
  propranolol (brand name Inderal)
  hydralazine (brand name Apresoline)
  furosemide (brand name Lasix)
- sedatives and sleep-inducing agents
- certain potent antiarthritic drugs, including but not limited to
  phenylbutazone (brand name Butazolidin and Azolid)
  indomethacin (brand name Indocin)

Pregnancy or Lactation

Information concerning the use of most drugs during pregnancy and when breast-feeding an infant is inconclusive or lacking. *The use of many drugs during this time can result in abnormal development of the fetus and infant.* The safest course of action is to avoid taking any unnecessary medications during pregnancy or while breast-feeding an infant.

It is vital that you tell your doctor if you are pregnant, if you plan to become pregnant, or if you are breast-feeding while taking any medication.

THE
GUIDE TO
GENERIC DRUGS

Now that you've obtained a good sense of the variables to consider when making a choice between a brand-name prescription drug and its generic substitute, you're ready to review the available alternatives.

The information provided for each drug in this section regarding use, when to avoid use, and the various side effects possible is not intended to be all-inclusive and should not be so construed. Only the most commonly occurring uses and the most important or frequent side effects are offered. For more specific or complete details, consult your doctor or pharmacist.

HOW TO USE THIS SECTION

Brand Name

While most drugs are marketed by only one brand name, usually belonging to the product's innovator, sometimes a drug may be co-marketed by two or more companies, each drug having a different name. These firms may be co-licensed to market a drug developed by a foreign company lacking an American sales force, or two domestic manufacturers may have co-developed a new pharmaceutical and have decided on a joint marketing venture. It is also possible for a drug, once its original patent expires, to be manufactured and heavily promoted by other big research-oriented pharmaceutical houses under their own brand names. This has the effect of establishing many brand names for a single entity. This practice is especially prevalent in the case of antibiotics.

In this section, under the heading Brand Name, you will find all popular brand names in common use in an effort to distinguish them from the many generic products available.

Dosage Form

Where applicable, the particular dosage forms and strengths discussed for each drug will be identified under this heading.

Use

This category states the main applications for each drug. Many pharmaceuticals are routinely put to more than one use. For example, the antihistamine diphenhydramine (brand name Benadryl) does double duty as a sleeping pill.

If more specific information about less common uses for these products is needed, consult your doctor, pharmacist, or any of the numerous consumer reference books available.

Avoid Use

There are many preexisting conditions that may preclude the use of a drug for an individual patient. Although not the norm, they are prevalent enough and their potential for harm is great enough to warrant special mention in this section.

If any of these warnings apply to you, consult your doctor or pharmacist to determine the suitability of taking that product.

Side Effects

Every drug has some possible adverse effects. These can range from a mild, barely noticeable annoyance to debilitating or life-threatening conditions.

A fairly inclusive listing is provided for each drug under this category, but more detailed information is available from your doctor, pharmacist, or medical literature.

Each drug's potential for side effects differs, depending both on the chemical entity and on each patient's reaction to that product. These factors may play a role in choosing between a brand-name drug or a generic alternative. Where appropriate, this will be discussed under the section Brand or Generic?

Brand or Generic?

Generalizations about generic drugs are not possible. Too many variables affect the manufacturing process, and there can be marked variance in the performance of the same drug as manufactured by different marketers. This has been taken into consideration for each drug being discussed in this section.

If any generalizations must be made, it is that tablets, the most frequently encountered drug dosage form, are probably the most difficult to manufacture. Due to the myriad ingredients and processes involved, it is unlikely that any two manufacturers approach tableting in precisely the same manner. This often makes bioequivalence an elusive goal. Time-release tablets require even more art in formulating and are almost never considered bioequivalent.

Capsules are somewhat easier to manufacture. But time-release capsules offer similar problems to time-release tablets, and the same attitude has been adopted at the FDA, which rarely considers them bioequivalent.

Syrups offer few problems in manufacture. Their production is generally straightforward, the main concerns being how well the active ingredient goes into solution and how to avoid contamination on the production line.

Creams and ointments, while requiring a degree of pharmaceutical elegance to appear esthetically pleasing, are fairly simple in approach and usually have little trouble meeting bioequivalence standards. Again, as with syrups, a primary concern is avoiding microbial contamination during the physical movement and blending of ingredients.

Computing Your Dollar Savings

Price is an obvious concern when choosing among drug products. But prices vary considerably among pharmacies, and it is impossible to come up with a "magic number" indicating the savings to be realized in each case no matter where you live and how you shop. However, by quoting potential generic savings as a percentage discount rather than as a dollar amount, much of the confusion arising from the considerable variation in prices found in store-to-store comparison shopping can be eliminated. Percentages, expressing a ratio between the price of brand and generic, tend to remain constant for a longer time than do specific dollar prices, which become obsolete almost as soon as they are published.

The Equation for Savings.   In order to compare the prices you find at the prescription counter into the percentage savings quoted in this section for each drug, merely plug those prices into the following formula:

$$\frac{\text{BRAND PRICE minus GENERIC PRICE}}{\text{BRAND PRICE}} \times 100 = \% \text{ SAVINGS}$$

Let's take a hypothetical example and use it in this formula.

You receive a prescription from your doctor for HydroDIURIL 50 mg (a brand-name diuretic) and proceed to compare the brand and generic price:

brand name drug—HydroDIURIL 50 mg   pharmacy price $6.00
generic substitute—hydrochlorothiazide 50 mg   pharmacy price $4.00

$$\text{FORMULA:} \quad \frac{\$6.00 \text{ minus } \$4.00}{\$6.00} \times 100 = ?\%$$

$$\frac{\$2.00}{\$6.00} \times 100 = 33\% \text{ savings}$$

In this example the generic drug offers a 33 percent savings over the brand-name product.

Price Fluctuations. The figures used to determine the potential generic savings quoted in this chapter are based on drug *costs* to the pharmacist. Although it is almost impossible to control or predict the retail prices of prescription drugs, we do know their approximate acquisition costs. Wide variations exist in pricing among pharmacies and geographic areas, but costs remain fairly constant.

Many pharmacists seek to recoup profits lost on "giveaway" brand-name drugs by increasing margins on generically filled prescriptions. Since we can never foretell this occurrence, discounts you are offered may not always match those quoted in this chapter.

Do not use the figures presented here as an absolute. They are given as a yardstick against which to measure your pharmacy. As much as a 10 or 20 percent difference from the percentage savings given here may be entirely legitimate. This can be due to the widely varying business expenses the pharmacist must recover via sale of products. Also, brand-name drug prices, which are used as the basis for figuring generic savings, may be abnormally low where you shop, depending on the policy of the particular store or the promotional status of various drugs at a given time. But if this chapter quotes a 50 percent discount as being possible with generic use and you realize only 10 percent, then you should question the pharmacist.

The savings figures here are not intended for a comparison among pharmacies. The calculations are based on price differentials occurring in the *same* store. The dollar gap between brand and generic in any one establishment, regardless of its image as a deep discounter or a full-service independent family pharmacy, will tend to reflect the percentages quoted for the drug listings that follow.

Yes, some pharmacies will be cheaper than others, but, as I've previously observed, bargain hunting for prescriptions all over town can be a way of shortchanging yourself in the long run. By patronizing one pharmacy only, you place your trust in a carefully selected family pharmacist. A druggist who knows you and your family could ultimately save you much more than the simple difference between what a product costs purchased from her or him or purchased from a cheaper outlet. And generic savings can still be substantial with your family pharmacist, but accrued in a safe way that maximizes the considerable benefits that grow out of a long-term professional service relationship.

Note that the prices used to determine the potential generic discounts given here are calculated on the use of "pure generic" substitutes rather than branded generics. Branded generics will usually offer intermediate savings. Prices for them can be expected to fall somewhere between the brand-name price and the generic savings quoted in this chapter.

Surveys have shown that generic prescription prices can fluctuate even more than those for brand-name drugs in various pharmacies. In addition to the many different prices charged by competing manufacturers for the same generic, other variables also enter into the computation of retail prescription prices. Rent, the kind of services offered, different formulas used to determine markup, and the considerable overhead of maintaining a professional staff all enter into determining the final price to the consumer. Many pharmacies use nonlicensed technicians or pharmacy student interns to perform most of the routine dispensing tasks, while other employers insist on hiring only licensed pharmacists.

FDA-Approved Bioequivalent Manufacturers

Each drug listed in this section includes the name of the manufacturers appearing in the FDA's guide to bioequivalent drug products—*Approved Prescription Drug Products with Therapeutic Equivalence Evaluations.*

This publication is the only universally accepted guide to the bioequivalence status of all drug products manufactured in the United States. With numerous supplements issued annually, the approved makers listed under each drug may change. The information in this section represents the latest data available at the time of publication.

HOW TO FIND YOUR DRUG

Many drugs manufactured by more than one company have differing brand names, but only one generic designation can be assigned to a product. For this reason all drugs in this section are listed by their generic name, with cross-references by their various brand names.

If your prescription is written generically, proceed directly to the full information found under that name in this section. If, on the other hand, your doctor has prescribed a drug by its brand name, look for that name in its alphabetical place in the section. You will find it as a cross reference, which will tell you where to turn for a full discussion of the generic product.

Again, remember that the information that follows is not intended to substitute for the advice of your physician and pharmacist. Rather, use it to educate yourself about the questions to be raised with your physician or pharmacist when it comes to assuring yourself of the use of a drug that is both effective and economical.

ACETAMINOPHEN/CODEINE

BRAND NAME:
Empracet with Codeine (Burroughs Wellcome)
Tylenol with Codeine (McNeil)

DOSAGE FORM:
Tablet 300 mg acetaminophen/15 mg codeine (or strength #2)
Tablet 300 mg acetaminophen/30 mg codeine (or strength #3)
Tablet 300 mg acetaminophen/60 mg codeine (or strength #4)

USE:
To relieve pain.

AVOID USE:
If allergic to acetaminophen or codeine or to any related drug.

SIDE EFFECTS:
Nausea; constipation; drowsiness; lightheadedness; dizziness.

$ BRAND OR GENERIC?
There are many FDA-approved bioequivalent generics, assuring a wide availability of products which should perform on par with the brand. In quantities of 30 tablets, the 15-mg(#2) tablet offers generic savings of about 20%; the 30-mg(#3) tablet should save slightly over 20% generically; the 60-mg(#4) strength shows a generic discount of over 30%. If used on a chronic basis in quantities of 100 tablets, generic savings approach 40% for the 15-mg(#2) and 30-mg(#3) tablet and over 40% for the 60-mg(#4) strength. Consult your doctor.

FDA-APPROVED BIOEQUIVALENT MANUFACTURERS:

Tablet 300 mg/15 mg (#2)

Barr	Lemmon
Chelsea	KV
Drummer/Phoenix	*McNeil
Duramed	Parke-Davis/W-L
Halsey	Roxane

Tablet 300 mg/30 mg (#3)

Barr	Lemmon
Boots	*McNeil
*Burroughs Wellcome	Parke-Davis/W-L
Carnrick/G. W. Carnrick	Pharm Basics
Chelsea	Purepac/Kalipharma
Cord	A. H. Robins
Drummer/Phoenix	Roxane
Duramed	Stanlabs/Simpak
Halsey	Towne Paulsen
ICN	Vangard Labs/MWM
KV	Vitarine/Phoenix
Lederle Labs	Zenith

Tablet 300 mg/60 mg (#4)

Barr
*Burroughs Wellcome
Chelsea
Cord
Drummer/Phoenix
Duramed
Halsey
KV
Lemmon

*McNeil
Parke-Davis/W-L
Pharm Basics
Purepac/Kalipharma
Roxane
Towne Paulsen
Vangard Labs/MWM
Zenith

ACETAZOLAMIDE

BRAND NAME:

Diamox (Lederle Labs)

DOSAGE FORM:

Tablet 250 mg

USE:

To reduce eye pressure associated with glaucoma; also as a diuretic.

AVOID USE:

In presence of low sodium and/or potassium blood levels; certain kidney and liver diseases; certain glaucomas; suprarenal gland failure; certain blood imbalances; if allergic to this drug, to sulfa drugs, or to any other related drug.

SIDE EFFECTS:

Infrequent but may include drowsiness; burning, itching or tingling of the skin; appetite loss; stomach upset; nausea; blood abnormalities; liver problems.

$ **BRAND OR GENERIC?**

Generic use presents little problem since slight variation in dosage has minimal effect. Savings with the generic product can approach 50%, making generic use a good choice. Since differences among generics have been documented, generic savings are worthwhile provided that the same manufacturer's product is used with each prescription refill.

FDA-APPROVED BIOEQUIVALENT MANUFACTURERS:

Ascot
Bolar
Lannett
*Lederle Labs
Vangard Labs/MWM

ACHROMYCIN V

SEE Tetracycline

ACTIDIL

SEE Tripolidine

ACTIFED

SEE Tripolidine/Pseudoephedrine

ACTIFED WITH CODEINE COUGH SYRUP

SEE Codeine/Pseudoephedrine/Tripolidine

ADAPIN

SEE Doxepin

ALDACTAZIDE

SEE Spirinolactone/Hydrochlorothiazide

ALDACTONE

SEE Spirinolactone

ALDOMET

SEE Methyldopa

ALLOPURINOL

BRAND NAME:
Lopurin (Boots)
Zyloprim (Burroughs Wellcome)

DOSAGE FORM:
Tablet 100 mg
Tablet 300 mg

USE:

To treat gout and high uric acid levels.

AVOID USE:

If a nursing mother; most children; if allergic to this drug or to any related drug.

SIDE EFFECTS:

Skin rash; hair loss; nausea; vomiting; abdominal pain; diarrhea.

$ BRAND OR GENERIC?

Several generics have recently entered the market since the expiration of Burroughs Wellcome's patent on the brand name Zyloprim. Boots Pharmaceutical, however, has been marketing Lopurin even prior to Zyloprim's loss of exclusive rights. This was possible because the British firm was actually the drug's developer and originally licensed Burroughs Wellcome to sell the product in the U.S.

In quantities of 100, the 100-mg strength of Lopurin should save more than 25% off the price of Zyloprim, while generics can yield discounts of around 40%.

The same quantity in the 300-mg tablet shows Lopurin saving almost 30% from the price of Zyloprim, and generics post savings of over 40%.

FDA-APPROVED BIOEQUIVALENT MANUFACTURERS:

Tablet 100 mg

Bolar	*Burroughs Wellcome
*Boots	Danbury
Chelsea	

Tablet 300 mg

Bolar	Chelsea
*Boots	Danbury
*Burroughs Wellcome	

AMBENYL COUGH SYRUP

SEE Bromodiphenhydramine/Codeine

AMCILL

SEE Ampicillin

AMINOPHYLLINE

BRAND NAME:

Aminophyllin (Searle)

DOSAGE FORM:
Tablet 100 mg
Tablet 200 mg

USE:
To relieve bronchial asthma.

AVOID USE:
Peptic ulcer; if allergic to aminophylline, to theophylline, or to any related drug.

SIDE EFFECTS:
Upset stomach; tension; restlessness; heart stimulation; loss of appetite; nausea; vomiting; dizziness; headache; insomnia; skin rash.

$ BRAND OR GENERIC?
Aminophylline is a generic term, but the product considered as the standard to which all others are compared is made by Searle under the name Aminophyllin (no "e" at the end). Aminophylline is erratically absorbed by the body when taken by mouth, making good tablet formulation essential. In light of the potential unpleasant side effects of this drug and the marginal dollar savings with generic use in small quantities, the brand product is a prudent choice. Generics can be had at up to 40% less than the brand, but savings are only worthwhile provided the same manufacturer's product can be used with each prescription refill.

FDA-APPROVED BIOEQUIVALENT MANUFACTURERS:

Tablet 100 mg

Duramed	Vangard Labs/MWM
Roxane	West-Ward
*Searle	

Tablet 200 mg

Cord	*Searle
Duramed	Vangard Labs/MWM
Roxane	West-Ward

AMITID

SEE Amitriptyline

AMITRIL

SEE Amitriptyline

AMITRIPTYLINE

BRAND NAME:
Amitid (E. R. Squibb)
Amitril (Parke-Davis/W-L)
Elavil (MSD/Merck)
Endep (Hoffmann-La Roche)

DOSAGE FORM:
Tablet 10 mg
Tablet 25 mg
Tablet 50 mg

USE:
To relieve depression.

AVOID USE:
During recovery from certain heart conditions; if taking a monoamine oxidase inhibitor drug; children under 12 years; if allergic to this drug or to any related drug.

SIDE EFFECTS:
Fast heartbeat, other heart irregularities; disorientation; anxiety; insomnia; dry mouth; blurred vision; skin rash; sedation; nausea; stomach upset; vomiting; dizziness; headache; changes in sex drive.

$ BRAND OR GENERIC?
Side effects seem to be less than with other drugs in this category (tricyclic antidepressants); but if there is a preexisting heart condition, the side effects can be much more serious. Being a film-coated tablet, amitriptyline is difficult to manufacture with consistent bio-equivalency. This is important, since blood levels of this drug can vary greatly in different individuals on the same dose, even if taking the same brand. Many generics are now considered bioequivalent by the FDA, although this was not always the case. Endep, although chemically equivalent to other amitriptylines, is a scored tablet (able to be split in half). Other brands do not have this feature and may not be suitable for generic interchange if the doctor specifies Endep.

Elavil is the most expensive brand in all three strengths. Price will be discussed by strength:

Tablet 10 mg Endep can be expected to save up to 17% over the price of Elavil. Amitid should yield up to a 20% savings, while Amitril should approach a 38% discount. Various generic products can be had at up to 56% savings over Elavil.

Tablet 25 mg Endep should average a 20% savings over Elavil, while Amitid should approach 34% off. A 43% discount is possible using Amitril, while various generics can save up to 73%.

Tablet 50 mg Savings with Endep approach 20%, while a 35% discount is possible with Amitid. Amitril should save up to 45%, and various generics should produce savings in excess of 80%.

FDA-APPROVED BIOEQUIVALENT MANUFACTURERS:

Tablet 10 mg

Barr	*MSD/Merck
Biocraft	Mylan
Chelsea	*Parke-Davis/W-L
Cord	Purepac/Kalipharma
Danbury	Roxane
*Hoffmann-La Roche	*E. R. Squibb
Ikapharm	Sidmak
Lederle Labs	Vangard Labs/MWM
MD	West-Ward

Tablet 25 mg

Barr	Mylan
Biocraft	*Parke-Davis/W-L
Chelsea	Pharm Basics
Cord	Purepac/Kalipharma
Danbury	Roxane
*Hoffmann-La Roche	*E. R. Squibb
Ikapharm	Sidmak
Lederle Labs	Vangard
MD	West-Ward
*MSD/Merck	

Tablet 50 mg

Barr	*MSD/Merck
Biocraft	Mylan
Chelsea	*Parke-Davis/W-L
Cord	Purepac/Kalipharma
Danbury	Roxane
*Hoffmann-La Roche	*E. R. Squibb
Ikapharm	Sidmak
Lederle Labs	Vangard Labs/MWM
MD	West-Ward

AMOXICILLIN

BRAND NAME:

Amoxil (Beecham)	Trimox (E. R. Squibb)
Larotid (Beecham)	Utimox (Parke-Davis/W-L)
Polymox (Bristol)	Wymox (Wyeth/AMHO)
Robamox (A. H. Robins)	

DOSAGE FORM:

Capsule 250 mg
Capsule 500 mg
Suspension 125 mg/teaspoonful (5 ml)
Suspension 250 mg/teaspoonful (5 ml)

USE:

As an antibiotic to treat various infections.

AVOID USE:

If allergic to penicillin and to related drugs.

SIDE EFFECTS:

Nausea; vomiting; diarrhea; skin reactions; mouth and tongue irritations; black "hairy" tongue.

$ BRAND OR GENERIC?

Some savings are possible with generic use, but you may be able to get a brand product just as cheaply. It pays to check the price with this drug, since many pharmacies get special deals on brand-name amoxicillin and can sell it almost as cheaply as a generic. Generics can save you over 40% if the brand is not discounted.

FDA-APPROVED BIOEQUIVALENT MANUFACTURERS:

Capsule 250 mg and 500 mg

*Beecham	Mylan
Biocraft	*Parke-Davis/W-L
*Bristol	*E. R. Squibb
John D. Copanos	*Wyeth/AMHO

Suspension 125 mg/5 ml and 250 mg/5ml

*Beecham	Mylan
Biocraft	*E. R. Squibb
*Bristol/B-M	*Wyeth Labs/AMHO
John D. Copanos	

AMOXIL

SEE Amoxicillin

AMPICILLIN

BRAND NAME:

Amcill (Parke-Davis/W-L)	Pensyn
Omnipen (Wyeth/AMHO)	Polycillin (Bristol)
Penbritin (Ayerst/AMHO)	Principen (E. R. Squibb)
Pfizerpen-A (Pfizer)	Totacillin (Beecham)

DOSAGE FORM:

Capsule 250 mg
Capsule 500 mg
Suspension 125 mg/teaspoonful (5 ml)
Suspension 250 mg/teaspoonful (5 ml)

USE:

As an antibiotic to treat various infections.

AVOID USE:

If allergic to penicillin or to any related drug.

SIDE EFFECTS:

Diarrhea; nausea; vomiting; skin reactions; mouth and tongue irritations; black "hairy" tongue.

$ BRAND OR GENERIC?

Some savings are possible with generic use, but with special deals available, pharmacies can often buy and sell a brand product almost as cheaply as the generic.

FDA-APPROVED BIOEQUIVALENT MANUFACTURERS:

Capsule 250 mg and 500 mg

*Ayerst/AMHO	Mylan
*Beecham	*Parke-Davis/W-L
Biocraft	*Pfizer
*Bristol	Purepac/Kalipharma
John D. Copanos	*E. R. Squibb
Drummer/Phoenix	*Wyeth/AMHO
Lederle Labs	Zenith

Suspension 125 mg/5 ml and 250 mg/5 ml

*Ayerst/AMHO	Mylan
*Beecham	*Parke-Davis/W-L
Biocraft	*Pfizer
*Bristol	Purepac/Kalipharma
*Bristol/Canada	*E. R. Squibb
John D, Copanos	*Wyeth/AMHO

ANDROID-F

SEE Fluoxymesterone

ANTABUSE

SEE Disulfiram

ANTEPAR

SEE Piperazine

ANTIVERT

SEE Meclizine

ANTURANE

SEE Sulfinpyrazone

APRESAZIDE

SEE Hydralazine/Hydrochlorothiazide

APRESOLINE

SEE Hydralazine

APRESOLINE-ESIDRIX

SEE Hydralazine/Hydrochlorothiazide

AQUATENSIN

SEE Methyclothiazide

ARALEN

SEE Chloroquine Phosphate

ARISTOCORT

SEE Triamcinolone Acetonide

ARLIDIN

SEE Nylidrin

ARMOUR THYROID

SEE Thyroid, Dessicated

ARTANE

SEE Trihexyphenidyl

ASPIRIN/CODEINE

BRAND NAME:
Empirin with Codeine (Burroughs Wellcome)

DOSAGE FORM:
Tablet 300 mg aspirin/15 mg codeine (or strength #2)
Tablet 300 mg aspirin/30 mg codeine (or strength #3)
Tablet 300 mg aspirin/60 mg codeine (or strength #4)

USE:
To relieve pain.

AVOID USE:
Various bleeding disorders; if on anticoagulant therapy; in presence of stomach ulcer; if allergic to aspirin or codeine, or to any related drug.

SIDE EFFECTS:
Nausea; constipation; drowsiness; dizziness; various skin reactions.

$ BRAND OR GENERIC?
Although no FDA bioequivalence guidelines are published for this product, generic performance should be on par with the brand. In quantities of 30 tablets, the 15-mg (#2) tablet offers generic savings of almost 30%; the 30-mg (#3) tablet should save over 30% generically; the 60-mg (#4) strength shows a generic discount of over 50%.

If used on a chronic basis in quantities of 100 tablets, generic savings approach 50% for the 15-mg(#2) and 30-mg(#3) tablet and up to 60% for the 60-mg(#4) strength. Consult your doctor.

FDA-APPROVED BIOEQUIVALENT MANUFACTURERS:
None

ATARAX

SEE Hydroxyzine Hydrochloride

ATIVAN

SEE Lorazepam

AVC

SEE Sulfanilamide/Aminacrine/Allantoin

AZO-GANTANOL

SEE Phenazopyridine/Sulfamethoxazole

AZO-GANTRISIN

SEE Phenazopyridine/Sulfisoxazole

AZOLID

SEE Phenylbutazone

AZULFADINE

SEE Sulfasalazine

AZULFADINE EN-TABS

SEE Sulfasalazine

BACTOCILL

SEE Oxacillin

BACTRIM

SEE Sulfamethoxazole/Trimethoprim

BACTRIM DS

SEE Sulfamethoxazole/Trimethoprim

BARBITA

SEE Phenobarbital

BEEPEN-VK

SEE Penicillin VK

BELLADONNA ALKALOIDS/PHENOBARBITAL

BRAND NAME:
Donnatal (A. H. Robins)

DOSAGE FORM:
Tablet
Elixir (Liquid)

USE:
To relieve stomach cramps, cramping of the intestines and bladder, and in combination with other drugs to treat ulcers.

AVOID USE:
Glaucoma; liver or kidney disease; urinary obstruction; gastrointestinal obstruction or paralysis; myasthenia gravis; certain problems with porphyrin metabolism; if allergic to any ingredient in this product.

SIDE EFFECTS:
Dry mouth; drowsiness; dizziness; changes in urinary frequency; headache; various eye problems; nausea; vomiting; various skin reactions; insomnia.

$ BRAND OR GENERIC?
This drug contains four different ingredients in very small quantities; tablet manufacture is difficult since consistency is hard to achieve. Any variation in tablet consistency may affect drug performance. The generic product does not represent a large savings, so there isn't even an economic incentive for its use.

The elixir form, while it is easier to manufacture and more reliable in performance, is not much cheaper in generic form, so the brand product would be the best choice here as well.

FDA-APPROVED BIOEQUIVALENT MANUFACTURERS:
None.
The FDA currently lists all brands of this product as ineffective. Bioequivalency ratings await completion of administrative proceedings.

BENADRYL

SEE Diphenhydramine

BENEMID

SEE Probenecid

BENTYL

SEE Dicyclomine

BENZTHIAZIDE

BRAND NAME:
Exna (A. H. Robins)

DOSAGE FORM:
Tablet 50 mg

USE:
To rid the body of excess fluid associated with various conditions; to control high blood pressure.

AVOID USE:
Lack of urine output; if a nursing mother; if allergic to this or to other sulfa drugs.

SIDE EFFECTS:
Loss of appetite; stomach upset; nausea; vomiting; cramps; various blood abnormalities; dizziness upon standing; various skin reactions; headache; muscle weakness or spasm; elevated blood sugar.

$ **BRAND OR GENERIC?**
Used on a long-term basis in large quantities, generic savings can yield up to a whopping 60%. However, the FDA considers this drug to have formulation problems. They do not at this time consider any products bioequivalent and interchangeable. For this reason savings from substitution are only worthwhile provided the same manufacturer's product can be used with each prescription refill. Consult your doctor first to make sure he or she approves of this strategy.

FDA-APPROVED BIOEQUIVALENT MANUFACTURERS:
None.
The FDA considers all brands of this product to have unresolved bioequivalency problems at this time.

BENZTROPINE

BRAND NAME:
Cogentin (MSD/Merck)

DOSAGE FORM:
Tablet 0.5 mg
Tablet 1 mg
Tablet 2 mg

USE:
To control Parkinson's disease used in combination with other drugs; also to treat extrapyramidal (involuntary movements such as tremors and muscle rigidity) symptoms due to certain tranquilizer drugs.

AVOID USE:
Children under 3 years old; if allergic to any form of this drug.

SIDE EFFECTS:
Dryness of mouth; blurred vision; nausea; nervousness; constipation; depression; skin rash; numbness of fingers.

$ **BRAND OR GENERIC?**
Because this drug is taken in relatively low doses (starting at ½ mg) and is increased in very small increments (also ½ mg), tablet consistency is very important. Although several generics are available at savings in excess of 40%, the FDA does not consider any of them to be bioequivalent, citing unresolved potential bioequivalence problems. Consult your doctor.

FDA-APPROVED BIOEQUIVALENT MANUFACTURERS:
None.
The FDA considers all brands of this drug to have potential bioequivalence problems.

BETAMETHASONE DIPROPIONATE

BRAND NAME:
Diprosone (Schering)

DOSAGE FORM:
Cream 0.05 %
Ointment 0.05 %

USE:
To relieve inflammation or itching of the skin.

AVOID USE:
If allergic to this or to any other corticosteroid drug.

SIDE EFFECTS:

Burning, itching, or irritation of the skin; loss of skin pigmentation; various other skin reactions.

$ BRAND OR GENERIC?

This drug has only recently become available generically. Although several companies market the substitute, it is manufactured for them by the same firm, Byk-Gulden. With discounts in excess of 40% for the 15-gm (½-ounce) tube and approaching 50% for the 45-gm (1½-ounce) size, the generic emerges as an excellent choice.

FDA-APPROVED BIOEQUIVALENT MANUFACTURERS:

E. Fougera/Byk-Gulden
Pharmaderm/Byk-Gulden
Savage Labs/Byk-Gulden
*Schering

BETAMETHASONE VALERATE

BRAND NAME:

Valisone (Schering)

DOSAGE FORM:

Cream 0.1 %
Ointment 0.1 %
Lotion 0.1 %

USE:

A corticosteroid used to relieve itching and inflammation of the skin.

AVOID USE:

If circulation is severely impaired; if extensive fungal infection is present; if tuberculosis of the skin is present; if recently vaccinated; if chickenpox is present; if allergic to betamethasone or other corticosteroids.

SIDE EFFECTS:

Burning sensation of the skin; itching; various other skin reactions.

$ BRAND OR GENERIC?

Several generics are FDA approved as bioequivalent. Since individuals respond differently to various corticosteroid creams, ointments, and lotions, it is difficult to distinguish between reactions to brand-name or a generic betamethasone.

In cream and ointment form, the 15-gm (½-ounce) tube offers generic savings approaching 50%. The 45-gm (1½-ounce) tube can save up to 54% in generic form.

The lotion, in a 60-cc (2-ounce) size, can yield generic discounts of up to 46%.

FDA-APPROVED BIOEQUIVALENT MANUFACTURERS:

Cream 0.1%

E. Fougera/Byk-Gulden   T. J. Roaco
Lemmon   Savage/Byk-Gulden
NMC   *Schering
Pharmaderm/Byk-Gulden   Thames

Ointment 0.1 %

E. Fougera/Byk-Gulden   Savage/Byk-Gulden
NMC   *Schering
Pharmaderm/Byk-Gulden

Lotion 0.1 %

E. Fougera/Byk-Gulden   Pharmaderm/Byk-Gulden
Lemmon   Savage/Byk-Gulden
National/Barre   *Schering

BETAPEN-VK

SEE Penicillin VK

BETHANECHOL

BRAND NAME:
Urecholine (MSD/Merck)

DOSAGE FORM:
Tablet 5 mg
Tablet 10 mg
Tablet 25 mg
Tablet 50 mg

USE:
To restore normal bladder or bowel function when urine is retained or bowel movement is impaired.

AVOID USE:
Overactive thyroid; pregnancy; stomach ulcer; bronchial asthma; slow heartbeat; low blood pressure; certain heart disease; epilepsy; Parkinson's disease; certain circulatory disorders; certain bladder or gastrointestinal wall problems and many other problems of these symptoms; if allergic to bethanechol or to any related drug.

SIDE EFFECTS:

Sweating; salivation; skin flushing; abdominal discomfort; headache; diarrhea; nausea; low blood pressure; gas; asthma.

$ BRAND OR GENERIC?

There is a tremendous price difference between brand and generic. The generic product is generally considered bioequivalent to the brand, with many FDA-approved manufacturers. The generic product is the best choice here and can offer the following savings in normal prescription quantities: in the 5-mg tablet, generic savings can be more than 50%; in the 10-mg tablet, savings are more than 70%; in the 25-mg tablet, up to 80%; in the 50-mg tablet, savings of more than 80% are possible.

FDA-APPROVED BIOEQUIVALENT MANUFACTURERS:

Tablet 5 mg

Bolar   Lannett
Chelsea   *MSD/Merck
Danbury   Vitarine/Phoenix
Glenwood

Tablet 10 mg

Ascot   Lannett
Bolar   *MSD/Merck
Chelsea   Norwich Eaton
Danbury   Sidmak
Glenwood   Vitarine/Phoenix

Tablet 25 mg

Ascot   Lannett
Bolar   *MSD/Merck
Chelsea   Sidmak
Danbury   Vitarine/Phoenix
Glenwood   Zenith

Tablet 50 mg

Bolar   *MSD/Merck
Danbury   Norwich Eaton

BONINE

SEE Meclizine

BRISTACYCLINE

SEE Tetracycline

BRISTAMYCIN

S<small>EE</small> Erythromycin Stearate

BROMODIPHENHYDRAMINE/CODEINE

BRAND NAME:
Ambenyl Cough Syrup (Marion)

DOSAGE FORM:
Syrup

USE:
To control cough due to colds and allergies.

AVOID USE:
Children under 2 years of age; during asthma attacks; certain glaucomas; prostate gland enlargement; certain ulcers; gastrointestinal obstruction; bladder obstruction; patients taking monoamine oxidase inhibitor drugs; if allergic to any ingredient in this product or to any related drug.

SIDE EFFECTS:
Drowsiness; mental confusion; nervousness; nausea; vomiting; diarrhea; blurred vision and other visual problems; difficult urination; constipation; nasal congestion; heart palpitations; headache; insomnia; various skin reactions including sensitivity to sunlight; anemia; low blood pressure; thickening of bronchial mucus; dry mouth, nose and throat; wheezing; tingling, heaviness and weakness of the hands.

$ BRAND OR GENERIC?
Good savings are possible with generic use. Since this is an expensive drug in brand-name form compared to other cough preparations, generic discounts, which can approach 40%, can also be substantial in dollars.

This product has recently been reformulated to conform to new FDA guidelines. With several generics now considered bioequivalent and many more sure to follow, they offer an intelligent alternative. Consult your doctor.

FDA-APPROVED BIOEQUIVALENT MANUFACTURERS:
Bay
*Marion
National/Barre

BROMPHENIRAMINE

BRAND NAME:
Dimetane (A. H. Robins)

DOSAGE FORM:

Tablet 4 mg
Tablet—Time-Release 8 mg
Tablet—Time-Release 12 mg

USE:

As an antihistamine to relieve symptoms of hay fever and allergic reactions, especially of the skin (itching, rash, hives).

AVOID USE:

Newborn infants; if allergic to this or to any related drug.

SIDE EFFECTS:

Drowsiness; dizziness; dry nose, mouth and throat; stomach upset; blurred vision; headache; skin rash; difficulty or pain when urinating.

$ BRAND OR GENERIC?

The recommendations for generic use vary with strengths and formulations. A special situation exists whereby the brand-name product, Dimetane, is marketed over the counter, while generic versions are sold by prescription only. This is possible because only the brand-name manufacturer, A. H. Robins, has sought OTC status from the FDA. This effects a change in the classic price relationship of the brand and generic drug for certain dosage forms. Some formulations are available in FDA-approved bioequivalent generics.

Tablet 4 mg   The FDA has certified many generics as bioequivalent to the brand. It is a plain tablet with no extended release properties, offering a few problems to generic formulators. The unusual aspect of the brand's price relationship to the generic is that the former is sold over the counter without need of a prescription while the latter is available by prescription only. This has the effect of making the generic about 37% more expensive than the brand.

The only possible advantage to generic use is if an insurance plan reimburses you for prescription drugs but not for over-the-counter products.

Tablet—Time-Release 8 mg   The FDA does not recognize generic equivalents of time-release formulations. The same situation applies here as with the 4-mg tablet; that is, the brand-name product is sold over the counter while the generic remains available by prescription only. The difference here is that the generic still saves up to 24% over the brand, despite its prescription-only status. Chronic use of this drug in large quantities could yield savings of over 60%. Insurance reimbursement for prescription drugs would also apply here for the generic, but not for the brand. Consult your doctor.

Tablet—Time-Release 12 mg   As with the 8-mg time-release tablet, the FDA does not certify any generics as bioequivalent to the brand. In normally prescribed quantities, a generic savings of up to 47% is possible. A truly staggering 70% savings can be had if used in quantities of 100, as might be the case for chronic use. Consult your doctor. Insurance company reimbursement for the generic product, which is sold on prescription, might be another reason to choose it over the brand-name drug, which is sold over the counter.

FDA-APPROVED BIOEQUIVALENT MANUFACTURERS:

Tablet 4 mg

Anabolic	Par
Barr	Phoenix
Chelsea	Pioneer
Cord	Private Formulations
Danbury	Purepac/Kalipharma
Drummer/Phoenix	*A. H. Robins
Lannett	Tablicaps
Newtron	Zenith

Tablet—Time-Release 8 mg and Tablet—Time-Release 12 mg

None

BROMPHENIRAMINE/PHENYLPROPANOLAMINE

BRAND NAME:
Dimetapp (A. H. Robins)

DOSAGE FORM:
Tablet (Time-Release)
Elixir

USE:
As a decongestant and antihistamine to relieve symptoms of colds and allergies.

AVOID USE:
If pregnant; if taking a monoamine oxidase inhibitor drug; bronchial asthma; children under 12; if allergic to any component of this product or to any related drug.

SIDE EFFECTS:
Various skin reactions; blood abnormalities; drowsiness; dizziness; drying of mucous membranes; increased frequency of or difficulty in urinating; thickening of bronchial secretions; heart palpitations; low or high blood pressure; nausea; vomiting; stomach upset; loss of appetite.

$ **BRAND OR GENERIC?**
Based on recommendations emerging from the FDA's DESI (Drug Efficacy Study Implementation) review, this product has recently been reformulated by the deletion of one ingredient (phenylephrine). A. H. Robins, maker of the brand name Dimetapp, has now chosen to sell their product over-the-counter, a departure from its former prescription-only status.

Generic makers, however, are still marketing the reformulated version as a prescription product. Since there has been no FDA recall of the old formula, existing stocks may be used up while the new formulation is phased in. For this reason, you have no guarantee of receiving the new products when your prescription is filled generically.

The tablet is designed as a time-release formulation. Time-release drugs, in general, are not considered bioequivalent and interchangeable by the FDA and this is no exception. Even with the over-the-counter status of the brand name Dimetapp, prescription generics still show a 50% savings in quantities of 24 tablets. Consult your doctor for guidance.

In the elixir form, generic use should pose no problems. Several generics are listed by the FDA as bioequivalent and more should soon follow. Even with the over-the-counter status enjoyed by the brand-name product, prescription generics still show a 20% savings.

Remember that if you receive reimbursement for prescription drugs under your medical insurance plan, the brand-name, over-the-counter Dimetapp will not be covered but prescription-only generics should qualify.

FDA-APPROVED BIOEQUIVALENT MANUFACTURERS:

Tablet (Time-Release)

None

Elixir

Bay
National/Barre

BROMPHENIRAMINE/PHENYLPROPANOLAMINE/CODEINE

BRAND NAME:

Dimetane-DC Cough Syrup (A. H. Robins)

DOSAGE FORM:

Syrup

USE:

As an antihistamine, a decongestant, and a cough suppressant to relieve upper respiratory symptoms due to allergy or the common cold.

AVOID USE:

Severe high blood pressure; severe coronary artery disease; in newborn or premature infants; if a nursing mother; if asthmatic or suffering from other lower respiratory ailments; if taking a monoamine oxidase inhibitor drug; if allergic to any ingredient in this product or to any related drug.

SIDE EFFECTS:

Dry mouth; nose and throat; stomach upset; nausea; vomiting; drowsiness; dizziness; headache; thickening of bronchial mucus; various skin reactions including sensitivity to sunlight; high or low blood pressure; heart rhythm irregularities; irritability; insomnia; difficult or increased frequency of urination; diarrhea; constipation; impaired coordination; loss of appetite; difficulty in breathing; wheezing; various blood abnormalities.

$ BRAND OR GENERIC?

The brand-name product has recently been reformulated to comply with new FDA guidelines emerging from the FDA's DESI (Drug Efficacy Study Implementation) review. As a result, all generics must also have their formulas revised to be considered interchangeable with the brand. Unfortunately, it may be some time before existing stocks of generics are used up and replaced with the most current formulation. It may be difficult to know which product you are really receiving.

Both formulations will work, however, and with generic savings averaging about 30%, it is an option worth consulting your doctor about. This product is usually given on a short-term basis; savings are not great unless the product is used for extended periods of time in large quantities.

FDA-APPROVED BIOEQUIVALENT MANUFACTURERS:

Bay
National/Barre
*A. H. Robins

BUTABARBITAL

BRAND NAME:

Butisol (Wallace/C-W)

DOSAGE FORM:

Tablet 15 mg
Tablet 30 mg

USE:

As a sedative or hypnotic.

AVOID USE:

Barbiturate allergy; impaired liver function; disturbance in porphyrin metabolism; certain respiratory diseases; if allergic to this drug or to any related drug.

SIDE EFFECTS:

Slight hangover; drowsiness; headache; nausea; vomiting.

$ BRAND OR GENERIC?

Many generic products are considered bioequivalent to the brand. Stick to the brand products, since this is an inexpensive drug and the savings are only about 10% with generic use.

FDA-APPROVED BIOEQUIVALENT MANUFACTURERS:

Tablet 15 mg

Chelsea	Marshall
Cord	Reid-Provident
Drummer/Phoenix	Towne Paulsen
Halsey	*Wallace/C-W
Lannett	West-Ward
Lemmon	

Tablet 30 mg

CM Bundy	Marshall
Chelsea	Reid-Provident
Cord	Towne Paulsen
Drummer/Phoenix	*Wallace/C-W
Halsey	West-Ward
Lannett	Zenith
Lemmon	

BUTALBITAL/ACETAMINOPHEN/CAFFEINE

BRAND NAME:
Esgic (Gilbert)
Fioricet (Sandoz)

DOSAGE FORM:
Tablet
Capsule

USE:
To relieve headache.

AVOID USE:
Disturbance in porphyrin metabolism; if allergic to any component of this product or to any related drug.

SIDE EFFECTS:
Rare, but may include drowsiness; nausea; dizziness; skin rash; constipation.

$ BRAND OR GENERIC?
Since side effects are few, some variation in tablet or capsule consistency among manufacturers may not be noticeable.

In tablet form, Fioricet is the most expensive alternative. Esgic saves about 18%, while generic discounts should approach 70%.

Fioricet is not available as a capsule. This leaves Esgic as the most expensive, with generics saving as much as 50%.

FDA-APPROVED BIOEQUIVALENT MANUFACTURERS:

Tablet

DM Graham
*Gilbert
Quantum
*Sandoz

Capsule

DM Graham
*Gilbert

BUTALBITAL/ASPIRIN/CAFFEINE

BRAND NAME:

Fiorinal (Sandoz)

DOSAGE FORM:

Tablet

Capsule

USE:

To relieve headache.

AVOID USE:

Disturbances in porphyrin metabolism; if allergic to any component of this product or to any related drug.

SIDE EFFECTS:

Rare, but may include drowsiness; nausea; dizziness; skin rash; constipation.

$ BRAND OR GENERIC?

Many generic products are considered bioequivalent to the brand. Since side effects are rare, some variation in tablet consistency among manufacturers may not be noticeable. If used on a short-term basis, there is not enough savings to warrant generic use. If used long-term, the generic is a good alternative, offering savings of up to 40%. Consult your doctor.

FDA-APPROVED BIOEQUIVALENT MANUFACTURERS:

Note: On November 4, 1983, the FDA removed from its approved list all products in this category containing phenacetin. Only those companies shown here have been approved in their new formulation. Sandoz, the brand-name manufacturer, was not among these companies at the time of this writing.

Tablet

Boots	Purepac/Kalipharma
Chelsea	Zenith
Cord	

Capsule

None

BUTAZOLIDAN

SEE Phenylbutazone

BUTISOL

SEE Butabarbital

CAFERGOT

SEE Ergotamine/Caffeine

CARAMIPHEN/PHENYLPROPANOLAMINE

BRAND NAME:
Tuss-Ornade (SK & F)

DOSAGE FORM:
Capsule—Time-Release
Liquid

USE:
As a cough suppressant and decongestant to relieve symptoms of the common cold.

AVOID USE:
Severe high blood pressure; bronchial asthma; certain heart disease; children under 15 pounds or under 6 months of age (applies to the liquid); children under 12 years old (applies to the capsule); if taking a monoamine oxidase inhibitor drug; if allergic to either ingredient in this product or to any related drugs.

SIDE EFFECTS:
Nausea; upset stomach; dizziness; drowsiness; rapid heartbeat; difficulty in urinating.

$ BRAND OR GENERIC?
This product is exempt from the FDA's bioequivalency approval process by a special court order. Using guidelines the FDA applies to other products, the

time-release capsule would not be bioequivalent in generic form, since all time-release products are considered to be inequivalent.

While not considered equivalent generically, the capsule can save up to 50%. Its use is worth consulting your doctor about.

The liquid poses no problem to bioequivalence for generics. It offers savings of up to 47% over the brand and would be the option to follow. Generic performance should be on par with the brand, even though the FDA has not been able to publish ratings on the various products available.

FDA-APPROVED BIOEQUIVALENT MANUFACTURERS:
   None

CARISOPRODOL

BRAND NAME:
   Rela (Schering)
   Soma (Wallace/C-W)

DOSAGE FORM:
   Tablet 350 mg

USE:
   As a muscle relaxant.

AVOID USE:
   Disturbances in porphyrin metabolism; children under 12 years; if allergic to this drug, to meprobamate or to any other related drug.

SIDE EFFECTS:
   Drowsiness; dizziness and dizziness upon standing; headache; various skin reactions; loss of coordination; depression; agitation; insomnia; nausea; vomiting; stomach upset; fast heartbeat; flushing of the face; hiccup; fainting.

$ BRAND OR GENERIC?
   Variation in dosage among different manufacturers is not likely to be noticeable. Several generic products are considered bioequivalent to the brand. Consult your doctor. Savings of up to 60% are possible with generic use. Both brand-name products are comparable in cost.

FDA-APPROVED BIOEQUIVALENT MANUFACTURERS:
   Bolar
   Chelsea
   Danbury
   *Schering
   *Wallace/C-W

CERESPAN

SEE Papaverine

CHLORAL HYDRATE

BRAND NAME:
Noctec (E. R. Squibb)

DOSAGE FORM:
Capsule 500 mg
Syrup 500 mg/5 ml

USE:
To induce sleep.

AVOID USE:
Liver and kidney problems; severe heart disease; certain stomach problems; if allergic to this drug or to any related drug.

SIDE EFFECTS:
Stomach upset; various skin reactions; unpleasant aftertaste; hangover; certain blood abnormalities; nausea; vomiting; diarrhea.

$ BRAND OR GENERIC?
Generic products are generally considered interchangeable with the brand. Stick to the brand product in both capsule and syrup, since this is an inexpensive drug. In capsule form there is a small savings of up to 20% possible with generic use. The syrup offers no appreciable savings in the generic form.

FDA-APPROVED BIOEQUIVALENT MANUFACTURERS:
Since this is a pre-1938 drug, the FDA has no approval procedure and does not rate generics for bioequivalency. Many states, however, do approve certain generic manufacturers.

CHLORAMPHENICOL

BRAND NAME:
Chloromycetin (Parke-Davis/W-L)

DOSAGE FORM:
Capsule 250 mg

USE:
As an antibiotic to treat various infections.

AVOID USE:

Should not be used where a safer alternative would be effective; if allergic to this drug or to any related drug.

SIDE EFFECTS:

This drug has many side effects, including some potentially dangerous ones. Adverse reactions include but are not limited to: various blood and bone marrow disorders; nausea; vomiting; tongue and mouth irritation; diarrhea; headache; mental depression or confusion; various skin reactions; a potentially fatal reaction in newborn and premature infants called gray syndrome.

$ BRAND OR GENERIC?

This drug is potentially very dangerous and is reserved for special situations. It is rapidly and well absorbed when taken orally so generic formulation is not difficult. Up to 65% savings are possible with the generic product, but due to the possible hazards with use of this drug, consult your doctor before making any decision.

FDA-APPROVED BIOEQUIVALENT MANUFACTURERS:

MK
*Parke-Davis/W-L
Rachelle
Zenith

CHLORDIAZEPOXIDE

BRAND NAME:

Librium (Roche)

DOSAGE FORM:

Capsule 5 mg
Capsule 10 mg
Capsule 25 mg

USE:

To relieve tension and anxiety.

AVOID USE:

If allergic to this drug or to any related drug.

SIDE EFFECTS:

Rare and few. Possible drowsiness; various skin reactions; lack of coordination; mental confusion; blood abnormalities; liver dysfunction.

$ BRAND OR GENERIC?

This is a widely used drug with few side effects. Variation in dosage has a minimal effect, making this a prime candidate for generic use. Many generic products are considered bioequivalent to the brand, and savings of up to 50% are possible with generic use.

FDA-APPROVED BIOEQUIVALENT MANUFACTURERS:

Capsule 5 mg, 10 mg, 25 mg

Abbott	Parke-Davis/W-L
Ascot	Pharm Basics
Barr	Purepac/Kalipharma
Chelsea	Rachelle
Cord	Richlyn
Drummer/Phoenix	*Roche
Halsey	Roxane
Lederle Labs	SK & F
Lemmon	Superpharm
MK	Vangard
M. M. Mast (10 mg only)	West-Ward
Mylan	Zenith

CHLORDIAZEPOXIDE/CLINIDIUM

BRAND NAME:

Librax (Roche)

DOSAGE FORM:

Capsule

USE:

To relieve "nervous stomach" and various other gastrointestinal disorders.

AVOID USE:

Glaucoma; enlarged prostate; certain bladder obstructions; if allergic to either component of this product or to any related drug.

SIDE EFFECTS:

Rare but may include: dry mouth; blurred vision; constipation; difficulty in urinating; drowsiness; loss of coordination; confusion; blood abnormalities; liver dysfunction; various skin reactions.

$ BRAND OR GENERIC?

Although not officially listed as bioequivalent by the FDA due to review under DESI (Drug Efficacy Study Implementation) program, the generic product offers over a 50% savings. With rare side effects, the safety of this product makes generic use worth consulting your doctor about.

FDA-APPROVED BIOEQUIVALENT MANUFACTURERS:

None

The FDA currently lists all brands of this product as ineffective. Bioequivalence ratings await completion of administrative procedures.

CHLORMEZANONE

BRAND NAME:
  Trancopal (Breon/Sterling)

DOSAGE FORM:
  Tablet 200 mg

USE:
  As an antianxiety agent.

AVOID USE:
  If allergic to chlormezanone or to any related drug.

SIDE EFFECTS:
  Drowsiness; dizziness; skin rash; flushing; nausea; dry mouth; retention of body fluids; mental depression; headache; inability to void; liver complications; confusion; weakness.

$ BRAND OR GENERIC?
  Although the FDA previously approved one generic as bioequivalent, none is approved now. However, with savings in excess of 60%, the generic is an alternative worth discussing with your physician. Slight variation among manufacturers should have little effect on performance.

FDA-APPROVED BIOEQUIVALENT MANUFACTURERS:
  None

CHLOROMYCETIN

  SEE Chloramphenicol

CHLOROQUINE PHOSPHATE

BRAND NAME:
  Aralen (Winthrop)

DOSAGE FORM:
  Tablet 150 mg base
  Tablet 300 mg base

USE:
  To treat or protect from infection by certain malarias; to treat certain amoebic infections.

AVOID USE:
  If certain eye problems exist; if pregnant; if allergic to this or to related drugs.

SIDE EFFECTS:

Headache; itching; stomach cramps; nausea; vomiting; diarrhea; low blood pressure; heart irregularities; visual disturbances; hearing impairments; various skin reactions; blood abnormalities.

$ BRAND OR GENERIC?

The FDA considers several generic products to be bioequivalent to the brand. A huge savings of up to 76% is possible with generic use. With the many potential side effects and risks in using this drug, it is of the utmost importance that its initial use be reliable and predictable. It is suggested that if a generic is used, make sure it is one appearing on the following list. The brand name Aralen is only marketed in the 300-mg strength.

Note: There are two methods of listing the strength of this product: milligrams of the total weight of chloroquine phosphate and milligrams of chloroquine base, which will be a lower number. In this manner, a product may be labeled Chloroquine phosphate 500 mg (equivalent to 300-mg chloroquine base).

FDA-APPROVED BIOEQUIVALENT MANUFACTURERS:

Tablet (equivalent 150 mg base)

Biocraft	Purepac/Kalipharma
Danbury	Richlyn
MD	West-Ward

Tablet (equivalent 300 mg base)

Danbury
*Winthrop

CHLOROTHIAZIDE

BRAND NAME:

Diuril (MSD/Merck)

DOSAGE FORM:

Tablet 250 mg
Tablet 500 mg

USE:

As a diuretic to control high blood pressure and fluid retention; also to treat certain heart problems.

AVOID USE:

No urine output; if pregnant; if a nursing mother; if allergic to this or to any sulfa drug.

SIDE EFFECTS:

Loss of appetite; stomach upset; nausea; vomiting; cramps; diarrhea; constipation; liver dysfunction (jaundice); weakness; burning sensations of the skin;

headache; various blood abnormalities; dizziness or dizziness upon standing; various skin reactions including sensitivity to sunlight; high blood sugar; high uric acid levels; inflammation of the pancreas; muscle spasm; low blood potassium levels; blurred vision.

$ BRAND OR GENERIC?

This drug is well absorbed by the body when taken by mouth, presenting few problems in tablet formulation. Many generics are considered bioequivalent to the brand. This is not a very potent drug and is rarely used in serious situations. Side effects are minimal. Expect generic savings to average about 35% for the 250-mg tablet and 40% for the 500-mg strength.

FDA-APPROVED BIOEQUIVALENT MANUFACTURERS:

Tablet 250 mg

Bolar	Lederle Labs
Camall	*MSD/Merck
Chelsea	Mylan
Danbury	West-Ward
Drummer/Phoenix	

Tablet 500 mg

Bolar	*MSD/Merck
Chelsea	Mylan
Lederle Labs	West-Ward

CHLOROTHIAZIDE/RESERPINE

BRAND NAME:

Diupres (MSD/Merck)

DOSAGE FORM:

Tablet 250 mg chlorothiazide/0.125 mg reserpine
Tablet 500 mg chlorothiazide/0.125 mg reserpine

USE:

To control high blood pressure (this two-component product contains reserpine to relieve the anxiety and tension often associated with this condition).

AVOID USE:

No urine output; if pregnant; if a nursing mother; electroshock therapy; peptic ulcer; certain colitis; mental depression; if allergic to either component of this product or to any related drug.

SIDE EFFECTS:

Loss of appetite; stomach upset; nausea; vomiting; cramps; dry mouth; increased salivation; constipation; diarrhea; liver dysfunction (jaundice); inflammation of the pancreas; increased stomach secretions and activity; dizziness; burning sensations of the skin; headache; sedation; depression; parkinsonism (usually reversible); nervousness; visual disturbances; hearing impairments; various blood abnormalities; various skin reactions including sensitivity to sunlight; flushing of the skin; dizziness upon standing; slowed heartbeat and other cardiac irregularities; nasal congestion; nosebleed; breathing difficulties; weight gain; lowered resistance to colds; high blood sugar and uric acid levels; muscle spasm and weakness; blurred vision; impotence or decreased sex drive.

$ BRAND OR GENERIC?

The generic product is not considered bioequivalent to the brand. It is a dual-component product with one drug, reserpine, contained in a fraction of a milligram amount. While there are possible savings of up to 40% with generic use, any variation in tablet consistency may affect drug performance and therefore the severity of potential side effects. The brand is the best choice. Consult your doctor.

FDA-APPROVED BIOEQUIVALENT MANUFACTURERS:
None

The FDA considers all brands of this product to have unresolved bioequivalency problems at this time.

CHLORPROMAZINE

BRAND NAME:
Thorazine (SK & F)

DOSAGE FORM:
Tablet 10 mg
Tablet 25 mg
Tablet 50 mg

USE:
To manage psychotic disorders; to control nausea and vomiting; to relieve hiccups; to manage certain behavioral problems in children.

AVOID USE:
Coma; bone marrow depression; use of large amounts of narcotics, barbiturates, alcohol; if allergic to this or to any related drug.

SIDE EFFECTS:
Drowsiness; liver dysfunction (jaundice); various blood abnormalities; heart irregularities; parkinsonlike reactions; a sometimes irreversible condition known as tardive dyskinesia; epileptic seizures; various skin reactions including sensitivity to sunlight; fullness and tenderness of the breasts; production of breast milk; menstrual irregularities; high or low blood sugar; dry mouth; nasal congestion; constipation; difficulty in urinating; visual disturbances; fever or lowered body temperature; increased appetite; weight gain; bone marrow depression.

$ BRAND OR GENERIC?

The effect of this drug varies widely from patient to patient even when the same dose is given. There are numerous and serious side effects possible, many being dose related. Bioequivalence of the generic product is not accepted. Savings with the generic can approach 70%, but all things considered, the brand is the best choice. If generic use is contemplated, savings may be worthwhile provided the same manufacturer's product can be used with each prescription refill. Consult your doctor.

FDA-APPROVED BIOEQUIVALENT MANUFACTURERS:

None

The FDA considers all brands of this product to have unresolved bioequivalency problems at this time.

CHLORPROPAMIDE

BRAND NAME:

Diabinese (Pfizer)

DOSAGE FORM:

Tablet 100 mg

Tablet 250 mg

USE:

As an antidiabetic agent to lower blood sugar.

AVOID USE:

In certain types of diabetes (juvenile, "brittle," or if complicated by certain other factors); during pregnancy; if there is liver, kidney, or thyroid function impairment; if allergic to this or to any sulfa drug.

SIDE EFFECTS:

Liver dysfunction (jaundice); various skin reactions; various blood abnormalities; loss of appetite; nausea; vomiting; stomach upset; weakness; burning sensations of the skin.

$ BRAND OR GENERIC?

Some generic products are considered bioequivalent to the brand by the FDA. Due to the price-competitive nature of this drug, many pharmacies sell the brand at a very low price, making generic use less attractive than otherwise. Although generic savings may be as much as 50%, check the price of the brand product first to make sure substitution is worthwhile. Also, consult your doctor.

FDA-APPROVED BIOEQUIVALENT MANUFACTURERS:

Tablet 100 mg

Barr	Chelsea
Bolar	Colmed

Cord	Par
Danbury	*Pfizer
Duramed	Sidmak
Lemmon	Superpharm
Mylan	Zenith

Tablet 250 mg

Barr	Lemmon
Bolar	Mylan
Chelsea	Par
Colmed	*Pfizer
Cord	Sidmak
Danbury	Superpharm
Drummer/Phoenix	Zenith
Duramed	

CHLORTHALIDONE

BRAND NAME:

Hygroton (USV)

DOSAGE FORM:

Tablet 25 mg

Tablet 50 mg

USE:

As a diuretic to control high blood pressure or reduce fluid retention.

AVOID USE:

Kidney or liver impairment; if pregnant; if a nursing mother; lack of urine output; if allergic to this drug or to any sulfa drug.

SIDE EFFECTS:

Loss of appetite; stomach upset; nausea; vomiting; cramps; diarrhea; constipation; liver dysfunction (jaundice); inflammation of the pancreas; dizziness; burning sensations of the skin; headache; various blood abnormalities; various skin reactions including sensitivity to sunlight; dizziness upon standing; high blood sugar and uric acid levels; muscle weakness or spasms; impotence.

$ BRAND OR GENERIC?

Some generic products are considered bioequivalent to the brand. Side effects, although they are potentially serious, are not common. Some product variation from manufacturer to manufacturer is acceptable, since the effective dose can vary widely among individuals. The generic offers up to a 40% savings, making it an excellent choice. Consult your doctor.

FDA-APPROVED BIOEQUIVALENT MANUFACTURERS:

Tablet 25 mg

Abbott	Lederle Labs
Ascot	Mylan
Barr	Parke-Davis/W-L
Boehringer Ingelheim	Superpharm
Bolar	*USV
Chelsea	Vangard Labs/MWM
Danbury	Zenith
KV	

Tablet 50 mg

Abbott	Lederle Labs
Ascot	Lemmon
Barr	Mylan
Bolar	Parke-Davis/W-L
Chelsea	Purepac/Kalipharma
Cord	Superpharm
Danbury	*USV
Drummer/Phoenix	Vangard Labs/MWM
KV	Zenith

CHLORZOXAZONE

BRAND NAME:

Paraflex (McNeil)

DOSAGE FORM:

Tablet 250 mg

USE:

As a muscle relaxant.

AVOID USE:

If allergic to this or to any related drug.

SIDE EFFECTS:

Possible upset stomach; intestinal or stomach bleeding; drowsiness; dizziness; various allergic skin reactions; possible liver damage.

$ BRAND OR GENERIC?

The side effects listed are not common; few adverse reactions have been reported. Many professionals consider this drug to be worthless and not a rational remedy for its intended use. For example, when combined with acetaminophen as a combination product (see chlorzoxazone with acetaminophen), many medical authorities suspect that it is the acetaminophen that gives relief and not the main ingredient, chlorzoxazone.

The generic should be just as effective as the brand, while offering impressive savings approaching 60%. Consult your doctor.

FDA-APPROVED BIOEQUIVALENT MANUFACTURERS:

Tablet 250 mg

Chelsea
Danbury
*McNeil
Par

CHLORZOXAZONE/ACETAMINOPHEN

BRAND NAME:
Parafon Forte (McNeil)

DOSAGE FORM:
Tablet

USE:
To relieve muscle pain and spasm.

AVOID USE:
If allergic to either chlorzoxazone or acetaminophen or to any related drug.

SIDE EFFECTS:
Possible upset stomach; intestinal or stomach bleeding; drowsiness; dizziness; various allergic skin reactions; possible liver damage.

$ BRAND OR GENERIC?
Generic products are not rated as bioequivalent by the FDA, but it is a drug with few side effects. With the difference in price approaching 60%, generic use is an option worth discussing with your doctor.

FDA-APPROVED BIOEQUIVALENT MANUFACTURERS:
None

The FDA currently lists all brands of this product as ineffective. Bioequivalency ratings await completion of administrative proceedings.

CHOLEDYL

SEE Oxtriphylline

CIN-QUIN

SEE Quinidine Sulfate

CLOMID

SEE Clomiphene

CLOMIPHENE

BRAND NAME:
Clomid (Merrell Dow)
Serophene (Serono)

DOSAGE FORM:
Tablet 50 mg

USE:
As a fertility drug to increase the chances for pregnancy.

AVOID USE:
Present or past liver disease or dysfunction; abnormal bleeding from the uterus or from undetermined origin; if pregnant; if allergic to this drug or to any related drug.

SIDE EFFECTS:
Flushing resembling "hot flashes" seen during menopause; abdominal pain or bloating; enlarged ovaries; tenderness of the breasts; abnormal uterine bleeding; nausea; vomiting; headache; dizziness, lightheadedness; increased frequency of urination; insomnia; nervousness; various skin reactions; depression; weight gain; fatigue; reversible hair loss; visual disturbances. The possibility of multiple births and birth defects exists.

$ **BRAND OR GENERIC?**
The FDA has until recently classified this drug as having potential bioequivalence problems. With only about a 13% savings possible with the use of Serophene, it would be prudent to stick with the originator, Clomid. Doctors are familiar with patient response to Clomid. In light of the many potential side effects and the possibility of birth defects resulting from the use of clomiphene, potential savings are just not worthwhile.

FDA-APPROVED BIOEQUIVALENT MANUFACTURERS:
*Merrell Dow
*Plantex/Ikapharm (Serono is this manufacturer's U.S. marketing group and its name appears on the product.)

CLOXACILLIN

BRAND NAME:
Cloxapen (Beecham)
Tegopen (Bristol)

DOSAGE FORM:
Capsule 250 mg
Capsule 500 mg
Suspension 125 mg/5 ml

USE:
As an antibiotic to treat various infections.

AVOID USE:
If allergic to penicillin or to any related drug.

SIDE EFFECTS:
Nausea; stomach upset; gas; diarrhea; various skin reactions.

$ BRAND OR GENERIC?
This drug is well absorbed in the body when taken orally, making formulation relatively trouble free. The FDA considers very few generics to be bioequivalent to the brand.

The 250-mg capsule form has two brand-name products, Tegopen and Cloxapen. Cloxapen saves up to 37% over Tegopen, while the generic can show savings of 44%.

The 500-mg capsule shows similar rankings in savings, with Cloxapen posting up to a 36% discount and the generic showing as much as a 50% savings.

In suspension form, only the brand Tegopen and one generic, Biocraft, are FDA-approved as bioequivalent. Expect savings of up to 40% with the generic.

FDA-APPROVED BIOEQUIVALENT MANUFACTURERS:

Capsule 250 mg and 500 mg

* Beecham
Biocraft
* Bristol

Suspension 125 mg/5 ml

Biocraft
* Bristol

CLOXAPEN

SEE Cloxacillin

CODEINE

BRAND NAME:
None

DOSAGE FORM:
   Tablet 15 mg
   Tablet 30 mg
   Tablet 60 mg

USE:
   To relieve pain.

AVOID USE:
   If allergic to codeine or to any related drug.

SIDE EFFECTS:
   Lightheadedness; dizziness; drowsiness; nausea; vomiting; euphoria; feelings of anxiety or physical discomfort; constipation; itching.

$ BRAND OR GENERIC?
   Available since 1886, this drug is still one of the most reliable and effective painkillers yet discovered. With minimal side effects, any manufacturer's products should be interchangeable. This drug's status as a pre-1938 product exempts it from most FDA regulations. For this reason, no bioequivalence data is published.
   Eli Lilly's brand is considered the standard to which others are compared. It is also the most expensive alternative. If used short-term in quantities of 30 tablets, expect to see generic savings of about 13% for the 15-mg tablet, 36% for the 30-mg strength, and up to 50% for the 60-mg tablet.
   If used chronically in quantities of 100, generic discounts can yield about 10% for the 15-mg strength, more than 40% for the 30-mg tablet, and up to 50% for the 60-mg dose.
   There is no real advantage to using Lilly's brand except that generic alternatives may not be as universally available as the Eli Lilly product.

FDA-APPROVED BIOEQUIVALENT MANUFACTURERS:
   This is a pre-1938 drug and is exempt from the FDA's bioequivalency approval process.

CODEINE/PSEUDOEPHEDRINE/TRIPOLIDINE

BRAND NAME:
   Actifed with Codeine Cough Syrup (Burroughs Wellcome)

DOSAGE FORM:
   Syrup

USE:
   To relieve cough, nasal congestion, and upper respiratory symptoms due to allergies or the common cold.

AVOID USE:

If asthmatic; in newborn or premature infants; severe high blood pressure; certain severe heart diseases; if taking a monoamine oxidase inhibitor drug; if a nursing mother; if allergic to any component of this product or to any related drugs.

SIDE EFFECTS:

Dry mouth, nose, and throat; drowsiness; dizziness; impaired coordination; various skin reactions and other allergic responses; increased sweating; chills; low blood pressure; headache; fast heartbeat and other related heart rhythm irregularities; various blood abnormalities; excitation; insomnia; burning sensations of the skin; blurred vision; ringing in the ears and other hearing problems; convulsions; hallucinations; stomach upset; nausea; vomiting; diarrhea; constipation; loss of appetite; difficult or frequent urination; menstrual irregularities; thickening of bronchial mucus; nasal congestion; slowed breathing.

$ **BRAND OR GENERIC?**

This product has recently been reformulated to reflect new FDA guidelines resulting from the Drug Efficacy Study Implementation (DESI) review that evaluated issues of safety and effectiveness.

While the brand-name product is almost exclusively available as the new formulation, it may take some time for existing generic stocks to be depleted and replaced with an equivalent formula. For this reason it may be difficult to know if you are receiving a generic that truly duplicates the brand-name product prescribed.

But this issue aside, a savings of about 30% is possible with generic use. Although only a few products are as yet considered bioequivalent and interchangeable by the FDA, this is probably because of the formula change rather than any issue of bioinequivalence. There just hasn't been enough time to process applications by all the generic manufacturers.

FDA-APPROVED BIOEQUIVALENT MANUFACTURERS:
Bay
*Burroughs Wellcome
National/Barre

COGENTIN

SEE Benztropine

COLBENEMID

SEE Colchicine

COLCHICINE

BRAND NAME:
None

DOSAGE FORM:
Tablet 0.6 mg

USE:
To relieve symptoms of acute gout attacks.

AVOID USE:
In presence of serious gastrointestinal, kidney or heart conditions; in presence of certain blood abnormalities; if pregnant; if allergic to this or to any related drug.

SIDE EFFECTS:
Nausea, vomiting, and diarrhea are usually evident at full therapeutic dosage. Long-term use may cause bone marrow depression; various blood abnormalities; hair loss; numbness or tingling of the hands and feet; skin rash; fever; liver damage.

$ BRAND OR GENERIC?
Since this drug is manufactured in a fraction of a milligram dose per tablet, quality control during production is essential for consistent performance. Unpleasant side effects are usually a necessary evil of this drug's full therapeutic effect. These factors make it doubly important to receive a top quality manufacturer's product.

This drug is usually prescribed in small quantities to be taken within a 24- to 48-hour period so generic savings are about 20%. But since dollar amounts are small, this does not add up to much. Although there is no product sold under a brand name, Lilly and Abbott, two brand-name manufacturers, sell their product for about the same price and are considered the standard to which others are compared. Since this drug was on the market before 1938, it is not subject to the FDA's bioequivalence evaluations.

FDA-APPROVED BIOEQUIVALENT MANUFACTURERS:
None

This is a pre-1938 drug and is exempt from the FDA's bioequivalency approval process.

COLCHICINE/PROBENECID

BRAND NAME:
Colbenemid (MSD/Merck)

DOSAGE FORM:
Tablet

USE:

To control chronic gouty arthritis when accompanied by recurrent gout attacks.

AVOID USE:

Blood abnormalities; uric acid kidney stones; children under two years; pregnant women; if currently experiencing a gouty attack; if allergic to colchicine or probenecid or to any related drug.

SIDE EFFECTS:

Headache; loss of appetite; nausea; vomiting; diarrhea; various allergic reactions including skin rashes, itching, and fever; flushing; dizziness; sore gums; various blood abnormalities; liver problems; hair loss.

$ BRAND OR GENERIC?

The potential for adverse reactions is great in this two-component product. While the milligram dose of probenecid is high, the dose of colchicine, at a fraction of a milligram, is low, making quality control difficult. The generic is not generally considered bioequivalent to the brand. Although the price difference can be as much as 40%, savings may only be worthwhile provided that the same manufacturer's product can be used with each prescription refill. Consult your doctor.

FDA-APPROVED BIOEQUIVALENT MANUFACTURERS:

None

The FDA considers all brands of this product to have unresolved bioequivalency problems at this time.

COMBID

SEE Prochlorperazine/Isopropamide

COMPAZINE

SEE Prochlorperazine

CONSTANT-T

SEE Theophylline

CORT-DOME

SEE Hydrocortisone

CORTISONE

BRAND NAME:
Cortone Acetate (MSD/Merck)

DOSAGE FORM:
Tablet 25 mg

USE:
As an antiinflammatory drug having a wide range of uses, including treatment of various endocrine disorders; certain arthritic and rheumatoid disorders; various allergic conditions; many eye disorders; skin problems; breathing difficulties; some blood disorders; certain cancers; and several intestinal diseases.

AVOID USE:
Widespread fungal infections of the blood; during use of live virus vaccines; if already receiving large amounts of this or a similar drug; if allergic to this or to other related steroid drugs.

SIDE EFFECTS:
Fluid retention and swelling; congestive heart failure (in certain predisposed patients); high blood pressure; potassium loss; muscle weakness; bone decomposition; loss of muscle mass; peptic ulcer with perforation or bleeding; inflammation of the pancreas; inflammation or ulceration of the esophagus; delayed wound healing; various skin reactions; increased sweating; convulsions; increased skull pressure; headache; vertigo; menstrual irregularities; growth suppression in children; Cushing's syndrome; loss of diabetic control; various eye disorders including glaucoma; increased appetite; decreased resistance to infection; various mental disturbances.

$ BRAND OR GENERIC?
This drug has the least antiinflammatory potency of any drug in its category (e.g., prednisone, prednisolone, methylprednisolone, triamcinolone, dexamethasone) but also has the most water and sodium-retaining potential. For this reason, it is not used as often as other, newer synthetic analogs. But this lack of relative potency also makes slight variations in bioavailability among various manufacturers' products less hazardous.

Since no manufacturer's tablet is rated as bioequivalent and interchangeable by the FDA, it seems inadvisable to use the brand name Cortone when generics save up to 80%.

FDA-APPROVED BIOEQUIVALENT MANUFACTURERS:
None

CORTONE ACETATE

See Cortisone

COUMADIN

SEE Warfarin

CRYSTODIGIN

SEE Digitoxin

CYCLANDELATE

BRAND NAME:
Cyclospasmol (Ives)

DOSAGE FORM:
Capsule 200 mg
Capsule 400 mg

USE:
As an antispasmodic to treat circulatory disorders.

AVOID USE:
If allergic to this drug or to any related drug.

SIDE EFFECTS:
Infrequent, but may include stomach upset; flushing; headache; fast heart-beat; weakness.

$ BRAND OR GENERIC?
This drug's high milligram dose, combined with a wide difference between the effective dose and a toxic one, allows for some variation among manufacturers without seriously compromising this product's effectiveness. Mild and infrequent side effects add to the pluses of using a generic. There is also a tremendous savings of up to 60% possible, making the generic product worth discussing with your doctor.

FDA-APPROVED BIOEQUIVALENT MANUFACTURERS:
The FDA currently lists all brands of this product as ineffective. Bioequivalency ratings await completion of administrative proceedings.

CYCLOPAR

SEE Tetracycline

CYCLOSPASMOL

SEE Cyclandelate

CYPROHEPTADINE

BRAND NAME:
Periactin (MSD/Merck)

DOSAGE FORM:
Tablet 4 mg
Syrup 2 mg/5 ml

USE:
To relieve a variety of allergic reactions, but mainly itching.

AVOID USE:
Glaucoma; urinary retention; peptic ulcer; certain bladder and intestinal obstructions; elderly or debilitated patients; bronchial asthma; newborn or premature infants; if a nursing mother; if taking a monoamine oxidase inhibitor drug; enlarged prostate; if allergic to this or to any related drug.

SIDE EFFECTS:
Drowsiness; dizziness, loss of coordination, mental confusion; insomnia; restlessness; burning sensations of the skin; various skin reactions including sensitivity to sunlight; inner ear disturbance; visual disturbances; low blood pressure; heartbeat irregularities; blood abnormalities; fatigue; stomach upset; loss of appetite; vomiting; diarrhea; constipation; difficult or frequent urination; early menstruation; dry mouth, nose, and throat; thickened bronchial mucus; headache; chills; nasal congestion.

$ BRAND OR GENERIC?
Many generic products are considered bioequivalent to the brand. Although potential side effects are many, few are usual, making generic use a good alternative. Expect up to a 50% savings with the tablet and up to 33% off on the syrup in generic form, making substitution an excellent choice. Consult your doctor.

FDA-APPROVED BIOEQUIVALENT MANUFACTURERS:

Tablet 4 mg

AM Therapeutics	KV
Ascot	MD
Bolar	*MSD/Merck
Camall	Mylan
Chelsea	Par
Cord	Pioneer
Danbury	Sidmak
Drummer/Phoenix	Superpharm
Duramed	Zenith

Syrup 2 mg/5 ml

Bay
*MSD/Merck
National/Barre

DARVOCET-N

SEE Propoxyphene Napsylate/Acetaminophen

DARVON

SEE Propoxyphene Hydrochloride

DARVON COMPOUND-65

SEE Propoxyphene/Aspirin/Caffeine

DECADRON

SEE Dexamethasone

DELTA-CORTEF

SEE Prednisolone

DELTASONE

SEE Prednisone

DEMEROL

SEE Meperidine

DEXAMETHASONE

BRAND NAME:
Decadron (MSD/Merck)

DOSAGE FORM:
Tablet 0.25 mg
Tablet 0.5 mg
Tablet 0.75 mg
Tablet 1.5 mg
Tablet 4 mg
Tablet 6 mg
Elixir 0.5 mg/5 ml

USE:
Most often as an antiinflammatory or to treat various allergic reactions.

AVOID USE:
Widespread fungal infection; if a nursing mother; if recently vaccinated with live virus; if allergic to this drug or to any related drug.

SIDE EFFECTS:
Salt and fluid retention; congestive heart failure (in predisposed individuals); high blood pressure; electrolyte imbalance; muscular weakness; bone decomposition; loss of muscle mass; peptic ulcer with possible bowel perforation; inflammation of the pancreas; ulcer and inflammation of the esophagus; various skin reactions; impaired healing of wounds; headache; vertigo; increased pressure on the skull; changes in menstrual cycle; symptoms of Cushing's syndrome; various hormonal problems including growth suppression in children; decreased tolerance to carbohydrates; diabetic symptoms or loss of diabetic control in those already diabetic; abnormal hair growth patterns; eye problems; increased appetite; weight gain; blood clots; nausea.

$ BRAND OR GENERIC?
A synthetic cortisone, this drug can have potentially serious side effects. Uniform dosage is mandatory as a means of controlling the side effects. Manufactured in very small milligram amounts, tablet consistency is a major consideration. Even though there is a tremendous difference in price of from 50% for the 0.25 tablet up to almost 80% for the 6 mg strength, between brand and generic, the generic product is not considered bioequivalent and contemplated use should first be discussed with your doctor. The elixir form, however, has several FDA-approved generic manufacturers, and savings with them can approach 36%.

FDA-APPROVED BIOEQUIVALENT MANUFACTURERS:

Tablet 0.25 mg, 0.5 mg, 0.75 mg, 1.5 mg, 4 mg, 6 mg

None
The FDA considers all brands of this product, in all tablet strengths, to have unresolved bioequivalency problems at this time.

Elixir 0.5 mg/5ml

| Bay | National/Barre |
| *MSD/Merck | Organon/Akzona |

DEXBROMPHENIRAMINE/PSEUDOEPHEDRINE

BRAND NAME:

Disophrol Chronotab (Schering)

Drixoral (Schering)

DOSAGE FORM:

Tablet—Time-Release

USE:

As an antihistamine and a decongestant to relieve symptoms of colds and allergies.

AVOID USE:

Lower respiratory tract symptoms; if taking a monoamine oxidase inhibitor drug; severe high blood pressure; certain heart diseases; overactive thyroid; if pregnant; if allergic to either component of this product or to any related drug.

SIDE EFFECTS:

Drowsiness; dizziness; anxiety; insomnia; various skin reactions; increased perspiration; dry mouth, nose, and throat; headache; cardiac rhythm irregularities; various blood abnormalities; stomach upset; nausea; vomiting; frequent or difficult urination; thickening of bronchial mucus.

$ BRAND OR GENERIC?

This product presents the consumer with a confusing situation. The two brand-name versions of this drug, Disophrol Chronotab and Drixoral, manufactured and marketed by the same company, Schering, are no longer sold by prescription. Even though available over-the-counter, they are still considerably more expensive than prescription generic products. Drixoral offers about a 20% savings over the identical Disophrol Chronotab, making it the only sensible choice for brand-name use.

Generics, none of which is considered bioequivalent, offer savings of about 30% to 40% in small quantities and from 65% to 70% in 100s. The range of savings depends on whether prices are compared to Drixoral or to the more expensive Disophrol Chronotab.

While the FDA does not usually consider time-release tablets to be bioequivalent—and this is no exception—the benign uses for this product would not make generic substitution harmful. Consult your doctor. If you are reimbursed for prescription drugs by an insurance plan, only the generic prescription drug would be covered.

FDA-APPROVED BIOEQUIVALENT MANUFACTURERS:
   None
   This is a time-release formulation and as such is not considered bioequivalent and interchangeable.

DEXCHLORPHENIRAMINE

BRAND NAME:
   Polaramine (Schering)

DOSAGE FORM:
   Tablet 4 mg
   Tablet 6 mg
   Syrup 2 mg/5 ml

USE:
   As an antihistamine to treat symptoms of various allergies.

AVOID USE:
   Newborn or premature infants; certain asthmatic conditions; if taking a monoamine oxidase inhibitor drug; if allergic to this or to any related antihistamine drug.

SIDE EFFECTS:
   Drowsiness; dizziness; ringing in the ears; inner ear disturbances; impaired coordination; nervousness; insomnia; various skin reactions including sensitivity to sunlight; increased sweating; dry mouth, nose, and throat; headache; heartbeat irregularities; low blood pressure; various blood abnormalities; stomach upset; nausea; vomiting; diarrhea; constipation; difficult or frequent urination; thickening of bronchial mucus; nasal congestion; menstrual irregularities.

$ BRAND OR GENERIC?
   The FDA has not certified any tablet strengths as bioequivalent to the brand. Savings of up to 51% are possible with generic use of the 4-mg tablet, while a discount approaching 61% can be realized with the 6-mg strength.
   In syrup form, the FDA has approved few generics, but their use could save as much as 23% over the brand. Consult your doctor.

FDA-APPROVED BIOEQUIVALENT MANUFACTURERS:

   Tablet 4 mg and 6 mg
   None

   Syrup 2 mg/5 ml
   Bay
   *Schering

DEXEDRINE

SEE Dextroamphetamine

DEXTROAMPHETAMINE

BRAND NAME:
Dexedrine (SK & F)

DOSAGE FORM:
Tablet 5 mg
Capsule—Time-Release 15 mg

USE:
To treat narcolepsy; to treat hyperactive children having attention span difficulties; as a short-term aid in weight loss.

AVOID USE:
Certain heart and circulatory disorders; high blood pressure; overactive thyroid; glaucoma; if there is a history of drug abuse; within 14 days following the use of a monoamine oxidase inhibitor drug; if suffering from anxiety or nervous tension; if allergic to this or to any related drug.

SIDE EFFECTS:
Rapid or irregular heartbeat; increased blood pressure; restlessness; dizziness; difficulty in sleeping; headache; euphoria; dry mouth; unpleasant taste; tremor; hives; changes in sex drive; possible psychotic experiences; diarrhea; constipation.

$ BRAND OR GENERIC?
This is a highly abused drug with great potential for physical dependence. In some states where the diagnosis must be written on the prescription form, it is no longer recognized for use in weight loss and a prescription written for such an indication cannot be dispensed by any pharmacist.

The brand-name tablet form of this drug is inexpensive. Since generic savings yield only about 16%, it is not much of a bargain. For children, when this drug is used for attention span disorders and to control hyperactive behavior, it would be prudent to stick to the brand-name product. This would assure dosage consistency each time a new prescription is filled, an important precaution for pediatric use.

In capsule form, savings are much more impressive. Generally used for adults, where precise dosage control is not as critical as with children, the generic can save up to 35%. The FDA, however, does not recognize any products as bioequivalent in this time-release formulation. Consult your doctor.

FDA-APPROVED BIOEQUIVALENT MANUFACTURERS:

Tablet 5 mg

Cord	Lannett
Ferndale	Lemmon

M. M. Mast   *SK & F
Purepac/Kalipharma   Vitarine/Phoenix
Rexar

Capsule—Time-Release 15 mg

None

DIABINESE

SEE Chlorpropamide

DIAMOX

SEE Acetazolamide

DIAZEPAM

BRAND NAME:
Valium (Hoffmann-La Roche)

DOSAGE FORM:
Tablet 2 mg
Tablet 5 mg
Tablet 10 mg

USE:
To relieve anxiety; to treat symptoms of acute alcohol withdrawal; to relieve muscle spasms; to control epileptic siezures in combination with other drugs.

AVOID USE:
Children under 6 months old; in acute narrow angle glaucoma; during the first trimester of pregnancy; if allergic to this drug or to any related drug.

SIDE EFFECTS:
Drowsiness; lack of coordination; mental confusion; constipation; visual disturbances; depression; headache; low blood pressure; liver dysfunction (jaundice); changes in sex drive; nausea; various skin reactions; slurred speech; muscle tremor; difficulty in urinating; dizziness; anxiety; hallucinations; insomnia; rage.

$ BRAND OR GENERIC?
For most uses of this drug, generics should serve just as well as the brand name Valium. However, when used to control epileptic seizures, any variation in bioavailability among manufacturers could have serious implications. In this case, it would be wise to discuss generic use with your doctor first.

In quantities of 30 tablets, the 2-mg and 5-mg strengths show generic savings approaching 40%, while the 10-mg tablet saves over 45%. Prescriptions of 100 tablets yield higher generic discounts of 50% or more in all three strengths.

Note: Since Valium is one of the nation's biggest selling and most well-known drugs, pharmacies often sell the brand at a discount. In this case, generic savings may be less than those quoted here.

FDA-APPROVED BIOEQUIVALENT MANUFACTURERS:
   None

Although several generic manufacturers have received the FDA's permission to market this drug, bioequivalency data were not yet published at the time of this writing.

DICLOXACILLIN

BRAND NAME:
   Dycill (Beecham)
   Dynapen (Bristol)
   Pathocil (Wyeth/AMHO)

DOSAGE FORM:
   Capsule 250 mg
   Capsule 500 mg
   Oral Suspension 62.5 mg/teaspoonful (5 ml)

USE:
   As an antibiotic to treat various infections.

AVOID USE:
   If allergic to any form of penicillin or cephalosporin drug or to any related drug.

SIDE EFFECTS:
   Nausea; vomiting; stomach upset; gas; diarrhea; various skin rashes; white blood cell suppression; possible superinfection.

$ BRAND OR GENERIC?
   This is a very expensive drug reserved for special situations when more widely used antibiotics are not effective. Available in both capsule and liquid form, savings with the generic can be quite impressive. Consult your doctor. Of the three brand-name products Dynapen consistently emerges as most expensive, with Pathocil and Dycill offering intermediate savings between Dynapen and the generic.

   Capsule 250 mg   Dynapen is the most expensive. Dycill and Pathocil can save up to 33%, while the generic offers a discount in the neighborhood of 65%.

   Capsule 500 mg   Again, Dynapen is the highest priced, with Dycill selling at about a 35% discount. Pathocil can save up to 30%, with generic products yielding a whopping 70% savings.

Oral Suspension 62.5 mg/teaspoonful (5 ml)   With only a few FDA-approved bioequivalent products in this category, the choice is quite narrow. Dynapen, again, is the most expensive. Pathocil can save up to 25% over Dynapen.

FDA-APPROVED BIOEQUIVALENT MANUFACTURERS:

Capsule 250 mg

*Beecham
 Biocraft
*Bristol
*Wyeth/AMHO

Capsule 500 mg

*Beecham
 Biocraft
*Wyeth/AMHO

Oral Suspension 62.5 mg/teaspoonful (5 ml)

*Bristol
*Wyeth/AMHO

DICYCLOMINE

BRAND NAME:
Bentyl (Merrell Dow)

DOSAGE FORM:
Capsule 10 mg
Tablet 20 mg

USE:
To relieve gastrointestinal conditions including irritable or spastic colon and mucous colitis.

AVOID USE:
Enlarged prostate; various intestinal and urinary obstructions; poor movement of the gastrointestinal tract; certain heart conditions; myasthenia gravis; certain colitis conditions; glaucoma; infants under 6 months old; if allergic to this or to any related drug.

SIDE EFFECTS:
Dry mouth; difficulty in urinating; blurred vision; heartbeat irregularities; various eye problems; headache; loss of taste; drowsiness; weakness; dizziness; nausea; vomiting; constipation; impotence; various allergic reactions including skin rash; decreased perspiration.

$ BRAND OR GENERIC?

In capsule form, manufacture is simple and quality control should be consistent. Tablets, although they are more difficult to make, should offer no problem, since both forms of generic are considered bioequivalent to the brand by many states. Side effects, although unpleasant, are not serious. Only a small savings is possible with generic use on a short-term basis, making the brand product a better choice. If used long-term, up to a 25% savings can be had with generic use.

FDA-APPROVED BIOEQUIVALENT MANUFACTURERS:

None

The FDA is awaiting revised labeling and additional information on this product's effectiveness.

DIETHYLPROPION

BRAND NAME:

Tenuate (Merrell Dow)

Tepanil (Riker/3M)

DOSAGE FORM:

Tablet 25 mg

Tablet 75 mg (time-release)

USE:

As a short-term diet aid.

AVOID USE:

Advanced arteriosclerosis; overactive thyroid; children under 12; glaucoma; adverse reaction to any other stimulant; heart disease; high blood pressure; preexisting anxiety; within 14 days of taking any monoamine oxidase inhibitor drug; if allergic to this or to any related drug.

SIDE EFFECTS:

Palpitations and other heartbeat irregularities; high blood pressure; restlessness; anxiety; insomnia; mental depression; headache; epileptic seizures (if already an epileptic); dry mouth; nausea; vomiting; upset stomach; disagreeable taste; diarrhea; constipation; various skin reactions; changes in sex drive; breast enlargement; menstrual irregularities; blood and bone marrow abnormalities; difficult breathing; hair loss; increased sweating.

$ BRAND OR GENERIC?

The 75-mg tablet is a time-release formulation and the generic product is not considered bioequivalent. The price difference between generic and brand approaches 50%, but unreliability of the dosage form would dictate use of the brand-name product. There is a slight difference in price between the two brand-name products, with a 14% edge going to Tenuate.

A 25-mg tablet is also available but used less frequently. Several generic tablets are considered bioequivalent by the FDA and would make more sense to use. In this strength, there is a difference of as much as 67% with generic use.

FDA-APPROVED BIOEQUIVALENT MANUFACTURERS:

Tablet 25 mg

Camall	MD
Chelsea	*Merrell Dow
Drummer/Phoenix	*Riker/3M
Lemmon	

Tablet—Time-Release 75 mg

None

The FDA does not consider time-release dosage forms as bioequivalent.

DIGITOXIN

BRAND NAME:
Crystodigin (Eli Lilly)
Purodigin (Wyeth/Amho)

DOSAGE FORM:
Tablet 0.05 mg
Tablet 0.1 mg
Tablet 0.15 mg
Tablet 0.2 mg

USE:
To treat various heart conditions by increasing the force of the heartbeat.

AVOID USE:
Certain rapid heartbeat conditions; if allergic to this or to related compounds.

SIDE EFFECTS:
Variation in dose can be life-threatening in both under- and overdosing. There is a very small margin between the effective dose and a toxic one. Potential side effects are usually related to overdosage. At normal drug levels these are limited to loss of appetite; nausea; vomiting; stomach upset; diarrhea.

$ BRAND OR GENERIC?
Although the two drugs are not interchangeable, the actions and side effects of digitoxin are almost identical to its close relative digoxin. Digitoxin's effects, however, are spread out over a longer period of time, making slight variations among different manufacturers less critical but still of concern.

But like digoxin, this is a drug given in a fraction of a milligram dose, making quality control during manufacture exceedingly difficult. The active ingredient comprises only about 1% of the total weight of each tablet.

Of the two brand-name products, only Eli Lilly's Crystodigin is available in every marketed strength. Wyeth's Purodigin is not sold in the lowest tablet dose (0.05 mg). Generics are only available in the 0.1-mg and 0.2-mg strengths. This may not always be an important consideration, but in order to achieve optimum therapeutic effects, it may become necessary to make very fine adjustments in dosage. If the doctor is to have confidence in knowing the exact response to minor dosing increments, it may be desirable to stick to Crystodigin.

Finally, although generics cost the pharmacist less than the brand, and in theory this should translate into a 30% discount for the 0.1-mg strength and almost a 50% savings on the 0.2-mg tablet, the chronic nature of conditions for which this drug is taken makes it a prime candidate for very low brand-name prices. Both Crystodigin and Purodigin should sell for the same price.

Before you consider a generic alternative, discuss the matter with your doctor and, if he or she is amenable, check your pharmacy's price first to make sure that savings actually accrue for the generic product.

FDA-APPROVED BIOEQUIVALENT MANUFACTURERS:

This is a pre-1938 drug and is exempt from the FDA's bioequivalency approval process.

DIGOXIN

BRAND NAME:

Lanoxin (Burroughs Wellcome)

DOSAGE FORM:

Tablet 0.125 mg

Tablet 0.25 mg

USE:

To strengthen the heartbeat; as an antiarrhythmic to treat various heart conditions.

AVOID USE:

Certain rapid heartbeat conditions; if allergic to this drug or to related compounds.

SIDE EFFECTS:

Variation in dose can be life-threatening in both under- and overdosing. There is a very small margin between the effective dose and a toxic one. Potential side effects are many and may include nausea; vomiting; diarrhea; vision problems; headache; heartbeat changes; and many other problems.

$ BRAND OR GENERIC?

Because this tablet is made in a fraction of a milligram dose, tablet consistency, which is critical, is difficult to achieve. The brand-name product is cheap, often sold at cost by pharmacies. There is little or no saving with the generic, so stick to the brand product.

FDA-APPROVED BIOEQUIVALENT MANUFACTURERS:

This is a pre-1938 drug and exempt from the FDA's bioequivalency approval process.

DIHYDROCODEINE/ASPIRIN/CAFFEINE

BRAND NAME:

Synalogos-DC (Ives)

DOSAGE FORM:

Capsule

USE:

To relieve pain.

AVOID USE:

If allergic to any ingredient in this product or to any related drug.

SIDE EFFECTS:

Lightheadedness; dizziness; drowsiness; nausea; vomiting; constipation; various skin reactions.

$ BRAND OR GENERIC?

Although the FDA does not list any generics as bioequivalent to the brand, the three ingredients in this product have been around for a long time and should present few surprises to formulators. With a 45% discount possible, generic use is a choice worth consulting your doctor about.

FDA-APPROVED BIOEQUIVALENT MANUFACTURERS:

None

DILANTIN

SEE Phenytoin

DIMETANE

SEE Brompheniramine

DIMETANE-DC COUGH SYRUP

SEE Brompheniramine/
  Phenylpropanolamine/
  Codeine

DIMETAPP

SEE Brompheniramine/
  Phenylpropanolamine

DIPHENHYDRAMINE

BRAND NAME:
  Benadryl (Parke-Davis/W-L)

DOSAGE FORM:
  Capsule 25 mg
  Capsule 50 mg
  Elixir 12.5 mg/5 ml

USE:
  As an antihistamine to relieve allergies, motion sickness, Parkinson's disease, and insomnia.

AVOID USE:
  Asthmatic attack; certain glaucomas; enlarged prostate; peptic ulcer; newborn or premature infants; if a nursing mother; if taking a monoamine oxidase inhibitor drug; if allergic to this drug or to other antihistamines.

SIDE EFFECTS:
  Drowsiness; dry mouth; blurred vision; various skin reactions; low blood pressure; stomach upset; problems with urination.

$ BRAND OR GENERIC?
  Many capsules and elixirs are considered bioequivalent by the FDA. If used to treat a serious condition, such as a bad allergic reaction, stick to the brand, since generic savings are not great. In other, less serious situations, the generic is acceptable and is a better choice if used long-term. The 25-mg capsule can save about 30% in generic form, while the 50-mg capsule can yield up to a 40% discount. The elixir form averages about 30% cheaper for the generic. Consult your doctor.

Note: Benadryl is now sold over-the-counter as the elixir and 25-mg capsule. While this could disqualify you from reimbursement under most medical insurance plans, savings of 30% or more are possible over its cost as a prescription product. This also means over-the-counter Benadryl costs less than most generics, which remain prescription-only.

FDA-APPROVED BIOEQUIVALENT MANUFACTURERS:

Capsule 25 mg

Anabolic
Barr
Bell
Bolar
Chelsea
Cord
Danbury
Drummer/Phoenix
Heather
ICN
Lannett
Lederle Labs
Lemmon
LNK International
MK
Newtron
*Parke-Davis/W-L
Private Formulations
Purepac/Kalipharma
Quantum
Richlyn
Superpharm
Towne Paulsen
Vangard Labs/MWM
Zenith

Capsule 50 mg

Anabolic
Barr
Bell
Bolar
Chelsea
Cord
Danbury
Drummer/Phoenix
Halsey
Heather
ICN
Lannett
Lederle Labs
Lemmon
LNK International
MK
Newtron
*Parke-Davis/W-L
Private Formulations
Purepac/Kalipharma
Quantum
Richlyn
Roxane
SK & F
Superpharm
Towne Paulsen
Vangard Labs/MWM
West-Ward
Zenith

Elixir

Bay
Bell
CM Bundy
C. R. Cenci
Halsey
KV
Lannett
Lederle Labs
Life
MK
Naska
National/Barre
*Parke-Davis/W-L
Pharms Assoc/Beach
Private Formulations
Purepac/Kalipharma
Roxane
Zenith

DIPHENOXYLATE/ATROPINE

BRAND NAME:

Lomotil (Searle)

DOSAGE FORM:

Tablet

USE:

To control diarrhea.

AVOID USE:

Children under 2 years; jaundice; certain colitis conditions; if allergic to either ingredient in this product or to any related drug.

SIDE EFFECTS:

Dryness of skin and mucous membranes; urine retention; flushing; stomach upset; nausea; vomiting; various skin reactions; swelling of the gums; sedation; rapid heartbeat; loss of appetite; dizziness; depression; breathing difficulties.

$ BRAND OR GENERIC?

Except in children from 2 to 12 years, side effects are rare. Many generic products are considered bioequivalent to the brand, and there is a staggering difference in price of up to 65%. Any possible variation in the generic product is in this case more than compensated for by the savings.

FDA-APPROVED BIOEQUIVALENT MANUFACTURERS:

Ascot	MD
Barr	Mylan
Boots	Parke-Davis/W-L
Chelsea	Pharm Basics
Cord	Private Formulations
Drummer/Phoenix	Roxane
Halsey	*Searle
Heather	Superpharm
ICN	Vangard
Inwood/Forest	Wallace/C-W
KV	West-Ward
Lannett	Zenith
Lederle Labs	

DIPROSONE

SEE Betamethasone Dipropionate

DIPYRIDAMOLE

BRAND NAME:

Persantine (Boehringer Ingelheim)

DOSAGE FORM:
   Tablet 25 mg
   Tablet 50 mg

USE:
   To relieve angina pectoris.

AVOID USE:
   If allergic to this drug or to any related drug.

SIDE EFFECTS:
   Few and rare: may include headache; dizziness; nausea; flushing; weakness; fainting; mild stomach or intestinal upset; skin rash; anginal pain.

$ **BRAND OR GENERIC?**
   Although not recognized as bioequivalent to the brand, there is up to a 65% savings possible when the generic is used. Since side effects are minimal, some variation in dose will not result in discomfort. The drug is used on a long-term basis only, so savings will really add up. Buying the generic in large quantities of from several hundred up to a thousand tablets at a time will reap the biggest discounts. To maximize generic consistency, making the substantial savings worthwhile, try to use the same manufacturer's product with each prescription refill.

FDA-APPROVED BIOEQUIVALENT MANUFACTURERS:
   None
   This product is exempt from FDA bioequivalency approval procedures under a special court order.

DISOPHROL CHRONOTAB

   SEE Dexbrompheniramine/
      Pseudoephedrine

DISOPYRAMIDE

BRAND NAME:
   Norpace (Searle)

DOSAGE FORM:
   Capsule 100 mg
   Capsule 150 mg

USE:
   As an antiarrhythmic.

AVOID USE:
   In presence of cardiogenic shock; with preexisting second- or third-degree heart block; if a nursing mother; if allergic to this or to any related drug.

SIDE EFFECTS:

Dry mouth, eyes, nose and throat; difficulty in urinating; constipation; diarrhea; vomiting; nausea; gas; blurred vision; dizziness; fainting; fatigue; muscle weakness; headache; aches and pains; impotence; congestive heart failure; fluid retention; weight gain; chest pain; loss of appetite; low blood pressure; various skin reactions; nervousness; low blood potassium levels; low blood sugar; insomnia; liver dysfunction; acute psychosis (rare).

$ BRAND OR GENERIC?

Since this drug has only recently become available generically, substitution savings are a little over 30%. As more manufacturers enter the generic market, savings should increase. The severity of the condition being treated, as well as the presence of preexisting illness, may affect the wisdom of using a generic substitute. Consult your doctor.

FDA-APPROVED BIOEQUIVALENT MANUFACTURERS:

Capsule 100 mg

Biocraft   Mylan
Danbury   *Searle

Capsule 150 mg

Biocraft   Mylan
Danbury   *Searle

DISULFIRAM

BRAND NAME:

Antabuse (Ayerst/AMHO)

DOSAGE FORM:

Tablet 250 mg
Tablet 500 mg

USE:

To enforce sobriety in alcoholics.

AVOID USE:

Certain heart disease; psychosis; if taking or have recently taken the following drugs: metronidazole, paraldehyde, alcohol, or any preparation containing alcohol such as cough syrups; if allergic to this or to any related drug.

SIDE EFFECTS:

Drowsiness; headache; lethargy; various skin reactions; tingling or numbness of the fingers and toes; various vision disturbances; metallic or garliclike taste; impotence.

$ BRAND OR GENERIC?

Because this drug is taken long-term for months or even years and it is purchased in quantities of at least 100 tablets, there is the potential for substantial savings with generic use. Although the FDA does not consider any generics to be bioequivalent and interchangeable, generic savings can still be worthwhile provided the same manufacturer's product can be used with each prescription refill. Consult your doctor.

Savings on the 250-mg tablet should approach 67% with generic use, while up to 60% off can be expected for the 500-mg generic.

FDA-APPROVED BIOEQUIVALENT MANUFACTURERS:
None

The FDA considers all brands of this product to have unresolved bioequivalency problems at this time.

DIUCARDIN

SEE Hydroflumethiazide

DIUPRES

SEE Chlorothiazide/Reserpine

DIURIL

SEE Chlorothiazide

DOLENE

SEE Propoxyphene Hydrochloride

DOLENE AP-65

SEE Propoxyphene/Acetaminophen

DONNATAL

SEE Belladonna Alkaloids/Phenobarbital

DORIDEN

SEE Glutethimide

DOXEPIN

BRAND NAME:
Adapin (Pennwalt)
Sinequan (Pfizer)

DOSAGE FORM:
Capsule 10 mg
Capsule 25 mg
Capsule 50 mg
Capsule 100 mg

USE:
As an antianxiety agent and antidepressant.

AVOID USE:
Glaucoma; problems with urine retention; in children under 12 years old; if using a monoamine oxidase inhibitor drug; if allergic to this or to any related drug.

SIDE EFFECTS:
Dry mouth; blurred vision; constipation; drowsiness; rapid heartbeat; low blood pressure; various gastrointestinal complaints; increased perspiration; dizziness; weakness; weight gain; fluid retention; burning sensations of the skin; flushing; ringing in the ears; decreased sex drive; various skin reactions; chills.

$ BRAND OR GENERIC?
This product is available under two brand names: Adapin and Sinequan. Although it is not considered a generic, a savings of about 20% is possible in all strengths of the product Adapin. If a prescription is written under the brand name Sinequan but the doctor indicates that generic substitution is permissible, Adapin would qualify as that alternative since it is bioequivalent and offers a savings.

FDA-APPROVED BIOEQUIVALENT MANUFACTURERS:

Capsule 10 mg, 25 mg, 50 mg, 100 mg

* Pennwalt
* Pfizer

DOXYCYCLINE

BRAND NAME:
Vibramycin (Pfizer)

DOSAGE FORM:
Capsule 50 mg
Capsule 100 mg
Tablet 100 mg

USE:
As an antibiotic to treat various infections.

AVOID USE:
In children under 8 years; if pregnant; if a nursing mother; if allergic to tetracycline or to any related drug.

SIDE EFFECTS:
Loss of appetite; nausea; vomiting; diarrhea; irritation of the tongue; various gastrointestinal complaints; yeast infections of the anogenital area; various skin reactions including sensitivity to sunlight; kidney dysfunction; allergic reactions including a worsening of preexisting systemic lupus erythematosis; increased pressure in the skull; various blood abnormalities.

$ BRAND OR GENERIC?
Major savings are possible with generics. Bioequivalence is approved for many, making it a good choice. Generic use of the 50-mg capsule can save up to 35%, while the 100-mg generic is almost 50% cheaper than the brand in both tablet and capsule form.

FDA-APPROVED BIOEQUIVALENT MANUFACTURERS:

Capsule 50 mg

Barr	Par
Chelsea	*Pfizer
Danbury	Purepac/Kalipharma
Faulding	Rachelle
Halsey	Superpharm
Heather	West-Ward
Lemmon	Zenith
Mylan	

Capsule 100 mg

Barr	Par
Chelsea	*Pfizer
Danbury	Purepac/Kalipharma
Drummer/Phoenix	Rachelle
Halsey	Superpharm
Heather	West-Ward
Lemmon	Zenith
Mylan	

Tablet 100 mg

Barr	Mylan
Chelsea	*Pfizer
Danbury	Rachelle
Heather	Superpharm
Lemmon	Zenith

DRIXORAL

SEE Dexbrompheniramine/
Pseudoephedrine

DURAPHYL

SEE Theophylline

DYCILL

SEE Dicloxacillin

DYNAPEN

SEE Dicloxacillin

DYPHYLLINE

BRAND NAME:
Lufyllin (Wallace/C-W)
DOSAGE FORM:
Tablet 200 mg
Tablet 400 mg
USE:
As a bronchodilator to treat bronchial asthma and bronchospasm.
AVOID USE:
If allergic to this or to any other xanthine-related drug.

SIDE EFFECTS:

Nausea; vomiting; stomach upset; diarrhea; headache; restlessness; insomnia; rapid or irregular heartbeat; increased blood sugar; convulsions; flushing; lowered blood pressure; rapid breathing; kidney dysfunction.

$ BRAND OR GENERIC?

While generic savings can be in excess of 60% for both strengths, the FDA considers this drug to have unresolved bioequivalence problems. The severity of the condition being treated can influence the advisability of generic use. Consult your doctor.

FDA-APPROVED BIOEQUIVALENT MANUFACTURERS:

None

The FDA currently considers all brands of this drug product to have potential bioequivalence problems.

EES

SEE Erythromycin Ethylsuccinate

ELAVIL

SEE Amitriptyline

ELDECORT

SEE Hydrocortisone

ELIXOPHYLLIN

SEE Theophylline

EMPIRIN WITH CODEINE

SEE Aspirin/Codeine

EMPRACET WITH CODEINE

SEE Acetaminophen/Codeine

E-MYCIN E

SEE Erythromycin Ethylsuccinate

ENDEP

SEE Amitriptyline

ENDURON

SEE Methyclothiazide

ENDURONYL

SEE Methyclothiazide/Deserpidine

ENDURONYL FORTE

SEE Methyclothiazide/Deserpidine

EPHEDRINE/HYDROXYZINE/THEOPHYLLINE

BRAND NAME:

Marax (Roerig)

DOSAGE FORM:

Tablet

Syrup

USE:

To relieve congestion and bronchospasm in bronchial asthma.

AVOID USE:

Heart disease; overactive thyroid gland; high blood pressure; pregnancy; if allergic to any component of this product or to any related drug.

SIDE EFFECTS:

Excitation; insomnia; rapid heartbeat and other cardiac irregularities; dry mouth, nose, and throat; headache; difficult urination; stomach upset; nausea; vomiting; sweating; vertigo.

$ BRAND OR GENERIC?

The generic tablet is not considered bioequivalent to the brand by the FDA. There is almost a 50% savings possible with generic use, but with three active ingredients, the generic may not give the consistent and predictable performance needed when this medication is called for. Unless used on a long-term basis where savings really add up, stick to the brand.

Several generic syrups are considered bioequivalent to the brand by some states, although not by the FDA. There was once a dye in the syrup that was implicated in allergic reactions, but this has been removed from the brand product. A clear, colorless syrup would indicate removal of this dye from generics. Generic use is a good alternative, offering savings approaching 40%. Consult your doctor.

FDA-APPROVED BIOEQUIVALENT MANUFACTURERS:

None

The FDA currently lists this product as ineffective. Bioequivalency ratings await completion of administrative proceedings.

EQUANIL

SEE Meprobamate

ERGOLOID MESYLATES

BRAND NAME:

Hydergine (Sandoz)

DOSAGE FORM:

Tablet—Oral 1 mg
Tablet—Sublingual (under the tongue) 0.5 mg
Tablet—Sublingual 1 mg

USE:

To treat senility.

AVOID USE:

Preexisting psychosis; if allergic to this or to any ergot drugs.

SIDE EFFECTS:

Minimal but may include occasional nasal congestion; nausea; stomach upset; vomiting; headache; some irritation under the tongue if taking the sublingual tablet.

$ BRAND OR GENERIC?

This drug is used mostly on a long-term basis. Tremendous savings are possible with generic use. The minimal occurrence of side effects helps to make generic use even more attractive.

Many sublingual (under the tongue) tablets and several oral (swallowed) generic tablets are considered bioequivalent to the brand by the FDA.

The generic oral 1-mg tablet represents a savings of up to 44%. The two strengths of sublingual tablet should realize generic savings of up to 63% in the 0.5-mg formulation and up to 74% in the 1-mg strength.

FDA-APPROVED BIOEQUIVALENT MANUFACTURERS:

Tablet—Oral 1 mg

Bolar	Danbury
Chelsea	*Sandoz

Tablet—Sublingual 0.5 mg

Barr	Lederle Labs
Bolar	Riker/3M
Chelsea	*Sandoz
Danbury	Vangard Labs/MWM
Drummer/Phoenix	Zenith
KV	

Tablet—Sublingual 1 mg

Barr	Lederle Labs
Bolar	Mead-Johnson/B-M
Chelsea	Riker/3M
Danbury	*Sandoz
Drummer/Phoenix	Vangard Labs/MWM
KV	Zenith

ERGOTAMINE/CAFFEINE

BRAND NAME:
Cafergot (Sandoz)

DOSAGE FORM:
Tablet

USE:
To treat or prevent migraine headache.

AVOID USE:
Certain circulatory ailments; some heart disease; high blood pressure; liver problems; kidney impairment; any severe infection; during pregnancy; if allergic to ergotamine or caffeine or to any related drug.

SIDE EFFECTS:
At normal dose levels side effects are uncommon but may include tingling and numbness of the fingers and toes; weakness; muscle pain; fast or slow heartbeat; nausea; vomiting; swelling and itching; chest pain; difficulty locating pulse.

$ BRAND OR GENERIC?

Although overdosage with this drug can be life-threatening, normal use presents little danger and few side effects. Since this drug is usually used on a long-term basis, generic savings, at up to 60%, are very impressive. Consult your doctor.

FDA-APPROVED BIOEQUIVALENT MANUFACTURERS:
Cord
Organon/Akzona
*Sandoz

ERYPAR

SEE Erythromycin Stearate

ERYTHROCIN

SEE Erythromycin Stearate

ERYTHROMYCIN ESTOLATE

BRAND NAME:
Ilosone (Dista/Lilly)

DOSAGE FORM:
Capsule 250 mg
Suspension 125 mg/5 ml
Suspension 250 mg/5 ml

USE:
As an antibiotic to treat various infections.

AVOID USE:
Liver disease; if allergic to this drug or to any related drug.

SIDE EFFECTS:
Stomach upset; abdominal cramps; nausea; vomiting; diarrhea; various skin reactions; certain liver problems; fungal infection; bacterial superinfection.

$ BRAND OR GENERIC?

Several generic products are FDA-certified as bioequivalent to the brand in capsule form, but only a few are listed for the suspension formulation.

The 250-mg capsule is capable of generating generic savings of over 25%.

The suspension product in the 125-mg/5-ml strength can realize generic savings of up to 36%, while the 250-mg/5-ml formulation can yield a discount of up to 44%.

FDA-APPROVED BIOEQUIVALENT MANUFACTURERS:

Capsule 250 mg

Barr	*Dista/Lilly
Danbury	Zenith

Suspension 125 mg/5 ml and 250 mg/5 ml

*Dista/Lilly
National/Barre

ERYTHROMYCIN ETHYLSUCCINATE

BRAND NAME:
EES (Abbott)
E-Mycin E (Upjohn)
Pediamycin (Ross/Abbott)
Wyamycin-E (Wyeth/AMHO)

DOSAGE FORM:
Tablet 400 mg
Suspension 200 mg/5 ml
Suspension 400 mg/5 ml
Granules 200 mg/5 ml

USE:
As an antibiotic to treat various infections.

AVOID USE:
If allergic to this or to any related drug.

SIDE EFFECTS:
Stomach upset; abdominal cramps; nausea; vomiting; diarrhea; various skin reactions; fungal infections; bacterial superinfection.

$ BRAND OR GENERIC?

Tablet 400 mg   There are few FDA-approved generics in this category. Up to a 25% discount over the brand name, EES, is possible with generic substitution.

Suspension 200 mg/5 ml   E-Mycin E is the most expensive. Other products yield savings of from 13% to 15%.

Suspension 400 mg/5 ml   Again, as in the lower strength suspension, E-Mycin E emerges as the most expensive product. Other FDA-approved products can save only about 10%.

Granules 200 mg/5 ml   This dosage form is a dry granulation to which the pharmacist adds water. Of the FDA-approved manufacturers, Pediamycin is the most expensive. EES is only about 5% cheaper, while the generic manufactured by Barr saves about 15%.

FDA-APPROVED BIOEQUIVALENT MANUFACTURERS:

Tablet 400 mg

* Abbott
Barr

Suspension 200 mg/5 ml; 400 mg/5 ml

* Abbott   Pharmafair
Dista/Lilly   * Ross/Abbott
KV   * Upjohn
National/Barre   * Wyeth/AMHO
Parke-Davis/W-L

Granules 200 mg/5 ml

* Abbott
Barr
* Ross/Abbott

ERYTHROMYCIN STEARATE

BRAND NAME:
  Bristamycin (Bristol)
  Erypar (Parke-Davis/W-L)
  Erythrocin (Abbott)
  Ethril (E. R. Squibb)
  Pfizer-E (Pfizer)
  Wyamycin-S (Wyeth/AMHO)

DOSAGE FORMS:
  Tablet 250 mg
  Tablet 500 mg

USE:
  As an antibiotic to treat various infections.

AVOID USE:
  If allergic to this drug or to any related drug.

SIDE EFFECTS:
  Stomach upset; abdominal cramps; nausea; vomiting; diarrhea; various skin reactions; fungal infections; bacterial superinfections.

$ BRAND OR GENERIC?

Although many generics are considered bioequivalent to the brand, there is not enough of a savings to warrant generic use. This is especially true since many pharmacies can offer the brand product almost as cheaply as the generic.

FDA-APPROVED BIOEQUIVALENT MANUFACTURERS:

Tablet 250 mg

*Abbott	*Parke-Davis/W-L
Barr	*Pfizer
*Bristol	Purepac/Kalipharma
Chelsea	*E. R. Squibb
Lederle Labs	*Wyeth/AMHO
Mylan	Zenith

Tablet 500 mg

*Abbott	*Pfizer
Chelsea	*E. R. Squibb
Lederle Labs	*Wyeth/AMHO
Mylan	Zenith
*Parke-Davis/W-L	

ESGIC

SEE Butalbital/Acetaminophen/Caffeine

ESIDRIX

SEE Hydrochlorothiazide

ESTROGENS, CONJUGATED

BRAND NAME:

Premarin (Ayerst/AMHO)

DOSAGE FORM:

Tablet 0.625 mg

Tablet 1.25 mg

Tablet 2.5 mg

USE:

To replace estrogen; to treat certain cancers.

AVOID USE:

Impaired liver function; most breast cancers and certain other cancers; blood clot disorders; undiagnosed abnormal genital bleeding; pregnancy; certain circulatory disorders; if allergic to this drug or to any related drug.

SIDE EFFECTS:

Numerous menstrual irregularities including breakthrough bleeding; vaginal yeast infection; breast tenderness, fullness, or secretion; nausea; vomiting; cramping; bloating; liver dysfunction (jaundice); loss of appetite; various skin reactions and changes in hair growth; various eye problems; headache; dizziness; depression; weight gain or loss; retention of water; changes in sex drive; possible cancer of the breast, cervix, vagina, uterus, and liver; gallbladder disease (postmenopausal); widespread blood clots and diseases associated with them; lesions of the liver; high blood pressure; decreased tolerance to glucose; high blood calcium levels (in patients with breast or bone cancers).

$ BRAND OR GENERIC?

The FDA currently considers this drug to have unresolved bioequivalence problems related to differences in levels of the drug in the blood produced by various tablets. Pending completion of revised USP standards of identification, no conjugated estrogens are currently considered bioequivalent and interchangeable.

The side effects of this drug are numerous and potentially unpleasant. The price difference between brand and generic for normal monthly quantities should average about 20% for the 0.625-mg tablet, 30% for the 1.25-mg strength, and as much as 40% for the 2.5-mg dosage. In light of the potential hazards of this medication and the status of unresolved bioequivalency, the brand-name drug is still the best choice.

FDA-APPROVED BIOEQUIVALENT MANUFACTURERS:

None.

There are unresolved bioequivalency issues at this time. The FDA is awaiting revised testing standards in order to accurately evaluate generic equivalency.

ETHRIL

SEE Erythromycin Stearate

EXNA

SEE Benzthiazide

EXSEL

SEE Selenium Sulfide

FASTIN

SEE Phentermine

FIORICET

SEE Butalbital/Acetaminophen/Caffeine

FIORINAL

SEE Butalbital/Aspirin/Caffeine

FLAGYL

SEE Metronidazole

FLUOCINOLONE

BRAND NAME:
Fluonid (Herbert/Allergan)
Synalar (Syntex)

DOSAGE FORM:
Cream 0.01%
Cream 0.025%
Ointment 0.025%
Solution 0.01%

USE:
As a topical cortisone to relieve skin inflammation and rash.

AVOID USE:
Chickenpox; vaccination rash or other viral disease of the skin; if allergic to this preparation or to other cortisones.

SIDE EFFECTS:
Burning sensation of the skin; itching; various other skin reactions.

$ BRAND OR GENERIC?
The FDA recognizes many generic products as bioequivalent. Substantial savings are possible when using the generic products. Consult your doctor.

Cream 0.01%   Available in two sizes, the smaller (15 gm or ½ ounce) is most expensive when bought as the brand Fluonid. The other brand, Synalar, offers a slight savings of about 8%. The generic can save over 50% and is an excellent choice. In the 60-gm size (about 2 ounces), the brand Fluonid is most expensive with the other brand-name product, Synalar, about 10% cheaper. Generics can save over 50% and are worth using.

Cream and Ointment 0.025%   Cream and ointment of equal strengths sell for about the same price. In the 15-gm (about ½-ounce) size, the brand Fluonid emerges as most expensive. The other brand, Synalar, can offer savings of up to 20%, while generics can offer a discount of up to 53%. In the 60-gm (2-ounce) size, Synalar is about 5% cheaper than Fluonid. Generics can offer a whopping 70% discount.

Solution 0.01%   In the 60-cc (2-ounce) size and the 20-cc size, the brand name Synalar is the most expensive, with Fluonid only about 7% less in price. The generic, however, can save up to a hefty 53% and is an excellent choice.

FDA-APPROVED BIOEQUIVALENT MANUFACTURERS:

Cream 0.01%

Bay	NMC
Clay-Park	Savage Labs/Byk-Gulden
E. Fougera/Byk-Gulden	*Syntex
Pharmaderm/Byk-Gulden	Thames
Pharmafair	

Cream 0.025%

Bay	Pharmaderm/Byk-Gulden
Clay-Park	Pharmafair
E. Fougera/Byk-Gulden	Savage Labs/Byk-Gulden
*Herbert/Allergan	*Syntex
NMC	Thames

Ointment 0.025%

Bay	Pharmafair
E. Fougera/Byk-Gulden	Savage Labs/Byk-Gulden
*Herbert/Allergan	*Syntex
Pharmaderm/Byk-Gulden	

Solution 0.01%

Bay	Pharmaderm/Byk-Gulden
E. Fougera/Byk-Gulden	Pharmafair
*Herbert/Allergan	Savage Labs/Byk-Gulden
National/Barre	*Syntex

FLUONID

SEE Fluocinolone

FLUOXYMESTERONE

BRAND NAME:
Android-F (Brown Pharm)
Halotestin (Upjohn)
Ora-Testryl (E. R. Squibb)

DOSAGE FORM:
Tablet 2 mg
Tablet 5 mg
Tablet 10 mg

USE:
As a male hormone (testosterone). In males, used to replace male hormone in many conditions of deficiency or absence and used to treat delayed puberty. In females, used to treat certain breast cancers.

AVOID USE:
In males with breast cancer or cancer of the prostate gland; pregnant women; anyone with serious heart, liver or kidney disease; if allergic to this drug or to any related drug.

SIDE EFFECTS:
Males   Enlargement of the breasts; increased frequency of erection; lowered sperm count.

Females   Menstrual irregularities; various virilizing characteristics such as deepening of the voice and clitoral enlargement.

Males and Females   Various skin and scalp reactions; retention of body fluid and various electrolytes; nausea; vomiting; liver abnormalities including jaundice; changes in sex drive; headache; mental depression; burning sensations of the skin; anxiety; allergic reactions.

$ BRAND OR GENERIC?
The FDA considers this drug to have bioequivalency problems. For this reason no product is certified as bioequivalent and interchangeable. When taking this drug, it is important to be maintained at a constant dosage level. This makes any fluctuation in tablet bioavailability extremely undesirable.

In the 2-mg tablet strength, only Halotestin is commercially available. This is a brand-name drug and there is no alternative but to pay the higher price. In the 5-mg dosage form, Ora-Testryl, a brand-name drug, is even more expensive than Halotestin. In this case up to a 22% savings can be had with use of Halotestin. It is in the 10-mg tablet strength that true generic competition appears. Halotestin emerges as the highest priced product, with generics yielding about a 45% savings. Curiously, Android-F, another brand-name drug, sells for even less than most generics, saving over 50% off the price of Halotestin.

FDA-APPROVED BIOEQUIVALENT MANUFACTURERS:
None
The FDA considers all brands of this product to have unresolved bioequivalency problems at this time.

FOLIC ACID

BRAND NAME:

Folvite (Lederle Labs)

DOSAGE FORM:

Tablet 1 mg

USE:

As a vitamin to treat certain anemias.

AVOID USE:

Not effective for pernicious, aplastic, or normocytic anemias; if allergic to this drug or to any related drug.

SIDE EFFECTS:

Possible allergic reactions.

$ BRAND OR GENERIC?

Since side effects are practically nonexistent, differences among generics should go unnoticed. Folic acid is very efficiently used by the body when taken orally, making tablet formulation straightforward.

Used in a dose of 1 mg, tablet consistency may be somewhat difficult to control, but slight variations are acceptable. There are many FDA-approved generics and no rationale exists for brand-name use, especially since there is a better than 70% savings generically. This drug is also available over the counter, without prescription, in a lower strength. Consult your doctor.

FDA-APPROVED BIOEQUIVALENT MANUFACTURERS:

Tablet 1 mg

Anabolic	Pharm Basics
Bolar	Phoenix
Boots	Private Formulations
Chelsea	Purepac/Kalipharma
Danbury	Richlyn
Drummer/Phoenix	Stanlabs/Simpak
Halsey	Tablicaps
ICN	Towne Paulsen
Lannett	Unit Dose
*Lederle Labs	Vangard Labs/MWM
Eli Lilly	West-Ward
Mission	Zenith
MK	

FOLVITE

SEE Folic Acid

FULVICIN

SEE Griseofulvin

FURADANTIN

SEE Nitrofurantoin

FUROSEMIDE

BRAND NAME:
Lasix (Hoechst-Roussel)

DOSAGE FORM:
Tablet 20 mg
Tablet 40 mg
Tablet 80 mg

USE:
As a potent diuretic to eliminate excess water; to control high blood pressure.

AVOID USE:
Women contemplating pregnancy; if urine output is impaired; if a nursing mother; if allergic to this drug or to sulfa drugs.

SIDE EFFECTS:
Loss of appetite, mouth irritation, stomach upset; nausea; vomiting; cramps; diarrhea; constipation; liver dysfunction (jaundice); inflammation of the pancreas; dizziness; burning sensations of the skin; headache; blurred vision; ringing in the ears or hearing loss; various blood abnormalities; various skin reactions including sensitivity to sunlight; dizziness upon standing; high blood sugar and uric acid levels; muscle spasm and weakness; bladder spasm; restlessness; thrombophlebitis.

$ BRAND OR GENERIC?
Several generics are FDA-certified as bioequivalent to the brand, with savings to be had approaching 30%. The generic product is a good choice, but check in your area first to make sure that the savings are worthwhile. Some pharmacies sell Lasix at a very low price. Consult your doctor.

FDA-APPROVED BIOEQUIVALENT MANUFACTURERS:

Tablet 20 mg

Chelsea	Mylan
Cord	Parke-Davis/W-L
*Hoechst-Roussel	Roxane
International Medication Systems	Superpharm
Kalapharm	Zenith
Lederle Labs	

Tablet 40 mg

Barr
Chelsea
Cord
Drummer/Phoenix
*Hoechst-Roussel
International Medication Systems
Kalapharm

Lederle Labs
Mylan
Parke-Davis/W-L
Roxane
Superpharm
Zenith

Tablet 80 mg

Cord
*Hoechst-Roussel

Lederle Labs
Parke-Davis/W-L

GANTANOL

SEE Sulfamethoxazole

GANTRISIN

SEE Sulfisoxazole

GARAMYCIN

SEE Gentamicin

GENTAMICIN

BRAND NAME:
Garamycin (Schering)

DOSAGE FORM:
Cream
Ointment

USE:
As an antibiotic to treat various bacterial infections.

AVOID USE:
If allergic to this drug or to any related drug.

SIDE EFFECTS:
Possible skin irritation.

$ BRAND OR GENERIC?

There are several FDA-approved bioequivalent generics available. Use of these can yield savings in excess of 50%. This drug is often used where other preparations have failed; use of a nonbioequivalent generic should be avoided.

FDA-APPROVED BIOEQUIVALENT MANUFACTURERS:

Cream

Clay-Park   Pharmafair
E. Fougera/Byk-Gulden   *Schering
NMC   Thames
Pharmaderm/Byk-Gulden

Ointment

Clay-Park   Pharmafair
Herbert/Allergan   *Schering
NMC   Thames

GLUTETHIMIDE

BRAND NAME:

Doriden (USV)

DOSAGE FORM:

Tablet 500 mg

USE:

To relieve insomnia.

AVOID USE:

Disturbance with porphyrin metabolism; in children; if allergic to this or to any related drug.

SIDE EFFECTS:

Skin rash; nausea; hangover; drowsiness; headache; vertigo; mental depression; lack of coordination; fluid retention; mental confusion; lightheadedness; stomach upset; vomiting; night sweating; dry mouth; impairment of memory; slurred speech; ringing in the ears; euphoria; excitation; impaired porphyrin metabolism; blood abnormalities.

$ BRAND OR GENERIC?

The generic can yield savings up to 60% and, with many generics considered bioequivalent to the brand, is the best choice. Consult your doctor. The tablet form has the potential for erratic absorption in the body, with wide variation in dose. (This drug also comes in capsule form by brand name only and is not available as a generic.) Generic savings are worthwhile provided the same manufacturer's product chosen from the list below is used with each prescription refill.

FDA-APPROVED BIOEQUIVALENT MANUFACTURERS:

Tablet 500 mg

Chelsea	Lannett
Cord	MD
Danbury	*USV
Drummer/Phoenix	

GLYCOPYRROLATE

BRAND NAME:
Robinul (A. H. Robins)
Robinul Forte (A. H. Robins)

DOSAGE FORM:
Tablet 1 mg
Tablet 2 mg

USE:
To treat stomach ulcer.

AVOID USE:
Glaucoma; urinary tract obstructions; various paralytic or obstructive conditions of the gastrointestinal tract; certain heart conditions; severe ulcerative colitis with or without toxic megacolon involvement; myasthenia gravis; if a nursing mother; if allergic to this or to any related drug.

SIDE EFFECTS:
Dry mouth; decreased sweating; difficulty in urinating; blurred vision; fast heartbeat; palpitations; visual disturbances; loss of taste; headache; mental confusion; drowsiness; excitation; insomnia; nausea; vomiting; constipation; impotence; various skin reactions; allergic responses.

$ BRAND OR GENERIC?
As with any anticholinergic drug, side effects can be very unpleasant but they are usually apparent only if the proper dosing is exceeded. When this level is adjusted, most side effects usually disappear.

With tablet strengths of only 1 and 2 milligrams, quality control in the manufacturing process is essential to maintain adequate dosage consistency. Even though several generics are considered bioequivalent, there is no guarantee that some differences among unlisted manufacturers will not exist. For this reason the 40% savings possible with generic use of both the 1-mg and 2-mg tablet are worthwhile provided that the same bioequivalent product is used with each prescription refill.

FDA-APPROVED BIOEQUIVALENT MANUFACTURERS:

Tablet 1 mg

Bolar
Danbury
*A. H. Robins

Tablet 2 mg

Bolar   Danbury
Chelsea   *A. H. Robins

GRIFULVIN V

SEE Griseofulvin

GRISACTIN

SEE Griseofulvin

GRISEOFULVIN

BRAND NAME:
Fulvicin (Schering)
Grifulvin V (Ortho)
Grisactin (Ayerst/AMHO)
Gris-PEG (Herbert/Allergan)

DOSAGE FORM:
Tablet—Microcrystalline 250 mg
Tablet—Microcrystalline 500 mg
Tablet—Ultramicrocrystalline 125 mg
Tablet—Ultramicrocrystalline 250 mg

USE:
As an antifungal.

AVOID USE:
Disturbances in porphyrin metabolism; certain liver problems; if allergic to this or to any related drug.

SIDE EFFECTS:
Various skin reactions; oral thrush (a yeast infection of the mouth); stomach upset; nausea; vomiting; diarrhea; headache; dizziness; fatigue; mental confusion; sensitivity to sunlight; burning sensations of the hands and feet.

$ **BRAND OR GENERIC?**

Tablet—Microcrystalline 250 mg   There are only two choices here: Fulvicin U/F 250 and Grifulvin V 250. Both are brand-name products and are approved as bioequivalent by the FDA. Grifulvin V 250 offers about a 10% discount over its competitor.

Tablet—Microcrystalline 500 mg   Fulvicin-U/F 500, Grifulvin V 500, and Grisactin 500 are all brand names and all FDA-certified as bioequivalent. Fulvicin-UF 500 and Grifulvin V 500 are the same price, but the best choice is Grisactin 500, which offers up to a 15% reduction in price.

Tablet—Ultramicrocrystalline 125 mg   The advantage of this dosage form over the previous ones is that since the active ingredient is ground to a finer consistency, the effective dose is almost doubled without any corresponding increase in milligram strength. It is a more efficient dosage form, offering three brand-name product choices, all FDA-approved as bioequivalent. They are Fulvicin PG 125, and Gris-PEG 125, which are the most expensive; and Grisactin Ultra 125, offering up to an 29% discount.

Tablet—Ultramicrocrystalline 250 mg   The same three brand-name products appearing in the 125-mg strength are available here as well. Fulvicin PG 250 is the most expensive, with Gris-PEG 250 offering up to a 10% savings. Grisactin Ultra 250 emerges as the best buy, with up to a 17% savings possible.

FDA-APPROVED BIOEQUIVALENT MANUFACTURERS:

Tablet—Microcrystalline 250 mg

* Ortho
* Schering

Tablet—Microcrystalline 500 mg

* Ayerst/AMHO
* Ortho
* Schering

Tablet—Ultramicrocrystalline 125 mg

* Ayerst/AMHO
* Herbert/Allergan
* Schering

Tablet—Ultramicrocrystalline 250 mg

* Ayerst/AMHO
* Herbert/Allergan
* Schering

GRIS-PEG

SEE Griseofulvin

GUAIFENESIN/CODEINE

BRAND NAME:
Robitussin A-C (A. H. Robins)

DOSAGE FORM:
Syrup

USE:
As a cough suppressant and expectorant.

AVOID USE:
If allergic to guaifenesin or codeine or to any related drug.

SIDE EFFECTS:
Nausea; stomach upset; constipation; sedation.

$ BRAND OR GENERIC?
Savings of up to 40% are possible with use of the generic alternative. However, the FDA does not list any manufacturers as bioequivalent and interchangeable. But this is mostly a function of current administrative proceedings and has little to do with the relative performance of various competing formulations. Consult your doctor.

FDA-APPROVED BIOEQUIVALENT MANUFACTURERS:
None

GUAIFENESIN/PSEUDOEPHEDRINE/CODEINE

BRAND NAME:
Robitussin-DAC (A. H. Robins)

DOSAGE FORM:
Syrup

USE:
As a cough suppressant, an expectorant, and a decongestant.

AVOID USE:
Severe high blood pressure or if receiving any medication to control high blood pressure; overactive thyroid; if receiving a monoamine oxidase inhibitor drug; if allergic to any component of this product or to any related drug.

SIDE EFFECTS:
Agitation; dizziness; insomnia; heart palpitations; nausea.

$ BRAND OR GENERIC?
Savings in excess of 30% are possible with use of the generic alternative. The FDA does not list any manufacturers as bioequivalent and interchangeable, but this is mostly a function of current administrative proceedings and has little to do

with the relative performance of various competing formulations. Consult your doctor.

FDA-APPROVED BIOEQUIVALENT MANUFACTURERS:
None

GUANETHIDINE

BRAND NAME:
Ismelin (Ciba/Ciba-Geigy)

DOSAGE FORM:
Tablet 10 mg
Tablet 25 mg

USE:
To treat high blood pressure.

AVOID USE:
If you have or suspect you have pheochromacytoma; if you have congestive heart failure; if taking or have taken within the last 2 weeks any monoamine oxidase inhibitor drug; if allergic to this or to any related drug.

SIDE EFFECTS:
Dizziness or dizziness on standing; weakness; fainting; slowed heartbeat; diarrhea; nausea; vomiting; aggravation or activation of peptic ulcer; impaired ejaculation; fluid retention and swelling; weight gain; difficult breathing; loss of urinary control; scalp hair loss; dry mouth; blurred vision; nasal congestion; muscle aches; skin rash; mental depression; tenderness of the salivary glands.

$ **BRAND OR GENERIC?**
This is a potent drug with potentially serious side effects. A decision to use a generic substitute should weigh this possibility against any potential savings. Consult your doctor.

Both the 10-mg and 25-mg tablets show generic savings approaching 40%. This drug has only recently become available generically and discounts should increase as more manufacturers enter the market.

FDA-APPROVED BIOEQUIVALENT MANUFACTURERS:

Tablet 10 mg and 25 mg

Bolar
*Ciba/Ciba-Geigy

HALOTESTIN

SEE Fluoxymesterone

HYCODAN

Sᴇᴇ Hydrocodone/Homatropine

HYCOMINE

Sᴇᴇ Hydrocodone/Phenylpropanolamine

HYDERGINE

Sᴇᴇ Ergoloid Mesylates

HYDRALAZINE

BRAND NAME:
Apresoline (Ciba/Ciba-Geigy)
DOSAGE FORM:
Tablet 10 mg
Tablet 25 mg
Tablet 50 mg
USE:
To control high blood pressure.
AVOID USE:
Coronary artery disease; certain types of rheumatic heart disease; if allergic to this or to any related drug.
SIDE EFFECTS:
Headache; fast heartbeat and other heart rhythm irregularities; loss of appetite; nausea; vomiting; diarrhea; anginal chest pain; nasal stuffiness; flushing; eye tearing and infection (conjunctivitis); burning sensations, numbness, and tingling of the extremities; fluid retention; dizziness; muscle tremor and cramping; mental depression; anxiety; various skin reactions and other allergic responses; constipation; difficulty in urinating; difficulty in breathing; slowing or stoppage of intestinal movement; enlarged spleen; lymph gland problems; liver dysfunction (hepatitis); various blood abnormalities; high or low blood pressure.
$ BRAND OR GENERIC?
A very hefty savings can be realized with generic use. Side effects, although potentially serious, usually disappear when dosage is reduced. The FDA has approved many generics as bioequivalent. The 10-mg tablet should show generic savings of up to 64%. The 25-mg strength can save as much as 70% generically, while up to 74% can be saved in the 50-mg strength.

FDA-APPROVED BIOEQUIVALENT MANUFACTURERS:

Tablet 10 mg

Barr	Par
Camall	Quantum
*Ciba/Ciba-Geigy	Superpharm
Cord	Zenith

Tablet 25 mg

Amide	Par
Ascot	Pharm Basics
Barr	Purepac/Kalipharma
Camall	Quantum
Chelsea	Richlyn
*Ciba/Ciba-Geigy	Sidmak
Cord	Superpharm
Danbury	Vangard Labs/MWM
Drummer/Phoenix	West-Ward
Lederle Labs	Zenith
Lemmon	

Tablet 50 mg

Amide	Par
Ascot	Pharm Basics
Barr	Purepac/Kalipharma
Camall	Quantum
Chelsea	Richlyn
*Ciba/Ciba-Geigy	Sidmak
Cord	Superpharm
Danbury	Vangard Labs/MWM
Drummer/Phoenix	West-Ward
Lederle Labs	Zenith

HYDRALAZINE/HYDROCHLOROTHIAZIDE

BRAND NAME:

Apresazide (Ciba/Ciba-Geigy)

Apresoline-Esidrix (Ciba/Ciba-Geigy)

DOSAGE FORM:

Capsule 25 mg hydralazine/25 mg hydrochlorothiazide

Capsule 50 mg hydralazine/50 mg hydrochlorothiazide

Capsule 100 mg hydralazine/50 mg hydrochlorothiazide

Tablet 25 mg hydralazine/15 mg hydrochlorothiazide

USE:

To control high blood pressure.

AVOID USE:

Coronary artery disease; certain rheumatic heart disease; lack of urine output; if a nursing mother; if allergic to either component of this product or to any sulfa drug.

SIDE EFFECTS:

Headache; palpitations; loss of appetite; stomach upset; nausea; diarrhea; cramps; constipation; liver dysfunction (jaundice or hepatitis); inflammation of the pancreas; dizziness or dizziness upon standing; numbness, tingling, or burning sensations of the skin; fast heartbeat; anginal chest pain; various blood abnormalities; various skin reactions and other allergic responses; high blood sugar and uric acid levels; muscle spasm and weakness; nasal congestion; flushing; eye tearing and infection (conjunctivitis); mental depression, disorientation or anxiety; difficulty in urinating; difficult breathing; slowing or stoppage of intestinal movement; lymph gland problems; high or low blood pressure.

$ BRAND OR GENERIC?

This product is a two-drug combination that comes in four different ratio strengths; three in capsule form and one in a tablet formulation.

The FDA recognizes several generic capsule formulations as bioequivalent to the brand, Apresazide. Savings of over 40% are possible.

In tablet form there are no generics considered bioequivalent to the brand Apresoline-Esidrix. Using generics that are marketed, although not considered bioequivalent, can net savings of up to 76%. Consult your doctor.

FDA-APPROVED BIOEQUIVALENT MANUFACTURERS:

Capsule—25 mg/25 mg; 50 mg/50 mg; 100 mg/50 mg

Bolar   Reid-Provident
*Ciba/Ciba-Geigy   Zenith

Tablet 25 mg/15 mg

*Ciba/Ciba-Geigy

HYDROCHLOROTHIAZIDE

BRAND NAME:

Esidrix (Ciba/Ciba-Geigy)
HydroDIURIL (MSD/Merck)
Oretic (Abbott)

DOSAGE FORM:

Tablet 25 mg
Tablet 50 mg

USE:

As a low-potency diuretic to control high blood pressure, excess water, and other related conditions.

AVOID USE:

Lack of urine output; if a nursing mother; if allergic to this drug or to any sulfa drug.

SIDE EFFECTS:

Loss of appetite; stomach upset; nausea; vomiting; cramps; diarrhea; constipation; liver dysfunction (jaundice); inflammation of the pancreas; dizziness; vertigo; burning sensations of the skin; headache; various blood abnormalities; dizziness upon standing; various skin reactions including sensitivity to sunlight; high blood sugar and uric acid levels; muscle spasm and weakness; blurred vision.

$ BRAND OR GENERIC?

Since side effects, although potentially serious, are not common and the drug's potency is not great, slight variations among manufacturers should go unnoticed. Many generics are considered bioequivalent to the brand by the FDA and emerge as the best choice. Savings for the 25-mg tablet average about 15% in quantities of 30, while the 50-mg dosage form yields generic discounts of up to 40% in the same quantity. Over 50% savings are possible when the 25-mg generic is purchased in 100s; more than 60% savings accrue for the 50-mg generic in 100s.

Of the three brand-name products, Esidrix, HydroDIURIL, and Oretic, the latter saves money over the other two. Expect only about a 10% savings for the 25-mg tablet in quantities of 30, but up to 30% in 100s. The 50-mg strength yields about a 20% discount in 30s and 30% in lots of 100.

Hydrochlorothiazide is a very popular drug, and many pharmacies use the brand as a giveaway, so check the brand price first to make sure you are really getting a bargain with the generic.

FDA-APPROVED BIOEQUIVALENT MANUFACTURERS:

Tablet 25 mg

*Abbott	*MSD/Merck
Ascot	Mylan
Barr	Parke-Davis/W-L
Bolar	Pharm Basics
Boots	Private Formulations
Camall	Purepac/Kalipharma
Chelsea	Reid-Provident
*Ciba/Ciba-Geigy	Richlyn
Cord	Roxane
Drummer/Phoenix	SK & F
Halsey	Superpharm
Inwood/Forest	Towne Paulsen
Lederle Labs	Vangard Labs/MWM
Lemmon	West-Ward
M.M. Mast	Zenith

Tablet 50 mg

*Abbott
Ascot
Barr
Bolar
Boots
Camall
Chelsea
*Ciba/Ciba-Geigy
Cord
Danbury
Drummer/Phoenix
Halsey
Heather
Inwood/Forest
Lederle Labs
Lemmon
M. M. Mast

*MSD/Merck
Mylan
Parke-Davis/W-L
Pharm Basics
Private Formulations
Purepac/Kalipharma
Quantum
Reid-Provident
Richlyn
Roxane
SK & F
Superpharm
Towne Paulsen
Vangard/MWM
West-Ward
Zenith

HYDROCHLOROTHIAZIDE/RESERPINE

BRAND NAME:
Hydropres (MSD/Merck)

DOSAGE FORM:
Tablet 25 mg hydrochlorothiazide/0.125 mg reserpine
Tablet 50 mg hydrochlorothiazide/0.125 mg reserpine

USE:
To control high blood pressure.

AVOID USE:
As initial therapy to control high blood pressure; if unable to urinate; if receiving electroshock therapy; in presence of active peptic ulcer or ulcerative colitis; if mentally depressed; if pregnant; if breast feeding; if allergic to either component of this product, to any sulfa drug, or to any other related drug.

SIDE EFFECTS:
Loss of appetite; increased gastrointestinal activity; increased salivation; stomach upset; nausea; dry mouth; vomiting; intestinal cramps; diarrhea; constipation; difficulty in urinating; liver dysfunction (jaundice); inflammation of the pancreas; dizziness or dizziness on standing; vertigo; fainting; drowsiness; tingling or burning sensation of the skin; headache; various blood abnormalities; various skin reactions including sensitivity to sunlight; flushing of the skin; various allergic responses; elevated blood sugar; increased uric acid blood levels; muscle spasm; muscle aches; weakness; restlessness; blurred vision; mental depression; nightmares; nervousness; agitation; confusion; hallucinations; parkinsonism;

slowed heartbeat; anginal chest pains; heart rhythm irregularities; nasal congestion; increased susceptibility to colds; weight gain; breast enlargement; production of milk; decreased sex drive or impotence.

$ BRAND OR GENERIC?

This product contains two active ingredients. One of them, reserpine, is included in a fraction of a milligram amount making it difficult to manufacture this tablet with consistent bioequivalence. In fact, the FDA does not consider any maker's product to be bioequivalent and interchangeable.

Generics, while saving up to 80% over the brand, should be used only after consulting your doctor. If your doctor allows substitution to take place, try to get the same manufacturer's product each time you refill your prescription.

FDA-APPROVED BIOEQUIVALENT MANUFACTURERS:
None

HYDROCHLOROTHIAZIDE/RESERPINE/ HYDRALAZINE

BRAND NAME:
Serapes (Ciba/Ciba-Geigy)

DOSAGE FORM:
Tablet

USE:
To control high blood pressure.

AVOID USE:
Mental depression; peptic ulcer; ulcerative colitis; electroshock therapy; various heart diseases; lack of urine output; if a nursing mother; if allergic to any ingredient in this product, to any related drug, or to any sulfa drug.

SIDE EFFECTS:
Excessive gastrointestinal secretions; stomach upset; nausea; vomiting; loss of appetite; diarrhea; constipation; liver dysfunction (jaundice and hepatitis); inflammation of the pancreas; dizziness; headache; dry mouth; numbness; tingling and burning sensations of the skin; various heart problems; drowsiness; mental depression; nightmares; nasal congestion, hearing impairments; glaucoma and other eye abnormalities; muscle tremor and cramping; various blood abnormalities; numerous skin reactions including sensitivity to sunlight; nosebleed; decreased sex drive or impotence; weight gain; breast enlargement; fluid retention; enlarged spleen; difficult breathing; difficulty in urinating; low or high blood pressure; high blood sugar and uric acid levels; muscle spasm and weakness.

$ BRAND OR GENERIC?

This is a three-component drug product formulated as a tablet. As such, it is very difficult to manufacture with good tablet consistency. The generic product is not considered bioequivalent to the brand. Even though there is up to an 80% difference in price, the potential hazards of taking an inferior product outweigh the benefits of the generic. Stick to the brand.

FDA-APPROVED BIOEQUIVALENT MANUFACTURERS:
None

The FDA considers all brands of this product to have unresolved bioequivalency problems at this time.

HYDROCODONE/ACETAMINOPHEN

BRAND NAME:
Vicodin (Knoll)

DOSAGE FORM:
Tablet

USE:
To relieve pain.

AVOID USE:
If a nursing mother; if allergic to either hydrocodone or acetaminophen or to any related drug.

SIDE EFFECTS:
Drowsiness; impairment of mental and physical performance; anxiety; dizziness; nausea; vomiting; constipation; difficulty in urinating; difficult breathing; physical dependence.

$ BRAND OR GENERIC?
Several generics are certified as bioequivalent by the FDA. They offer savings approaching 33% for short-term, small-quantity use and up to 44% when bought in quantities of 100 tablets.

FDA-APPROVED BIOEQUIVALENT MANUFACTURERS:

Tablet

Barr	D. M. Graham
B. F. Ascher	*Knoll
Central	

HYDROCODONE/HOMATROPINE

BRAND NAME:
Hycodan (Dupont)

DOSAGE FORM:
Syrup

USE:

To relieve cough.

AVOID USE:

Glaucoma; if allergic to either hydrocodone or homatropine.

SIDE EFFECTS:

Drowsiness; dizziness; nausea; vomiting; constipation; itching.

$ BRAND OR GENERIC?

Even though this product is usually used on a short-term basis, perhaps 4 or 5 days, to provide temporary cough control, potential savings are still enough to warrant generic use. With generic discounts of up to 44%, this is a very worthwhile alternative. No bioequivalence problems have been encountered with the FDA-approved products listed.

FDA-APPROVED BIOEQUIVALENT MANUFACTURERS:

Bay
*Dupont
Halsey
National/Barre

HYDROCODONE/PHENYLPROPANOLAMINE

BRAND NAME:

Hycomine (Endo)

DOSAGE FORM:

Syrup 5 mg hydrocodone/5 ml : 25 mg phenylpropanolamine/5 ml

Pediatric Syrup 2.5 mg hydrocodone/5 ml : 12.5 mg phenylpropanolamine/5 ml

USE:

To control cough and nasal congestion.

AVOID USE:

Glaucoma; certain gastrointestinal obstruction; if a nursing mother; if taking a monoamine oxidase inhibitor drug; overactive thyroid gland; certain breathing problems; heart disease; high blood pressure; diabetes; certain skull lesions; if allergic to either ingredient in this product or to any related drug.

SIDE EFFECTS:

Drowsiness; impairment of mental and physical performance; anxiety; dizziness; blurred vision; breathing difficulties; low blood pressure; palpitations and fast heartbeat; difficulty in urinating; nausea; vomiting; physical dependence; sweating; headache; various skin reactions.

$ BRAND OR GENERIC?

Syrups present few problems to formulation, and generic performance should be on par with the brand. Savings can be good with generic use, approaching

45%. The FDA does not recognize any generic products as bioequivalent to the brand, so check with your doctor before any substitution takes place.

FDA-APPROVED BIOEQUIVALENT MANUFACTURERS:
None

HYDROCORTISONE

BRAND NAME:
Cort-Dome (Miles)
Eldecort (Elder)
Hytone (Dermik/Rorer-Amchem)
Nutracort (Owen)
Synacort (Syntex)

DOSAGE FORM:
Cream 1%
Ointment 1%
Lotion 1%

USE:
To relieve skin inflammation and rash.

AVOID USE:
Chickenpox, vaccination rash or other viral diseases of the skin; if allergic to this drug or to any related drug.

SIDE EFFECTS:
Burning sensation of the skin; itching; various other skin reactions.

$ BRAND OR GENERIC?
This drug has been around a long time and manufacturers are experienced in its formulation. Numerous generic products are considered by the FDA to be bioequivalent to the brand. A moderate savings of up to 35% is possible with both the cream and ointment, making the generic a good choice. The lotion also has many FDA-approved generic products and can yield even better savings, approaching 44%.

FDA-APPROVED BIOEQUIVALENT MANUFACTURERS:

Cream 1%

Ambix/Organics	*Elder
Bay	G and W
Biocraft	Herbert/Allergan
Byk-Gulden	Ingram
C and M Pharmacal	Lemmon
Clay-Park	*Miles
*Dermik/Rorer-Amchem	NMC

*Owen	*Syntex
Pharmafair	Syosset
Rowell	Thames
Stanlabs/Simpak	Towne Paulsen
Stiefel	Westwood

Ointment 1%

Ambix/Organics	*Dermik/Rorer-Amchem
Bay	NMC
Byk-Gulden	Pfipharmecs/Pfizer
C and M	Thames
Clay-Park	

Lotion 1%

Clay-Park	*Miles
Coopercare	National/Barre
*Dermik/Rorer-Amchem	*Owen
Heran	Rowell
Key	

HYDRODIURIL

SEE Hydrochlorothiazide

HYDROFLUMETHIAZIDE

BRAND NAME:
Diucardin (Ayerst/AMHO)
Saluron (Bristol)

DOSAGE FORM:
Tablet 50 mg

USE:
As a diuretic to rid the body of excess fluid associated with congestive heart failure, liver problems, steroid and estrogen therapy, certain kidney ailments; to control high blood pressure.

AVOID USE:
Lack of urine output; if a nursing mother; if allergic to this or to other sulfa drugs.

SIDE EFFECTS:
Loss of appetite; stomach upset; nausea; vomiting; cramps; diarrhea; constipation; liver dysfunction (jaundice); inflammation of the pancreas; dizziness and

dizziness upon standing; burning sensations of the skin; headache; various blood abnormalities; various skin reactions including sensitivity to sunlight; high blood sugar and uric acid levels; muscle spasm and weakness.

$ BRAND OR GENERIC?

The FDA lists several generics as bioequivalent to the brand. However, a special situation exists whereby one of the brand-name products, Diucardin, offers up to a 35% discount over Saluron, the other brand-name drug. The FDA-approved bioequivalent generics offer a savings of up to 50%.

FDA-APPROVED BIOEQUIVALENT MANUFACTURERS:
* Ayerst/AMHO
  Bolar
* Bristol
  Chelsea
  Par

HYDROFLUMETHIAZIDE/RESERPINE

BRAND NAME:

Salutensin (Bristol)

DOSAGE FORM:

Tablet

USE:

To control high blood pressure.

AVOID USE:

Low or no urine output; active peptic ulcer; ulcerative colitis; severe depression; if receiving electroconvulsive therapy; if a nursing mother; if allergic to either hydroflumethiazide or reserpine or to any related drug.

SIDE EFFECTS:

Loss of appetite; stomach upset; nausea; vomiting; dry mouth; increased intestinal movement; cramps; diarrhea; constipation; liver dysfunction (jaundice); inflammation of the pancreas; high blood sugar; increased salivation; weight gain; blurred vision; headache; dizziness and dizziness upon standing; burning sensations of the skin; drowsiness; nasal stuffiness; breathing difficulties; changes in sex drive or impotence; nightmares; glaucoma and other visual disturbances; various blood abnormalities; various heart problems; hearing loss or deafness; muscle weakness and spasm; decreased resistance to colds; various skin reactions including sensitivity to sunlight; mental depression; nosebleed.

$ BRAND OR GENERIC?

This is a very poor candidate for generic use. Although generic savings can approach 60%, the FDA does not consider any products bioequivalent.

Reserpine is included in a fraction of a milligram dose, making quality control during manufacture a difficult procedure. It is hard enough to control a patient on a fixed combination drug product without adding to it the variables inherent in unapproved generic products.

If, after consulting with your physician, a decision is made to use a generic substitute, savings may be worthwhile provided the same manufacturer's product can be used with each prescription refill.

FDA-APPROVED BIOEQUIVALENT MANUFACTURERS:
None

The FDA considers all brands of this product to have unresolved bioequivalency problems at this time.

HYDROPRES

SEE Hydrochlorothiazide/Reserpine

HYGROTON

SEE Chlorthalidone

HYDROXYZINE HYDROCHLORIDE

BRAND NAME:
Atarax (Roerig)

DOSAGE FORM:
Tablet 10 mg
Tablet 25 mg
Tablet 50 mg
Syrup 10 mg/5 ml

USE:
To relieve anxiety, tension, agitation, apprehension, confusion; to treat various allergic conditions.

AVOID USE:
Early pregnancy; if a nursing mother; if allergic to this or to any related drug.

SIDE EFFECTS:
Drowsiness; dry mouth.

$ BRAND OR GENERIC?
This is a widely used drug having minimal side effects. Many generics are considered by the FDA to be bioequivalent to the brand. Excellent savings are possible, with approved generics performing on par with the brand.

With use of generics savings of up to 57% are possible for the 10-mg tablet; as much as 63% off the brand price for the 25-mg tablet; up to a 66% savings for the 50-mg tablet; about 45% savings for the syrup.

FDA-APPROVED BIOEQUIVALENT MANUFACTURERS:

Tablet 10 mg, 25 mg, 50 mg

Barr	Par
Chelsea	Purepac/Kalipharma
Cord	*Roerig
Danbury	Superpharm
Drummer/Phoenix	Zenith
KV	

Syrup

Bay	National/Barre
KV	*Roerig

HYDROXYZINE PAMOATE

BRAND NAME:
Vistaril (Pfizer)

DOSAGE FORM:
Capsule 25 mg

Capsule 50 mg

USE:
To relieve anxiety, tension, agitation, apprehension, confusion; to treat various allergic conditions such as itching.

AVOID USE:
Early pregnancy; if a nursing mother; if allergic to this drug or to any related drug.

SIDE EFFECTS:
Drowsiness; dry mouth.

$ BRAND OR GENERIC?
This is a widely used drug, with many FDA-approved bioequivalent generics. It is efficiently utilized by the body when taken orally, so capsule formulation presents few problems.

Truly astounding savings are possible with generic use. Both the 25-mg and 50-mg capsule offer discounts of over 70%.

FDA-APPROVED BIOEQUIVALENT MANUFACTURERS:

Capsule 25 mg and 50 mg

Barr	Chelsea
Bolar	Danbury (50 mg only)

Drummer/Phoenix
Duramed
Lemmon (25 mg only)
Par

*Pfizer
Vangard Labs/MWM
Zenith

HYTONE

SEE Hydrocortisone

IBUPROFEN

BRAND NAME:
Motrin (Upjohn)
Rufen (Boots)

DOSAGE FORM:
Tablet 400 mg
Tablet 600 mg

USE:
As an antiinflammatory; to relieve pain.

AVOID USE:
If a nursing mother; if allergic or sensitive to aspirin or allergic to any related drug.

SIDE EFFECTS:
Nausea; stomach upset or pain; heartburn; diarrhea; vomiting; constipation; dizziness; headache; nervousness; ringing in the ears; decreased appetite; fluid retention and swelling; ulcer or bleeding of the stomach or duodenum; liver dysfunction (jaundice, hepatitis); inflammation of the pancreas; mental depression, confusion, hallucinations; burning sensations of the skin; hearing loss; blurred vision and other eye problems; various skin reactions and other allergic responses; hair loss; various blood abnormalities; nosebleed; breast enlargement; low blood sugar; various heart problems; various kidney dysfunctions; dry eyes and mouth; ulcerated gums; inflammation of the nasal membranes.

$ BRAND OR GENERIC?
Of the two brand-name products, Rufen saves about 30% over Motrin in both the 400-mg and 600-mg tablet strengths. The generic offers over a 50% savings across the board.

Pharmacies will often sell Motrin very cheaply because it is such a well-known drug. If this is the case, generic savings may be less than those quoted here.

Recently Advil and Nuprin, 200-mg-strength tablets, have been approved for over-the-counter sale without a prescription. They also offer about a 10% savings over Rufen and a 30% savings over Motrin on a milligram-for-milligram basis.

FDA-APPROVED BIOEQUIVALENT MANUFACTURERS:

Tablet 400 mg and 600 mg
Barr
*Boots
*Upjohn

ILOSONE

SEE Erythromycin Estolate

IMIPRAMINE

BRAND NAME:
Janimine (Abbott)
Tofranil (Geigy/Ciba-Geigy)

DOSAGE FORM:
Tablet 10 mg
Tablet 25 mg
Tablet 50 mg

USE:
To relieve depression; to treat bed-wetting in children over 6 years old.

AVOID USE:
Following certain heart disease; within 14 days of taking a monoamine oxidase inhibitor drug; if a nursing mother; if allergic to this or to any related drug.

SIDE EFFECTS:
Dry mouth; blurred vision and other eye problems; constipation; difficulty in urinating; paralysis of the small intestine; mental disorientation; confusion, anxiety, or hallucinations; dizziness upon standing; tremors; high blood pressure; various heart problems including fast heartbeat and heart rhythm irregularities; numbness, tingling, and burning sensations of the extremities; loss of coordination; ringing in the ears; parkinsonlike symptoms; various skin reactions including sensitivity to sunlight; bone marrow and blood abnormalities; nausea; vomiting; loss of appetite; stomach upset; diarrhea; irritation of the tongue or mouth; peculiar taste; black tongue; breast enlargement in males; breast enlargement and formation of milk in females; changes in sex drive or impotence; swelling of the testicles; high or low blood sugar levels; liver dysfunction (jaundice or hepatitis); loss or gain in weight; sweating; flushing; drowsiness; headache; hair loss.

$ BRAND OR GENERIC?

There have been problems reported with certain generic tablets that have changed upon aging during normal storage conditions. This problem has been corrected, and many generic tablets are now considered by the FDA to be bioequivalent to the brand. Some truly astounding savings are possible with generic use. Expect to see savings on the 10-mg tablet in excess of 70%. The 25-mg generic should yield a discount of close to 80%, while the 50-mg tablet should save in excess of 80%.

Of special note is Abbott's brand of imipramine, Janimine. This brand-name product can save over 60% from the price of Tofranil in all strengths, while offering a wider availability than most generic brands.

FDA-APPROVED BIOEQUIVALENT MANUFACTURERS:

Tablet 10 mg

*Abbott	*Geigy/Ciba-Geigy
Biocraft	Lederle Labs
Bolar	Par
Chelsea	Roxane
Cord	SK & F
Drummer/Phoenix	Vangard Labs/MWM

Tablet 25 mg

*Abbott	Lederle Labs
Biocraft	Par
Bolar	Pharm Basics
Chelsea	Roxane
Cord	SK & F
Drummer/Phoenix	Vangard Labs/MWM
*Geigy/Ciba-Geigy	West-Ward

Tablet 50 mg

*Abbott	*Geigy/Ciba-Geigy
Biocraft	Lederle Labs
Bolar	Par
Chelsea	Roxane
Cord	Vangard Labs/MWM
Drummer/Phoenix	West-Ward

INDERAL

Sᴇᴇ Propranolol

INDOCIN

Sᴇᴇ Indomethacin

INDOMETHACIN

BRAND NAME:
Indocin (MSD/Merck)

DOSAGE FORM:
Capsule 25 mg
Capsule 50 mg

USE:
To relieve pain, stiffness, and swelling associated with various arthritic conditions.

AVOID USE:
Aspirin allergy or sensitivity; irritation or ulceration of the stomach or other areas of the gastrointestinal tract; during pregnancy; if a nursing mother; children 14 years old and under; if allergic to other related antiarthritic drugs.

SIDE EFFECTS:
Nausea; vomiting; stomach upset; heartburn; diarrhea; constipation; headache; dizziness; drowsiness; fatigue; vertigo; ringing in the ears; loss of appetite; bloating; gas; peptic ulcer; bleeding and ulceration of the gastrointestinal tract; rectal bleeding and inflammation; anxiety; muscle weakness or involuntary movements; insomnia; mental confusion and psychotic episodes; blurred vision and other eye problems; hearing disturbances and deafness; liver dysfunction (jaundice, hepatitis); burning sensations of the skin; fainting; aggravation of epilepsy and parkinsonism; high blood pressure; fast heartbeat; palpitations and other cardiac problems; fluid retention and swelling; weight gain; flushing; sweating; high blood sugar and potassium levels; various skin reactions and other allergic responses; difficult breathing; hair loss; bone marrow and blood abnormalities; vaginal bleeding; various kidney problems; nosebleed; breast enlargement and tenderness.

$ BRAND OR GENERIC?
This drug has a potential for serious side effects. It is usually prescribed if other, more innocuous drug therapies have failed. This drug is rarely taken on a long-term basis, with most courses of treatment spanning no more than two weeks. With the many potential side effects and the small quantities of drug needed, the most prudent choice is to stick to the brand-name product, Indocin.

Generic savings for those products available and considered bioequivalent by the FDA can be as high as 36% for the 25-mg strength and 50% for the 50-mg formulation.

If you do choose a generic alternative, make sure it appears on the FDA's list of bioequivalent products that follows.

FDA-APPROVED BIOEQUIVALENT MANUFACTURERS:

Capsule 25 mg and 50 mg

Chelsea	Par
Lederle Labs	Parke-Davis/W-L
*MSD/Merck	Roxane
Mylan	Zenith

IODOCHLORHYDROXYQUIN/HYDROCORTISONE

BRAND NAME:
Vioform HC (Ciba)

DOSAGE FORM:
Cream
Ointment

USE:
To treat various eczemas, skin rashes, and certain fungal infections including athlete's foot.

AVOID USE:
Eye growths; tuberculosis of the skin; various viral infections of the skin; if allergic to either component of this product or to any related drug.

SIDE EFFECTS:
Rash; burning sensation of the skin; itching and various other skin reactions.

$ BRAND OR GENERIC?
A tremendous price difference makes the generic product a very attractive choice. Although not officially recognized as bioequivalent to the brand, generic formulation presents little difficulty and should prove as effective as the brand-name product. With a discount of up to 62%, it is worth consulting your doctor about generic use.

FDA-APPROVED BIOEQUIVALENT MANUFACTURERS:
None

ISMELIN

SEE Guanethidine

ISONIAZID

BRAND NAME:
Nydrazid (E. R. Squibb)

DOSAGE FORM:
Tablet 100 mg
Tablet 300 mg

USE:
To treat or prevent tuberculosis.

AVOID USE:
If there is a history of liver disease; if allergic to this drug or to any related drug.

SIDE EFFECTS:

Nerve tissue injury of the hands and feet characterized by numbness, tingling, aching, and burning; possible liver complications (hepatitis, jaundice); nausea; vomiting; stomach upset; various blood abnormalities; vitamin B_6 deficiency; various skin rashes; possible fever; pain in the muscles or joints; various eye abnormalities; possible convulsions.

$ BRAND OR GENERIC?

Although the potential side effects of this drug can be severe, they tend to be dose-related, occurring at the higher range of dosage levels.

With many generics considered bioequivalent by the FDA, substitution is a viable alternative, with good response and avoidance of dangerous side effects dependent on careful monitoring of drug therapy by the doctor.

Squibb's Nydrazid is the most expensive brand of isoniazid in the 100-mg strength. Eli Lilly's tablet, although marketed by generic name, is considered a brand-name product and can save over 30%, while various generics offer a discount of over 50%.

In the 300-mg strength, Squibb does not market Nydrazid. Generics offer over a 50% discount in this strength tablet.

FDA-APPROVED BIOEQUIVALENT MANUFACTURERS:

Tablet 100 mg

Anabolic	Panray/Ormont
Barr	Pharmavite Pharms
Bell	Phoenix
Bolar	Purepac/Kalipharma
Chelsea	Richlyn
Danbury	*E. R. Squibb
Duramed	Stanlabs/Simpak
Halsey	Towne Paulsen
Lannett	Vitarine/Phoenix
*Eli Lilly	West-Ward
Mallinckrodt	Zenith
M K	

Tablet 300 mg

Barr	Halsey
Bolar	*Eli Lilly
Chelsea	Mallinckrodt
Ciba/Ciba-Geigy	Panray/Ormont
Danbury	Stanlabs/Simpak
Dow	Vitarine/Phoenix
Duramed	West-Ward

ISORDIL

SEE Isosorbide Dinitrate

ISOSORBIDE DINITRATE

BRAND NAME:
Isordil (Ives/AMHO)
Sorbitrate (Stuart/ICI AM)

DOSAGE FORM:
Tablet—Oral 5 mg
Tablet—Oral 10 mg
Tablet—Sublingual (under the tongue) 2.5 mg
Tablet—Sublingual 5 mg
Capsule—Time-Release 40 mg
Tablet—Time-Release 40 mg
Tablet—Chewable 10 mg

USE:
To increase blood and oxygen supply to the heart when an insufficiency exists, as in angina pectoris.

AVOID USE:
If allergic to this drug or to any related drug.

SIDE EFFECTS:
Flushing and redness of the skin, headache, dizziness, weakness. These are usually temporary and disappear.

$ BRAND OR GENERIC?
Oral tablet   These are taken on a regular, long-term basis to protect around-the-clock against angina attack. There is a tremendous savings of up to 70% with generic use. Although no generics are approved by the FDA, many states consider some generic products bioequivalent to the brand.

Sublingual (under the tongue) tablet   This is usually used when immediate relief is needed during an angina attack or before activity that is likely to provoke one. Many states consider some generic products bioequivalent to the brand. This drug must be reliable and predictable in its effect, and for this reason the brand is the best choice. The generic can offer over a 60% savings, and if you cannot pass up these savings, consult with your doctor and at least use the same manufacturer with each prescription refill. The FDA has not approved any generics as bioequivalent at this time.

Capsule—time-release and tablet—time-release   Since it is used on a prophylactic basis to protect against angina attacks, the generic capsule and tablet are a good choice and can offer a price reduction of up to 65%. This is a time-release formulation and is not considered bioequivalent in generic form. But the savings are so great that if the same generic product is used each time the prescription is refilled, an acceptable level of performance should be possible. It is worth discussing with your doctor.

Chewable tablet   These are reserved for use in situations much like the sublingual tablet, where immediate, reliable, and predictable relief is needed. Therefore, the same reasoning dictates the brand-name product as the better choice. The FDA has not approved any generics as bioequivalent to the brand.

FDA-APPROVED BIOEQUIVALENT MANUFACTURERS:
None
The FDA is awaiting revised labeling and additional information on this product's effectiveness.

ISOXSUPRINE

BRAND NAME:
Vasodilan (Mead-Johnson/B-M)

DOSAGE FORM:
Tablet 10 mg
Tablet 20 mg

USE:
As a vasodilator to improve circulation.

AVOID USE:
Immediately after childbirth; during arterial bleeding; if allergic to this drug or to any related drug.

SIDE EFFECTS:
Rare, but may include nausea; vomiting; dizziness; weakness; fast heartbeat; palpitation; low blood pressure; skin rash; chest pain.

$ **BRAND OR GENERIC?**
This drug shows few side effects, making variations among different manufacturers difficult to detect. Generic bioequivalence of some manufacturers is accepted in many states, although the FDA has not commented on this drug. Used mostly long-term, the savings with generic use can be truly astounding: in excess of 80%. Consult your doctor.

FDA-APPROVED BIOEQUIVALENT MANUFACTURERS:
None
The FDA is currently waiting for revised labeling and other product information. Bioequivalency ratings await completion of administrative proceedings.

JANIMINE

SEE Imipramine

KAOCHLOR

SEE Potassium

KAOCHLOR-EFF

SEE Potassium

KATO

SEE Potassium

KAY CIEL

SEE Potassium

KENACORT

SEE Triamcinolone

KENALOG

SEE Triamicinolone Acetonide

K-LOR

SEE Potassium

KLOR-CON

SEE Potassium

KLOR-10%

SEE Potassium

KLORVESS

SEE Potassium

K-LYTE

SEE Potassium

K-LYTE/CL

SEE Potassium

KWELL

SEE Lindane

LANOXIN

SEE Digoxin

LAROTID

SEE Amoxicillin

LASIX

SEE Furosemide

LEDERCILLIN VK

SEE Penicillin VK

LEVOTHROID

SEE L-Thyroxine

LIBRAX

SEE Chlordiazepoxide/Clinidium

LIBRIUM

SEE Chlordiazepoxide

LINDANE

BRAND NAME:
Kwell (Reed & Carnrick)
Scabene (Stiefel)

DOSAGE FORM:
Lotion 1%
Shampoo 1%

USE:
To treat scabies and various lice infestations.

AVOID USE:
If allergic to this compound or to any related drug.

SIDE EFFECTS:
Eczemalike skin eruptions; possible central nervous system toxicity expecially in infants, children, and pregnant women.

$ BRAND OR GENERIC?
Although potential side effects can be severe and manufacturers spell out these warnings in bold-face type, these reactions are uncommon. Most patients experience no untoward effects if they follow directions faithfully.

Among brand-name products Scabene represents about a 10% discount over Kwell in the shampoo and almost 20% off Kwell's price in the lotion. Generics should save 30% in the shampoo and 40% for the lotion. Unfortunately, actual dollar savings are not that great due to the relatively low price of this product.

FDA-APPROVED BIOEQUIVALENT MANUFACTURERS:

Lindane Lotion 1%

Barnes-Hind	*Reed & Carnrick
Bay	*Stiefel
National/Barre	

Lindane Shampoo 1%

Barnes-Hind	*Reed & Carnrick
Bay	*Stiefel
National/Barre	

LOMOTIL

SEE Diphenoxylate/Atropine

LOPURIN

SEE Allopurinol

LORAZEPAM

BRAND NAME:
Ativan (Wyeth)

DOSAGE FORM:
Tablet 0.5 mg
Tablet 1 mg
Tablet 2 mg

USE:
To relieve anxiety.

AVOID USE:
In acute narrow-angle glaucoma; in certain states of mental depression or psychosis; during the first 3 months of pregnancy; if allergic to this drug or to any related drug.

SIDE EFFECTS:
Drowsiness; dizziness; unsteadiness upon standing or walking; disorientation; mental depression; nausea; indigestion; altered appetite; headache; sleeping difficulties; agitation; various skin reactions; blurred vision or other disturbances of eye function.

$ **BRAND OR GENERIC?**
Generic use of this product offers excellent opportunities for savings over the brand. Used mostly as an anti-anxiety agent, slight potential differences in bioavailability among competing manufacturers' products should have minimal effect on this drug's performance. Since this drug has only recently become available generically, the FDA has not yet published bioavailability data at the time of this writing.

In quantities of 30 tablets, generic prescription prices are lower than the brand name Ativan by about 45% for the 0.5-mg tablet, 50% for the 1-mg strength, and up to 54% for the 2-mg product. Quantities of 100 tablets show slightly higher generic savings of about 55% in all 3 strengths.

Since the brand name Ativan has only recently lost its exclusive marketing rights, generics should eventually show even higher savings as more generic competitors enter the marketplace.

FDA-APPROVED BIOEQUIVALENT MANUFACTURERS:
None

L-THYROXINE

BRAND NAME:
Levothroid (Armour)
Synthroid (Flint)

DOSAGE FORM:
Tablet 0.025 mg
Tablet 0.05 mg
Tablet 0.1 mg
Tablet 0.125 mg
Tablet 0.15 mg
Tablet 0.2 mg
Tablet 0.3 mg

USE:
To replace thyroid hormone when an insufficiency exists.

AVOID USE:
Overactive thyroid gland; certain heart ailments; in cases of untreated adrenal gland insufficiency; if used to lose weight and thyroid gland is normal; if allergic to this or to any related drug.

SIDE EFFECTS:
Many are possible but they usually occur only when the dose is too high. They will disappear when the proper drug level is achieved. They may include sweating; heart palpitation; leg cramps; weight loss; skin reactions.

$ BRAND OR GENERIC?
This tablet is given in a fraction of a milligram dose, making formulation an exacting process. Any variation in tablet consistency can result in very unpleasant side effects. While price savings can be greater than 50% with generic use, bioequivalence is not accepted. The brand product is the best choice by far.

FDA-APPROVED BIOEQUIVALENT MANUFACTURERS:
None

LUFYLLIN

SEE Dyphylline

LUMINAL OVOIDS

SEE Phenobarbital

MACRODANTIN

SEE Nitrofurantoin

MANDELAMINE

SEE Methenamine Mandelate

MARAX

SEE Ephedrine/Hydroxyzine/Theophylline

MECLIZINE

BRAND NAME:
Antivert (Roerig)
Bonine (Pfipharmecs/Pfizer)

DOSAGE FORM:
Tablet 12.5 mg
Tablet 25 mg
Tablet (Chewable) 25 mg

USE:
To control nausea, vomiting, diarrhea, or motion sickness.

AVOID USE:
Children under 12 years old; if allergic to this or to any related drug.

SIDE EFFECTS:
Rare, but may include drowsiness; dry mouth; blurred vision.

$ BRAND OR GENERIC?
This drug has few side effects at normal dosage levels. Tablet formulation is not difficult, making generic performance on par with the brand. Up to a 40% savings over the price of Antivert is possible with generic use of all strengths, including the chewable tablet, if taken long-term in large quantities.

There is another alternative to prescription use of this drug. Bonine is the same product but available over-the-counter in a 25-mg chewable tablet, without a prescription. Consumer packages of 8 tablets are about 50% cheaper than a corresponding quantity of Antivert 25 mg by prescription. However, when normal prescriptive quantities of 30 are reached, Bonine's advantage diminishes to about 10%. A bottle of 100 Bonine tablets should save about 15% over the price of an equivalent amount of Antivert 25 mg. If you have medical insurance which covers prescription drugs, you will probably only be reimbursed for Antivert.

FDA-APPROVED BIOEQUIVALENT MANUFACTURERS:

Tablet 12.5 mg

Bolar	Par
C. M. Bundy	*Roerig
Camall	Unit Dose Labs
Chelsea	Vangard Labs/MWM
KV	Zenith

Tablet 25 mg

Anabolic	Par
C. M. Bundy	*Roerig
Camall	Unit Dose Labs
Chelsea	Vangard Labs/MWM
KV	Zenith

Tablet (Chewable) 25 mg

Anabolic
*Roerig
Zenith

MEDROL

SEE Methylprednisolone

MEDROXYPROGESTERONE

BRAND NAME:
Provera (Upjohn)

DOSAGE FORM:
Tablet 10 mg

USE:
To correct certain menstrual irregularities.

AVOID USE:
Blood clotting problems; liver problems; breast or genital cancers; undiagnosed vaginal bleeding; to prevent abortion; as a test for pregnancy; during the first 4 months of pregnancy; if allergic to this or to any related drug.

SIDE EFFECTS:
Breast tenderness and secretion; various skin reactions; acne; hair loss; unusual hair growth; blood clots; changes in menstrual cycle and flow including breakthrough bleeding or spotting; fluid retention; weight gain or loss; liver dys-

function (jaundice); various allergic responses; mental depression; insomnia; nausea; various eye problems; increased blood pressure; changes in sex drive; headache; dizziness; appetite changes.

$ BRAND OR GENERIC?

There is up to a 45% savings with generic use, but since the FDA has not approved any generics, and since this drug is used in potentially serious situations, absolute quality control is a must, making the brand product the best choice.

FDA-APPROVED BIOEQUIVALENT MANUFACTURERS:

None

The FDA considers all brands of this product to have unresolved bioequivalency problems at this time.

MELLARIL

SEE Thioridazine

MEPERIDINE

BRAND NAME;

Demerol (Winthrop/Sterling)

DOSAGE FORM:

Tablet 50 mg

Tablet 100 mg

USE:

To relieve pain.

AVOID USE:

If taking or have taken within the last 14 days a monoamine oxidase inhibitor drug; if allergic to meperidine or to any related drug.

SIDE EFFECTS:

Lightheadedness; dizziness; drowsiness; nausea; vomiting; sweating; dry mouth; constipation; euphoria; headache; hallucinations (temporary); visual disturbances; flushing of the face; heart rhythm irregularities; drop in blood pressure; fainting; difficulty in urinating; various skin reactions; agitation; muscle tremors and twitching; weakness; difficult breathing.

$ BRAND OR GENERIC?

Since this drug is used to relieve severe pain, the risk that a substitute may not perform as well as the brand must be carefully balanced against potential savings. Consult your doctor.

For the 50-mg tablet strength, generics save about 40%. The one exception is Halsey's generic (also known as Pethadol), which shows only intermediate savings of 20% over Demerol.

The 100-mg strength yields higher generic savings of about 50%. Again, Halsey's Pethadol saves less, at about a 30% discount over the brand.

FDA-APPROVED BIOEQUIVALENT MANUFACTURERS:

Tablet 50 mg

Barr   *Winthrop/Sterling
Halsey   Wyeth/AMHO

Tablet 100 mg

Barr
Halsey
*Winthrop/Sterling

MEPROBAMATE

BRAND NAME:
Equanil (Wyeth/AMHO)
Miltown (Wallace/C-W)

DOSAGE FORM:
Tablet 200 mg
Tablet 400 mg

USE:
To relieve anxiety and tension.

AVOID USE:
Certain porphyrin abnormalities; children under 6 years of age; if allergic to meprobamate or to related drugs such as carisoprodol.

SIDE EFFECTS:
Drowsiness; dizziness; loss of coordination; slurred speech; headache; weakness; vertigo; burning sensations of the skin; excitement or overstimulation; nausea; vomiting; diarrhea; various heart rhythm irregularities; low blood pressure; fainting; various skin reactions and other allergic responses; various blood abnormalities.

$ BRAND OR GENERIC?
Most generic products are considered bioequivalent to the brand. Generics should save up to 75%, while Equanil yields more than a 40% discount over Miltown.

FDA—APPROVED BIOEQUIVALENT MANUFACTURERS:

Tablet 200 mg

Anabolic
Barr
Bell
Chelsea
Danbury
Drummer/Phoenix
Halsey
ICN
Lannett
MK
Parke-Davis/W-L
Pharm Basics

Purepac/Kalipharma
Quantum
Reid-Provident
Richlyn
SK & F
Stanlabs/Simpak
Towne Paulsen
*Wallace/C-W
West-Ward
*Wyeth/AMHO
Zenith

Tablet 400 mg

Anabolic
Barr
Bell
Boots Pharmaceutical
Chelsea
Cord
Danbury
Drummer/Phoenix
Ferndale
First Texas/Scherer
Halsey
Heather
ICN
Lannett
Lederle Labs
Lemmon
Mallard
MK

Mylan
Parke-Davis/W-L
Pharm Basics
Pharmavite Pharms
Private Formulations
Purepac/Kalipharma
Quantum
Reid-Provident
Richlyn
SK & F
Stanlabs/Simpak
Tablicaps
Towne Paulsen
Vangard Labs/MWM
*Wallace/C-W
West-Ward
*Wyeth/AMHO
Zenith

MEQUIN

SEE Methaqualone

METAHYDRIN

SEE Trichlormethiazide

METHAQUALONE

BRAND NAME:
Mequin (Lemmon)
Parest (Parke-Davis/W-L)
Quāālude (Lemmon)

DOSAGE FORM:
Tablet 150 mg
Tablet 300 mg
Capsule 200 mg
Capsule 400 mg

USE:
As a sleeping aid.

AVOID USE:
Women who are or may become pregnant; children under 12 years of age; if allergic to methaqualone or to any related drug.

SIDE EFFECTS:
Headache; hangover; dizziness; numbness; stomach upset; nausea; dry mouth; vomiting; sweating with or without a bad odor; skin eruptions; itching; diarrhea; bone marrow depression.

$ **BRAND OR GENERIC?**
Both Mequin and Quāālude are tablets. They were manufactured by the same company and equal in price until methaqualone was withdrawn from the market in 1983. The form of methaqualone in these brands is the base form (not a hydrochloride salt) and 90% is absorbed within 2 hours, with onset occurring within 10 to 20 minutes and lasting 5 to 8 hours.

Parest was manufactured in capsule form as the hydrochloride salt of methaqualone. It is absorbed faster than the tablet. A 400-mg capsule is equivalent to 350 mg of the base. Parest was half the cost of Mequin and Quāālude.

FDA-APPROVED BIOEQUIVALENT MANUFACTURERS:
None
This drug was withdrawn from the market in 1983.

METHENAMINE MANDELATE

BRAND NAME:
Mandelamine (Parke-Davis/W-L)

DOSAGE FORM:
Tablet 250 mg
Tablet 500 mg

USE:
To treat various urinary tract infections.

AVOID USE:
Certain severe impairments of liver or kidney function; if allergic to this drug or to any related drug.

SIDE EFFECTS:
Stomach irritation; nausea; vomiting; various skin reactions; formation of crystals in the urine.

$ BRAND OR GENERIC?
Because this is a pre-1938 drug, it is not subject to the FDA bioequivalency approval process. Side effects are few and safety is not a problem. This drug's high milligram dose, combined with a wide difference between the effective dose and a toxic one, allows some variation among manufacturers without seriously compromising product effectiveness. Major savings with generic use, approaching 70%, make it worthwhile to forsake the brand-name Mandelamine for less expensive substitutes.

FDA-APPROVED BIOEQUIVALENT MANUFACTURERS:
This is a pre-1938 product and is not subject to the FDA's bioequivalency approval process.

METHOCARBAMOL

BRAND NAME:
Robaxin (A. H. Robins)

DOSAGE FORM:
Tablet 500 mg
Tablet 750 mg

USE:
To relieve muscle spasm and pain.

AVOID USE:
Pregnant women; if a nursing mother; children under 12 years of age; if allergic to this drug or to any related drug.

SIDE EFFECTS:
Lightheadedness; dizziness; sedation; nausea; various allergic skin reactions; nasal congestion; eye irritation; blurred vision; headache; fever.

$ BRAND OR GENERIC?
Many generic products are considered bioequivalent by the FDA. This drug's high milligram dose, combined with a wide difference between the effective dose and a toxic one, allows for some variation among manufacturers without compro-

mising product effectiveness. The 500-mg tablet offers generic savings in excess of 40%, while the 750-mg formulation yields a discount of over 50% generically.

FDA-APPROVED BIOEQUIVALENT MANUFACTURERS:

Tablet 500 mg

Ascot	Mylan
Barr	Par
Bolar	Purepac/Kalipharma
Boots	Reid-Provident
Chelsea	Richlyn
Cord	*A. H. Robins
Danbury	Roxane
Drummer/Phoenix	Superpharm
Ferndale	Tablicaps
Heather	Upsher-Smith
Inwood/Forest	West-Ward
KV	Zenith
Lederle Labs	

Tablet 750 mg

Ascot	Mylan
Barr	Par
Bolar	Purepac/Kalipharma
Boots	Reid-Provident
Chelsea	Richlyn
Cord	*A. H. Robins
Danbury	Roxane
Drummer/Phoenix	Superpharm
Heather	Tablicaps
Inwood/Forest	Upsher-Smith
KV	West-Ward
Lannett	Zenith
Lederle Labs	

METHOCARBAMOL/ASPIRIN

BRAND NAME:
Robaxisal (A. H. Robins)

DOSAGE FORM:
Tablet

USE:
To relieve muscle spasm and pain.

AVOID USE:
Pregnant women; if a nursing mother; children under 12 years of age; if allergic to either component of this product or to any related drug.

SIDE EFFECTS:

Dizziness; lightheadedness; nausea; drowsiness; blurred vision; headache; fever; various allergic skin reactions; stomach irritation or ulceration; vomiting; constipation; diarrhea; asthma.

$ BRAND OR GENERIC?

While there are numerous generics approved with the single ingredient, methocarbamol, this dual-component product with the second ingredient, aspirin, has very few FDA-approved generic manufacturers. Use of approved generics should show savings of 30%, while other nonbioequivalent generics can save up to 40%. The best choice here is to stick to the approved product.

FDA-APPROVED BIOEQUIVALENT MANUFACTURERS:

* A. H. Robins
Zenith

METHYCLOTHIAZIDE

BRAND NAME:

Aquatensin (Wallace/C-W)
Enduron (Abbott)

DOSAGE FORM:

Tablet 2.5 mg
Tablet 5 mg

USE:

As a diuretic to rid the body of excess fluid; to manage high blood pressure; to treat congestive heart failure.

AVOID USE:

Certain kidney problems; if a nursing mother; if allergic to this or to other sulfa-related drugs.

SIDE EFFECTS:

Loss of appetite; stomach upset; nausea; vomiting; cramps; diarrhea; constipation; liver dysfunction (jaundice); inflammation of the pancreas; dizziness or dizziness upon standing; vertigo; burning sensations of the skin; headache; various blood abnormalities; skin reactions including sensitivity to sunlight; high blood sugar, uric acid or calcium levels; muscle weakness or spasm.

$ BRAND OR GENERIC?

This drug is considered to be one of the less potent agents in this category. It is not used in severe conditions requiring excessive diuresis (elimination of body water). Used on a long-term basis, savings with generic use can really add up.

The 2.5-mg tablet has only one brand-name product, Enduron. Generics should save up to 30%.

Aquatensin, available only in 5-mg tablet strength, is about 20% more expensive than Enduron, the other brand-name product. Generics will yield over a 40% savings compared to Aquatensin.

FDA-APPROVED BIOEQUIVALENT MANUFACTURERS:

Tablet 2.5 mg

*Abbott	Mylan
Bolar	Zenith
Chelsea	

Tablet 5 mg

*Abbott	Mylan
Bolar	*Wallace/C-W
Chelsea	Zenith
Colmed	

METHYCLOTHIAZIDE/DESERPIDINE

BRAND NAME:
Enduronyl (Abbott)
Enduronyl Forte (Abbott)

DOSAGE FORM:
Tablet 5 mg methyclothiazide/0.25 mg deserpidine
Tablet 5 mg methyclothiazide/0.5 mg deserpidine

USE:
To control high blood pressure.

AVOID USE:
Inadequate kidney function; mental depression; active peptic ulcer; ulcerative colitis; if a nursing mother; if receiving electroconvulsive therapy; if allergic to either ingredient in this product, to any sulfa drug, or to any other related drug.

SIDE EFFECTS:
Stomach upset; nausea; vomiting; loss of appetite; constipation; diarrhea; dizziness or dizziness on standing; drowsiness; depression; headache; nightmares; hearing loss; tingling or burning sensations of the skin; various blood abnormalities; various skin reactions including sensitivity to sunlight; heart rhythm irregularities; pseudoanginal symptoms; increased blood sugar; high uric acid levels; muscle weakness and spasm; nasal congestion; changes in sex drive; dry mouth; various eye problems; liver dysfunction (jaundice); inflammation of the pancreas; various eye problems.

$ **BRAND OR GENERIC?**
Because this two-ingredient product contains one component, deserpidine, in a fraction of a milligram dose, quality control is of tantamount importance in en-

suring therapeutic consistency. It is difficult and often ill-advised to control hypertension with a fixed-ratio multicomponent drug product. Adding to this the uncertainty of not knowing which generic you may receive each time your prescription is refilled, it just doesn't seem to justify the risks, even though there is a possible 25% to 30% savings.

FDA-APPROVED BIOEQUIVALENT MANUFACTURERS:
None

The FDA considers all brands of this product to have unresolved bioequivalency problems at this time.

METHYLDOPA

BRAND NAME:
Aldomet (MSD/Merck)

DOSAGE FORM:
Tablet 250 mg
Tablet 500 mg

USE:
To control high blood pressure.

AVOID USE:
In cases of active liver disease (hepatitis, cirrhosis); if previous therapy with this drug has caused liver disorders; if allergic to this drug or to any related drug.

SIDE EFFECTS:
Sedation, drowsiness, headache, and weakness may occur temporarily during the first few weeks of therapy or can continue longer; lightheadedness; tingling or burning sensations of the skin; parkinsonism; Bell's palsy; mental confusion; nightmares; mild psychoses (reversible); depression; slowed heartbeat; aggravation of angina pectoris; dizziness on standing; water retention and weight gain; nausea; vomiting; constipation; diarrhea; dry mouth; nasal stuffiness; irritation of the tongue; inflammation of the pancreas; liver dysfunction (jaundice); abnormal liver function tests; bone marrow depression; various anemias; various allergic reactions such as fever, lupuslike symptoms, and inflammation of the heart; various skin reactions; enlargement of the breasts; production of breast milk; menstrual irregularities; decreased sex drive or impotence; muscle and joint pain.

$ BRAND OR GENERIC?
Since this drug has only recently gone off patent, there are few generic products available. Currently generics yield about a 20% savings over the price of the brand in both the 250-mg and 500-mg strengths. But as more competitors enter the marketplace, this discount should increase.

FDA-APPROVED BIOEQUIVALENT MANUFACTURERS:

Tablet 250 mg

Chelsea   *MSD/Merck
Cord   Mylan

Tablet 500 mg

Chelsea   *MSD/Merck
Cord   Mylan

METHYLPHENIDATE

BRAND NAME:
  Ritalin (Ciba/Ciba-Geigy)

DOSAGE FORM:
  Tablet 5 mg
  Tablet 10 mg
  Tablet 20 mg

USE:
  As a stimulant used to treat hyperactive children, narcolepsy, and senile behavior.

AVOID USE:
  Children under 6 years old; glaucoma; preexisting states of anxiety, tension,
and agitation; in those with motor tics; in patients with a family history of or
diagnosed Gilles de la Tourette's syndrome; if allergic to this or to any related
drug.

SIDE EFFECTS:
  Nervous tension; sleeplessness; various skin reactions; loss of appetite; nausea;
rapid heartbeat; stomach pain; dizziness; headache; certain blood abnormalities;
high or low blood pressure or pulse; weight loss; hair loss.

$ **BRAND OR GENERIC?**
  Since many of the side effects associated with this drug are dose related, generic savings are only worthwhile provided the same manufacturer's product can
be used with each prescription refill.
  Few generics are approved as bioequivalent by the FDA. Use of this product
can yield savings in the 60% range in all strengths. Mostly used on a long-term
basis, considerable savings will accrue with generic use. Consult your doctor.

FDA-APPROVED BIOEQUIVALENT MANUFACTURERS:

Tablet 5 mg, 10 mg, 20 mg

*Ciba/Ciba-Geigy
 MD

METHYLPREDNISOLONE

BRAND NAME:
Medrol (Upjohn)

DOSAGE FORM:
Tablet 4 mg

USE:
As cortisone replacement therapy in certain endocrine gland disorders; for various arthritic conditions; certain collagen diseases; some skin conditions; allergic states; some eye disorders; certain lung diseases; some cancers.

AVOID USE:
Fungal infections of the blood; if allergic to this or to any related drug.

SIDE EFFECTS:
Fluid retention; potassium loss; high blood pressure; muscle weakness; bone decomposition; loss of muscle mass; peptic ulcer; ulceration of the esophagus; inflammation of the pancreas; delayed wound healing; facial redness or rash; sweating; increased skull pressure; convulsions; headache; vertigo; growth suppression in children; Cushing's syndrome; diabetic decontrol; menstrual irregularities; glaucoma and other eye problems; various skin reactions and other allergic responses.

$ **BRAND OR GENERIC?**
Bioequivalence approval of the generic is pending. The price savings with generic use can be as high as 55%. If used short-term for a serious condition, the brand is the best choice. Long-term therapy will yield major savings with generic use, making an alternative worth consulting your physician about.

FDA-APPROVED BIOEQUIVALENT MANUFACTURERS:
None

Bioequivalence ratings are awaiting results of studies of prednisone, a similar drug that has known bioequivalence problems.

METICORTEN

SEE Prednisone

METOCLOPRAMIDE

BRAND NAME:
Reglan (A. H. Robins)

DOSAGE FORM:

Tablet 10 mg

USE:

To treat delayed gastric emptying.

AVOID USE:

In presence of gastrointestinal hemorrhage, obstruction or perforation; in patients with pheochromacytoma; in epileptics; if taking any other drug likely to cause extrapyramidal reactions; if allergic to this drug or to any related drug.

SIDE EFFECTS:

Restlessness; drowsiness; fatigue; lassitude; insomnia; headache; dizziness; nausea; extrapyramidal reactions; parkinson-like reactions; anxiety; diarrhea; depression.

$ BRAND OR GENERIC?

Since the brand name Reglan has just recently gone off-patent, only a few generics have been approved by the FDA. But these are rated as bioequivalent to the brand so substitution should pose no problem.

Generic use saves in excess of 40% over the brand-name product. As more generic competitors enter the marketplace, savings should increase even more.

FDA-APPROVED BIOEQUIVALENT MANUFACTURERS:

Biocraft
Colmed
Quantum
*A. H. Robins

METRONIDAZOLE

BRAND NAME:

Flagyl (Searle)
Metryl (Lemmon)
Protostat (Ortho)

DOSAGE FORM:

Tablet 250 mg
Tablet 500 mg

USE:

To treat various trichomonal, amoebic, or bacterial infections.

AVOID USE:

During the first 3 months of pregnancy; if taking alcohol at the same time; if a nursing mother; if allergic to this or to any related drug.

SIDE EFFECTS:

Nausea; headache; loss of appetite; vomiting; diarrhea; stomach upset; abdominal cramps; constipation; convulsive seizures; numbness or burning sensations of an extremity; unpleasant metallic taste; irritation of the mouth and tongue; furry tongue; yeast infection of the mouth or vagina; low white blood cell count; dizziness; loss of coordination; mental depression; insomnia; irritability; weakness; various skin reactions; flushing; nasal congestion; dry mouth; fever; kidney dysfunction; decreased sex drive.

$ BRAND OR GENERIC?

Many generic products are FDA-approved as bioequivalent. Three brand-name products are available and there are some price variations among them.

The 250-mg-strength tablet is generally used in quantities of 21, over a 7-day period. Flagyl emerges as the most expensive. Protostat can save up to 24%, while Metryl offers up to a 60% discount. Generics, however, can yield savings approaching 75%.

The 500-mg tablet is usually dispensed in quantities of only 4 tablets to be taken at once, or split into two divided doses on the same day. Flagyl again emerges as the most expensive, with Protostat offering a discount of about 23%. Metryl can save as much as 48%, while generics offer savings approaching 60%.

FDA-APPROVED BIOEQUIVALENT MANUFACTURERS:

Tablet 250 mg and 500 mg

Barr	*Ortho
Chelsea	Par
Cord	Savage
Danbury	*Searle
Halsey	Sidmak
*Lemmon	Superpharm
LNK (250-mg strength only)	Zenith

METRYL

SEE Metronidazole

MILTOWN

SEE Meprobamate

MOTRIN

SEE Ibuprofen

MYCIFRADIN

SEE Neomycin

MYCOLOG-II

SEE Nystatin/Triamcinolone

MYCOSTATIN

SEE Nystatin
SEE Nystatin Oral
SEE Nystatin Vaginal

MYSOLINE

SEE Primidone

NALDECON

SEE Phenylpropanolamine/
   Phenylephrine/Phenyltoloxamine
   Chlorpheniramine

NAQUA

SEE Trichlormethiazide

NEOMYCIN

BRAND NAME:
   Mycifradin (Upjohn)
DOSAGE FORM:
   Tablet 500 mg
USE:
   As an antibiotic to sterilize the bowel before and after certain surgical proce-
dures; to keep in check certain bacteria present when cirrhosis of the liver occurs;
to control certain infectious diarrhea.

AVOID USE:

Intestinal obstruction; if allergic to this or to any related drug.

SIDE EFFECTS:

Since very little of this drug (about 3%) is absorbed into the body when taken orally, side effects are not usual. Upon prolonged use, however, hearing disorders and even deafness can occur. Large doses can produce a malabsorption syndrome affecting the way the body uses the food it takes in. Other possible side effects may include nausea, vomiting, diarrhea, and liver problems.

$ BRAND OR GENERIC?

This drug is reserved for special situations, generally being used for a maximum of three days and only under a doctor's direct supervision. Taken at normal dosage levels, side effects are minimal since most of the drug's effect is localized in the intestines, with very little getting into the general blood circulation. It is only when too high a dose is given or when duration of therapy is too long that some of the potentially dangerous side effects come into play.

Several generics are approved by the FDA as bioequivalent. Pfizer's neomycin can net savings approaching 50% over Eli Lilly's or Squibb's products, the two most expensive and comparably priced branded generics.

Nonbranded generics, marketed by numerous smaller manufacturers, can yield savings of up to 67% and should offer performance on a par with other, more expensive alternatives.

FDA-APPROVED BIOEQUIVALENT MANUFACTURERS:

Tablet 500 mg

Biocraft	Roxane
Lannett	E. R. Squibb
Eli Lilly	*Upjohn
Pfizer	Vitarine/Phoenix

NEMBUTAL

SEE Pentobarbital

NILSTAT

SEE Nystatin
SEE Nystatin Oral
SEE Nystatin Vaginal

NITROBID

SEE Nitroglycerin
SEE Nitroglycerin Ointment

NITROFURANTOIN

BRAND NAME:

Furadantin (Norwich Eaton)
Macrodantin (Norwich Eaton)

DOSAGE FORM:

Tablet 50 mg ⎫
Tablet 100 mg⎭ Known by brand name Furadantin

Capsule 50 mg ⎫
Capsule 100 mg⎭ Known by brand name Macrodantin

USE:

To treat certain urinary tract infections.

AVOID USE:

Little or no urine output; certain kidney problems; infants under one month;
pregnant women at term; if allergic to this drug or to any related drug.

SIDE EFFECTS:

Loss of appetite; nausea; vomiting; diarrhea; abdominal pain; liver dysfunction (jaundice, hepatitis); various skin reactions; potentially serious allergic responses including lung complications that mimic many symptoms of pneumonia;
various blood abnormalities; numbness, tingling or burning pain of the extremities; headache; dizziness; drowsiness; visual problems; loss of hair (temporary);
various superinfections.

Note: The capsule form known by the brand name Macrodantin tends to
cause less stomach upset than tablets and generic capsules.

$ BRAND OR GENERIC?

Tablet Several generics are considered bioequivalent to the brand by the
FDA. Generic use offers tremendous savings. The 50-mg tablet can save over 50%,
while a discount of almost 75% is possible with the 100-mg tablet.

Capsule Since Macrodantin is still protected by patent, no generic products
are allowed to be sold as yet. But a confusing situation exists whereby many manufacturers market a capsule that contains not the macrocrystalline active ingredient found in the brand-name product but the microcrystalline form similar to
the tablet formulation. In fact, Norwich Eaton, maker of Macrodantin, does not
even market a microcrystalline capsule form of the drug. Many doctors and pharmacists were erroneously substituting generic capsules for Macrodantin until
Norwich Eaton sent a bulletin around to health professionals warning them that
no alternative to Macrodantin can be marketed generically. Since no price com-

parison can be offered to a brand-name product, and no real rationale exists for prescribing a generic capsule, this section is included to clarify a confusing state of affairs.

FDA-APPROVED BIOEQUIVALENT MANUFACTURERS:

Tablet 50 mg and 100 mg

Bolar	*Norwich Eaton
Chelsea	Quantum
Drummer/Phoenix	Towne Paulsen (100-mg strength only)
Lannett	Zenith

Capsule 50 mg and 100 mg

None

NITROGLYCERIN

BRAND NAME:
Nitro-Bid (Marion)
Nitroglycerin (Eli Lilly)
Nitroglyn (Key)
Nitrospan (USV)
Nitrostat (Parke-Davis/W-L)
Nitrostat SR (Parke-Davis/W-L)

DOSAGE FORM:
Capsule—Time-Release 2.5 mg
　　　　　　　　　　6.5 mg
　　　　　　　　　　9 mg
Tablet—Sublingual (under the tongue) 0.15 mg (1/400 grain)
　　　　　　　　　　　　　　　　　0.3　 mg (1/200 grain)
　　　　　　　　　　　　　　　　　0.4　 mg (1/150 grain)
　　　　　　　　　　　　　　　　　0.6　 mg (1/100 grain)

USE:
To treat anginal pain.

AVOID USE:
Certain heart disease; severe anemia; closed-angle glaucoma; if prone to light-headedness upon standing; if allergic to this or to any related drug.

SIDE EFFECTS:
Headache; drop in blood pressure when standing up; nausea; vomiting; various skin reactions; dizziness; flushing of the face; palpitation.

$ BRAND OR GENERIC?
Nitroglycerin capsules are a time-release formulation and, as such, generics are not considered bioequivalent to the brand product. Since each manufacturer

takes a different approach to formulating a time-release dosage form, the characteristics of various products differ. This capsule, however, is taken on a protective basis to guard against an angina attack. Quick action is not the purpose of this product. Although various brands may differ somewhat, they all do the job. Since there is almost an 80% savings with the generic product, it emerges as the best choice. Among brand products, Nitroglyn is the cheapest and offers up to a 70% savings over Nitro-Bid and Nitrospan, the most expensive brands. Nitrostat saves about 30%. Discuss alternatives with your doctor.

The sublingual tablet is meant to provide immediate relief and has just two competitors on the market, Lilly's Nitroglycerin and Parke-Davis's Nitrostat. Both are considered brand-name pharmaceuticals and retail for about the same price. There is, however, one distinction that gives an edge to the Parke-Davis product: All nitroglycerins are volatile—that is they tend to lose potency rapidly, especially when exposed to the atmosphere. Nitrostat's formulation includes polyethylene glycol, a stabilizer that slows this loss and is responsible for its extended shelf life of 5 years as opposed to Lilly's 2-year expiration date.

FDA-APPROVED BIOEQUIVALENT MANUFACTURERS:

Capsule—Time-Release

None

The FDA is awaiting revised labeling and additional information on this product's effectiveness.

Tablet—Sublingual

This is a pre-1938 drug and is exempt from the FDA's bioequivalency approval process.

NITROGLYCERIN OINTMENT

BRAND NAME:
  Nitro-Bid (Marion)
  Nitrol (Kremers-Urban)
  Nitrostat (Parke-Davis/W-L)

DOSAGE FORM:
  Ointment 2%

USE:
  To treat anginal pain.

AVOID USE:
  If allergic to this or to related nitrate drugs.

SIDE EFFECTS:

Headache (temporary); low blood pressure; increased heart rate; flushing; dizziness; nausea; skin reactions (in area of ointment application).

$ **BRAND OR GENERIC?**

Because this drug is exempt by court order from the FDA's bioequivalency ratings, guidance in selecting a generic substitute is limited.

Being an ointment, formulation variables can influence the absorption of nitroglycerin through the skin enough to warrant careful consideration when effecting generic interchange. The three brand-name products all describe their ointment base as having the same ingredients, although methods of blending and percentages of each component are not divulged. Consult your doctor.

All brands come in two sizes: a 30-gram (1-ounce) tube (except for Nitro-Bid, which markets a 20-gram size) and a 60-gram quantity.

In the 30-gram tube, Nitrol and Nitro-Bid are the most expensive, with Nitrostat saving about 10%. The generic offers savings in excess of 30%.

The 60-gram size shows Nitrol about 7% more expensive than the other two brand names, with generics offering discounts of up to 33%.

FDA-APPROVED BIOEQUIVALENT MANUFACTURERS:

None

This product is exempt from FDA-bioequivalency approval procedures under a special court order.

NITROGLYN

SEE Nitroglycerin

NITROL

SEE Nitroglycerin Ointment

NITROSPAN:

SEE Nitroglycerin

NITROSTAT

SEE Nitroglycerin; Nitroglycerin Ointment

NITROSTAT SR

SEE Nitroglycerin

NOCTEC

SEE Chloral Hydrate

NORFLEX

SEE Orphenadrine

NORPACE

SEE Disopyramide

NUTRACORT

SEE Hydrocortisone

NYDRAZID

SEE Isoniazid

NYLIDRIN

BRAND NAME:
Arlidin (USV)

DOSAGE FORM:
Tablet 6 mg
Tablet 12 mg

USE:
To treat various circulatory disorders.

AVOID USE:
Certain heart disease; thyroid disease; if allergic to this or to any related drug.

SIDE EFFECTS:
Trembling; nervousness; dizziness; nausea; vomiting; weakness; palpitations.

$ BRAND OR GENERIC?

Tremendous savings are possible with generic use. Although the FDA is currently withholding bioequivalency ratings, many states do not accept generic equivalents. Users of this drug experience few side effects, making it a prime candidate for generic use, with savings in excess of 80% possible. Consult your doctor.

FDA-APPROVED BIOEQUIVALENT MANUFACTURERS:
None

The FDA currently lists this product as ineffective. Bioequivalency ratings await completion of administrative proceedings.

NYSTATIN

BRAND NAME:

Mycostatin (E. R. Squibb)
Nilstat (Lederle Labs)

DOSAGE FORM:

Cream 100,000 units/gm
Ointment 100,000 units/gm

USE:

As an antifungal to treat Candida infections of the skin and mucous membranes.

AVOID USE:

If allergic to nystatin or to any related drug.

SIDE EFFECTS:

Possible skin irritation.

$ BRAND OR GENERIC?

This product comes in two sizes of tubes: 15 gm (½ ounce) and 30 gm (1 ounce). Generic use can save over 50% for the small size and can approach 70% for the larger quantity. The brand-name Nilstat only comes in the smaller size tube but saves about 15% over the other brand-name, Mycostatin.

FDA-APPROVED BIOEQUIVALENT MANUFACTURERS:

Cream

Byk-Gulden	Miles
Clay-Park	NMC
*Lederle Labs	*E. R. Squibb
Lemmon	Thames

Ointment

Byk-Gulden	*Lederle Labs
Clay-Park	*E. R. Squibb

NYSTATIN ORAL

BRAND NAME:
Mycostatin (E. R. Squibb)
Nilstat (Lederle Labs)

DOSAGE FORM:
Oral Tablet 500,000 units
Oral Suspension 100,000 units/ml

USE:
To treat Candida infections of the intestine (oral tablet): to treat Candida infections of the mouth (oral suspension).

AVOID USE:
If allergic to nystatin or to any related drug.

SIDE EFFECTS:
None is usual. High doses may cause diarrhea; stomach upset; nausea; vomiting.

$ **BRAND OR GENERIC?**
Good savings are possible with generic use. Since little of the drug is absorbed into the body, exerting mainly a local effect on the gastrointestinal tract, side effects are rare. The generic alternative is the best choice for this drug, with savings of better than 46% possible for the tablets and up to 57% for the oral suspension.

FDA-APPROVED BIOEQUIVALENT MANUFACTURERS:

Oral Tablet 500,000 units

Chelsea	Par
Drummer/Phoenix	Quantum
*Lederle Labs	*E. R. Squibb

Oral Suspension 100,000 units/ml

Bay	Pharmaderm/Byk-Gulden
E. Fougera/Byk-Gulden	Pharmafair
*Lederle Labs	Savage Labs/Byk-Gulden
National/Barre	*E. R. Squibb

NYSTATIN/TRIAMCINOLONE

BRAND NAME:
Mycolog-II (E. R. Squibb)

DOSAGE FORM:
Cream
Ointment

USE:

To treat various skin conditions such as inflammation, Candida and bacterial skin infections.

AVOID USE:

Tuberculosis of the skin; viral skin conditions; most fungal skin growths; if allergic to this or to any related drug.

SIDE EFFECTS:

Burning sensation of the skin; itching; dryness of the skin; various other skin reactions.

$ BRAND OR GENERIC?

Until recently, this product has not been rated for bioequivalence by the FDA due to its inclusion in the DESI review program. With the removal of two ingredients, neomycin and gramicidin, this preparation has been upgraded from the status of "ineffective" to the category of "safe and effective." Considerable savings are possible with generic use, ranging from up to 50% with the 15-gm (½ ounce) tube to as much as 65% for the 60-gm (2-ounce) size.

FDA-APPROVED BIOEQUIVALENT MANUFACTURERS:

Cream

Clay-Park
NMC
*E. R. Squibb

Ointment

None

NYSTATIN VAGINAL

BRAND NAME:

Mycostatin (E. R. Squibb)
Nilstat (Lederle Labs)

DOSAGE FORM:

Vaginal tablets 100,000 units

USE:

To treat fungal infections of the vagina.

AVOID USE:

If allergic to nystatin or to any related drug.

SIDE EFFECTS:

Possible vaginal irritation.

$ BRAND OR GENERIC?

Savings of over 40% are possible with generic use. Bioequivalence for many generic products is accepted by the FDA.

FDA-APPROVED BIOEQUIVALENT MANUFACTURERS:
  Chelsea
  Drummer/Phoenix
  E. Fougera/Byk-Gulden
  Holland-Rantos
  *Lederle Labs
  Lemmon
  Quantum
  *E. R. Squibb

OMNIPEN

SEE Ampicillin

ORA-TESTRYL

SEE Fluoxymesterone

ORETIC

SEE Hydrochlorothiazide

ORINASE

SEE Tolbutamide

ORNADE

SEE Phenylpropanolamine/Chlorpheniramine

ORPHENADRINE

BRAND NAME:
  Norflex (Riker/3M)
DOSAGE FORM:
  Tablet—Time-Release 100 mg

USE:

As a muscle relaxant.

AVOID USE:

Glaucoma; certain esophageal disorders; some prostate conditions; difficulty in urinating; myasthenia gravis; if allergic to this or to any related drug.

SIDE EFFECTS:

Dry mouth; blurred vision; various visual problems; drowsiness; weakness; headache; dizziness; confusion (particularly in the elderly); hallucinations; fainting; palpitation or fast heartbeat; nausea; vomiting; stomach irritation; constipation; difficulty in urinating; aplastic anemia; various skin reactions and other allergic responses.

$ BRAND OR GENERIC?

Side effects, when they occur, are mostly due to higher than usual dosage levels. At normal levels side effects are rare, allowing for some variation among manufacturers without seriously compromising product performance.

This is a time-release tablet, making generic duplication very difficult. Time-release formulations are not normally considered bioequivalent due to the many different approaches possible in manufacturing this type of product, but in this case a few generic manufacturers have demonstrated the bioequivalence of their products. Use of these generics can yield savings as high as 76%. Although generally used on a short-term basis, dollar savings are very high due to the expensive nature of the brand-name drug.

FDA-APPROVED BIOEQUIVALEN⎯ MANUFACTURERS:

Ascot
Bolar
*Riker/3M

OXACILLIN

BRAND NAME:

Bactocill (Beecham)
Prostaphlin (Bristol)

DOSAGE FORM:

Capsule 250 mg
Capsule 500 mg
Powder for oral solution 250 mg/5 ml

USE:

As an antibiotic to treat various infections.

AVOID USE:

If allergic to this drug or to any penicillin.

SIDE EFFECTS:
Skin rash; mouth or tongue irritation; monilia (fungal) infection of the mouth or anus; upset stomach; nausea; vomiting; diarrhea; various blood abnormalities.

$ BRAND OR GENERIC?
The FDA has certified several generic products as bioequivalent to the brand. Generic savings can be quite high.

In capsule form, the 250-mg strength will yield over a 60% savings generically, while the 500-mg capsule can net better than 40% off the brand price.

In the powder-for-oral-solution formulation, up to 60% can be slashed from the price of the brand.

There is also another alternative. Bactocill (Beecham) is considered to be a branded generic. This means that it is manufactured by a major pharmaceutical house and can be expected to maintain a very high quality. Although not available in liquid form (even though it is posted on the FDA list), it is marketed in capsule form. Both the 250-mg and 500-mg strength can save over 40%.

FDA-APPROVED BIOEQUIVALENT MANUFACTURERS:

Capsule 250 mg, capsule 500 mg, powder for oral solution 250 mg/5ml

* Beecham
  Biocraft
* Bristol

OXTRIPHYLLINE

BRAND NAME:
Choledyl (Parke-Davis/W-L)

DOSAGE FORM:
Tablet 100 mg
Tablet 200 mg
Elixir 100 mg/5 ml

USE:
To treat breathing difficulties associated with certain asthmas, bronchitis, and emphysema.

AVOID USE:
If allergic to this drug, to theophylline, or to any other related drug.

SIDE EFFECTS:
Stomach upset; nausea; rapid or irregular heartbeat; excitation; anxiety.

$ BRAND OR GENERIC?
Due to the enteric coating on the tablet formulation, bioequivalence is difficult to attain for generic products. The FDA has certified few generic tablets or elixirs as bioequivalent to the brand.

Generic savings can be as high as 26% with the 100-mg tablet, 34% for the 200-mg strength, and up to 24% in the elixir form. Consult your doctor.

FDA-APPROVED BIOEQUIVALENT MANUFACTURERS:

Tablet 100 mg and 200 mg

Bolar
*Parke-Davis/W-L

Elixir 100 mg/5 ml

Bay
*Parke-Davis/W-L

OXYCODONE/ACETAMINOPHEN

BRAND NAME:
Percocet-5 (DuPont)

DOSAGE FORM:
Tablet

USE:
To relieve severe pain.

AVOID USE:
In children; if allergic to oxycodone, to acetaminophen, or to any related drug.

SIDE EFFECTS:
Lightheadedness; dizziness; drowsiness; nausea; vomiting; constipation; euphoria; skin rash.

$ **BRAND OR GENERIC?**
This is a very strong pain reliever. If you need this drug, you may be in no frame of mind to go bargain hunting. If it is used for a short period of time for temporary relief of pain, quantities will be small and potential savings may not be as important as getting quick, reliable relief. Expect savings on the order of 30% with generic use.

If, on the other hand, this product is needed for chronic pain on a long-term basis in quantities of 100 tablets, generic savings can exceed 50%. For long-term use the generic alternative is the best by far.

FDA-APPROVED BIOEQUIVALENT MANUFACTURERS:
Barr
*DuPont
Halsey
Roxane

OXYCODONE HYDROCHLORIDE/OXYCODONE TEREPTHALATE/ASPIRIN

BRAND NAME:
Percodan (DuPont)

DOSAGE FORM:
Tablet

USE:
To relieve severe pain.

AVOID USE:
In children; if allergic to either component of this product or to any related drug.

SIDE EFFECTS:
Lightheadedness; dizziness; drowsiness; nausea; vomiting; constipation; euphoria; itching.

$ BRAND OR GENERIC?
This is a very strong pain reliever. If you need this drug, you may be in no frame of mind to go bargain hunting. If used for a short period of time for temporary relief of pain, quantities will be small and potential savings may not be as important as getting quick, reliable relief. Expect savings on the order of 30% with generic use.

If, on the other hand, this product is needed for chronic pain relief on a long-term basis in quantities of 100 tablets, generic savings can exceed 50%. For long-term use the generic alternative is the best by far.

FDA-APPROVED BIOEQUIVALENT MANUFACTURERS:
Barr
*DuPont
Halsey
Roxane

OXYTETRACYCLINE

BRAND NAME:
Terramycin (Pfizer)

DOSAGE FORM:
Capsule 250 mg

USE:
As an antibiotic to treat various infections.

AVOID USE:
During the second half of pregnancy; in infants and children up to 8 years old; if allergic to this or to any related drug.

SIDE EFFECTS:

Stomach upset; nausea; vomiting; diarrhea; tongue inflammation; possible yeast infection of the rectum or genital area; various skin reactions including sensitivity to sunlight; numerous allergic responses; various blood abnormalities.

$ BRAND OR GENERIC?

Despite the long list of possible side effects, most are rare. As with most antibiotics taken by mouth, the dosage prescribed is usually in excess of the level actually needed to treat the infection. For this reason some variation in potency among various generics is not a major consideration.

The FDA has approved several generics as bioequivalent, assuring nearly universal availability. Generic savings approaching 75% are possible, stating a rather convincing case for using an alternative to the brand-name product.

FDA-APPROVED BIOEQUIVALENT MANUFACTURERS:
    MK
  *Pfizer
    Proter/Italy
    Purepac/Kalipharma
    Richlyn
    West-Ward

PANMYCIN

SEE Tetracycline

PANWARFIN

SEE Warfarin

PAPAVERINE

BRAND NAME:
    Pavabid (Marion)
    Cerespan (USV)

DOSAGE FORM:
    Capsule—Time-Release 150 mg

USE:
    To improve circulation in various heart and circulatory conditions.

AVOID USE:
    If allergic to this drug or to any related drug.

SIDE EFFECTS:

Rare, but may include nausea; stomach upset; loss of appetite; constipation; drowsiness; skin rash; diarrhea; vertigo; sweating; headache.

$ BRAND OR GENERIC?

Since this is a time-release capsule, generic products are not considered bioequivalent to the brand. The different in price between brand and generic is truly staggering at up to 70%. The generic product may do the job very adequately, and since this drug is used long-term, the potential for savings more than justifies generic use. Consult your doctor.

FDA-APPROVED BIOEQUIVALENT MANUFACTURERS:

This is a pre-1938 drug and is exempt from the FDA's bioequivalency approval process.

PARAFLEX

SEE Chlorzoxazone

PARAFON FORTE

SEE Chlorzoxazone/Acetaminophen

PAREGORIC

BRAND NAME:

None

DOSAGE FORM:

Tincture (concentrated liquid)

USE:

To control diarrhea.

AVOID USE:

If you have diarrhea due to poisoning; in infants; if allergic to this or to other opium- or morphine-derived drugs.

SIDE EFFECTS:

Lightheadedness; dizziness; drowsiness; nausea; vomiting; sweating; various skin reactions; breathing difficulties; dry mouth; constipation; difficulty in urinating; facial flushing.

$ BRAND OR GENERIC?

Since this drug dates back to 1885, there is no brand-name product. The manufacturer considered to be the highest priced is Eli Lilly, but there is no real advantage to using Lilly's product since tinctures are simple to manufacture and bioavailability should not vary among makers. Use of other manufacturers' products yields savings up to 24%.

FDA-APPROVED BIOEQUIVALENT MANUFACTURERS:

This is a pre-1938 drug and is exempt from the FDA's bioequivalency approval process.

PAREST

SEE Methaqualone

PATHIBAMATE

SEE Tridihexethyl/Meprobamate

PATHOCIL

SEE Dicloxacillin

PAVABID

SEE Papaverine

PBZ

SEE Tripelennamine

PEDIAMYCIN

SEE Erythromycin Ethylsuccinate

PENAPAR-VK

SEE Penicillin VK

PENBRITIN

SEE Ampicillin

PENICILLIN G POTASSIUM

BRAND NAME:
Pentids (E. R. Squibb)
Pfizerpen G (Pfizer)

DOSAGE FORM:
Tablet 200,000 units (125 mg)
Tablet 400,000 units (250 mg)
Syrup 200,000 units (125 mg/5 ml)
Syrup 400,000 units (250 mg/5 ml)

USE:
As an antibiotic to treat various infections.

AVOID USE:
If allergic to penicillin or to any related drug.

SIDE EFFECTS:
Nausea; vomiting; stomach upset; diarrhea; a superinfection called black hairy tongue; various skin reactions and many possible allergic responses; various blood abnormalities; mouth or tongue irritation.

$ **BRAND OR GENERIC?**
In tablet form there can be some savings using a generic product, but often, due to special purchasing arrangements, a pharmacy can sell the brand almost as cheaply as the generic. Ask the price of the brand before you allow the prescription to be filled generically.

In the syrup form it almost never pays to use a generic, since the prices for brands and generics differ very little.

FDA-APPROVED BIOEQUIVALENT MANUFACTURERS:

Tablet 200,000 units (125 mg)

Biocraft	Purepac/Kalipharma
Mylan	*E. R. Squibb
*Pfizer	Wyeth/AMHO

Tablet 400,000 units (250 mg)

Biocraft	*E. R. Squibb
Mylan	Wyeth/AMHO
*Pfizer	Zenith
Purepac/Kalipharma	

Syrup 200,000 units (125 mg)/5 ml

Biocraft
Mylan
*E. R. Squibb

Syrup 400,000 units (250 mg)/5 ml

Biocraft	Purepac/Kalipharma
Mylan	*E. R. Squibb
*Pfizer	

PENICILLIN VK

BRAND NAME:

Beepen-VK (Beecham)
Betapen-VK (Bristol)
Ledercillin VK (Lederle Labs)
Penapar VK (Parke-Davis/W-L)
Pen-Vee K (Wyeth/AMHO)
Pfizerpen VK (Pfizer)
Robicillin VK (A. H. Robins)
Uticillin VK (Upjohn)
V-Cillin K (Eli Lilly)
Veetids (E. R. Squibb)

DOSAGE FORM:

Tablet 250 mg
Tablet 500 mg
Oral Solution 125 mg/5 ml
Oral Solution 250 mg/5 ml

USE:

As an antibiotic to treat various infections.

AVOID USE:

If allergic to penicillin or to any related drug.

SIDE EFFECTS:

Nausea; vomiting; stomach upset; diarrhea; various skin reactions and many possible allergic responses; a superinfection called black hairy tongue; various blood abnormalities; mouth or tongue irritation.

$ BRAND OR GENERIC?

In tablet form there can be some savings using the generic product, but often, due to special purchasing arrangements, a pharmacy can sell the brand almost as cheaply as the generic. Ask the price of the brand before you allow the prescription to be filled generically. In the oral-solution form it almost never pays to use the generic, since the prices for brands and generics differ very little.

FDA-APPROVED BIOEQUIVALENT MANUFACTURERS:

Tablet 250 mg and 500 mg

*Beecham	*Bristol
Biocraft	John D. Copanos

*Lederle Labs	Purepac/Kalipharma
*Eli Lilly	*E. R. Squibb
Mylan	*Upjohn
*Parke-Davis/W-L	*Wyeth/AMHO
*Pfizer	Zenith

Oral Solution 125 mg/5 ml; 250 mg/5 ml

*Beecham	Mylan
Biocraft	*Parke-Davis/W-L
*Bristol	*Pfizer
John D. Copanos	Purepac/Kalipharma
*Lederle Labs	*E. R. Squibb
*Eli Lilly	*Wyeth/AMHO

PENSYN

SEE Ampicillin

PENTAERYTHRITOL TETRANITRATE

BRAND NAME:
Peritrate (Parke-Davis/W-L) [refers to Tablet]
Peritrate SA (Parke-Davis/W-L) [refers to Time-Release Tablet]

DOSAGE FORM:
Tablet 10 mg
Tablet 20 mg
Time-Release Tablet 80 mg

USE:
To relieve chest pain associated with coronary artery disease.

AVOID USE:
If allergic to this drug or to any related drug.

SIDE EFFECTS:
Skin rash; headache; stomach upset; flushing; dizziness; weakness.

$ BRAND OR GENERIC?
Tablet 10 mg and 20 mg A major price difference exists between brand and generic. Taken as a precautionary measure to prevent anginal pain, the generic product should perform as well as the brand while offering up to a 63% savings.

Time-Release Tablet The generic product is not considered bioequivalent to the brand since it is a time-release formulation. Since this drug is used as a precautionary therapy, the generic product may do just as good a job as the brand.

With huge savings of up to 70% possible, it is worth discussing generic use with your doctor.

FDA-APPROVED BIOEQUIVALENT MANUFACTURERS:
None

This product is exempt from the FDA's bioequivalency approval procedures under a special court order.

PENTIDS

SEE Penicillin G Potassium

PENTOBARBITAL

BRAND NAME:
Nembutal (Abbott)

DOSAGE FORM:
Capsule 50 mg
Capsule 100 mg

USE:
As a sleep aid, sedative, or preanesthetic.

AVOID USE:
Problems with porphyrin metabolism. If allergic to this or to any related drug.

SIDE EFFECTS:
Drowsiness; agitation; lack of coordination; various skin reactions; nausea, vomiting; anemia; difficult or slowed breathing; low blood pressure; dizziness; liver problems; nightmares; hallucinations; various allergic responses; slowed heartbeat; fainting; constipation; headache; fever; liver damage; physical dependence.

$ BRAND OR GENERIC?
Although many side effects are possible, they seldom occur. This drug does, however, have a high degree of addiction potential and it is not unusual to increase the dosage over long periods of use in order to maintain the same level of effect. Under these conditions users tend to have problems with side effects and psychological complications.

Used according to recommended directions, approved generic substitutes perform on par with the brand-name product. Many generics are FDA-approved as bioequivalent, and savings with these products should add up to 24% in the 50-mg strength and as much as 40% for the 100-mg capsules.

FDA-APPROVED BIOEQUIVALENT MANUFACTURERS:

Capsule 50 mg

*Abbott
Lannett
Zenith

Capsule 100 mg

*Abbott   Purepac/Kalipharma
Anabolic   Quantum
Bell   Stanlabs/Simpak
Chelsea   Towne Paulsen
Halsey   Vitarine/Phoenix
ICN   Wyeth/AMHO
Lannett   Zenith
Parke-Davis/W-L

PEN-VEE K

SEE Penicillin VK

PERCOCET-5

SEE Oxycodone/Acetaminophen

PERCODAN

SEE Oxycodone Hydrochloride/Oxycodone Terepthalate/Aspirin

PERIACTIN

SEE Cyproheptadine

PERITRATE

SEE Pentaerythritol Tetranitrate

PERITRATE SA

SEE Pentaerythritol Tetranitrate

PERSANTINE

SEE Dipyridamole

PFIZER-E

SEE Erythromycin Stearate

PFIZERPEN-A

SEE Ampicillin

PFIZERPEN G

SEE Penicillin G Potassium

PFIZERPEN VK

SEE Penicillin VK

PHENAZOPYRIDINE

BRAND NAME:
Pyridium (Parke-Davis/W-L)
DOSAGE FORM:
Tablet 100 mg
Tablet 200 mg
USE:
As a urinary analgesic to relieve pain, burning, urgency.
AVOID USE:
Certain kidney problems; severe hepatitis; if allergic to this or to any related drug.

SIDE EFFECTS:
Stomach upset; colors urine red-orange; headache; skin rash.

$ **BRAND OR GENERIC?**
Many states consider some generics bioequivalent to the brand, and good savings are possible with their use. However, this drug is used short-term (several days) and in situations requiring immediate relief from an intensely painful condition. It is best to get predictable, reliable results and pay a little more for the brand. If it is used for more than 2 or 3 days, the 100-mg tablet saves as much as 50% generically, while the 200-mg dose can save you up to 67%.

FDA-APPROVED BIOEQUIVALENT MANUFACTURERS:
This is a pre-1938 drug and is exempt from the FDA's bioequivalency approval process.

PHENAZOPYRIDINE/SULFAMETHOXAZOLE

BRAND NAME:
Azo-Gantanol (Hoffmann-La Roche)

DOSAGE FORM:
Tablet

USE:
As an antiinfective and analgesic to treat urinary tract infections.

AVOID USE:
Children under 12 years; near the end of pregnancy; if a nursing mother; certain kidney problems; severe hepatitis; if allergic to either component of this product or to any sulfa drug or to any other related drug.

SIDE EFFECTS:
Red-orange urine color; numerous skin reactions and allergic responses; sensitivity to sunlight; nausea; vomiting; abdominal pain; diarrhea; loss of appetite; liver damage and dysfunction (hepatitis, jaundice); inflammation of the pancreas; mouth irritation; headache; numbness and tingling of the extremities; mental depression; loss of coordination; hallucinations; convulsions; ringing in the ears; insomnia; kidney damage; little or no urine output; fever; chills; joint pain; bone marrow depression.

$ **BRAND OR GENERIC?**
Due to revised labeling and additional information required by the FDA, no bioequivalence data are available for comparison among different manufacturers of this drug.

In a quantity of 12 tablets, the maximum recommended amount for one round of therapy, generic savings can approach 47%. If your doctor prescribes a greater quantity, generic savings can increase to 60%.

FDA-APPROVED BIOEQUIVALENT MANUFACTURERS:
None

The FDA is awaiting revised labeling and additional information on this product's effectiveness.

PHENAZOPYRIDINE/SULFISOXAZOLE

BRAND NAME:
Azo-Gantrisin (Hoffmann-La Roche)

DOSAGE FORM:
Tablet

USE:
As an antiinfective and analgesic to treat urinary tract infections.

AVOID USE:
Children under 12 years; near the end of pregnancy; if a nursing mother; certain kidney problems; severe hepatitis; if allergic to either component of this product or to any sulfa drug or to any other related drug.

SIDE EFFECTS:
Red-orange urine color; numerous skin reactions and allergic responses; sensitivity to sunlight; increased heart rate; fainting; nausea; vomiting; abdominal pain; diarrhea; mouth irritation; gas; enlargement of the salivary glands; gastrointestinal bleeding; inflammation of the pancreas; liver damage and dysfunction (hepatitis, jaundice); formation of crystals in the urine; kidney damage; little or no urine output; various blood abnormalities; chest pain; muscle pain; joint pain; headache; dizziness; burning sensation of the skin; convulsions; hearing loss; ringing in the ears; loss of coordination; psychosis; hallucinations; depression; anxiety; fluid retention; drowsiness; weakness; flushing; insomnia.

$ BRAND OR GENERIC?
In quantities of 20 tablets, the maximum recommended amount for one round of therapy, generic savings can approach 36%. If your doctor prescribes a greater quantity, generics can save up to 60%.

FDA-APPROVED BIOEQUIVALENT MANUFACTURERS:
None

PHENDIMETRAZINE

BRAND NAME:
Plegine (Ayerst/AMHO)

DOSAGE FORM:
Tablet 35 mg

USE:
As a short-term diet aid.

AVOID USE:
Certain circulatory disease; some heart ailments; severe high blood pressure; overactive thyroid; if taking a monoamine oxidase inhibitor drug or any other stimulant drug; if nervous or agitated; if there is a history of drug abuse; children under 12 years old; if allergic to this or to related compounds.

SIDE EFFECTS:
Agitation; insomnia; dizziness; sweating; palpitation or fast heartbeat; elevated blood pressure; dry mouth; nausea; increased urination; changes in sex drive; flushing; headache; blurred vision; diarrhea; constipation; stomach pain.

$ BRAND OR GENERIC?
Studies have shown that weight loss with this drug when combined with a plan for dietary management did not differ much from the same diet plan when combined with a harmless placebo (unmedicated preparation). It would logically follow that use of a brand versus generic substitute would have little bearing on the outcome of drug therapy.

The FDA recognizes numerous generics as bioequivalent to the brand. With a whopping 80% savings possible, use of a generic alternative seems to be the logical choice.

FDA-APPROVED BIOEQUIVALENT MANUFACTURERS:
Anabolic
* Ayerst/AMHO
Barr
Camall
Chelsea
Cord
Drummer/Phoenix
Ferndale
Inwood/Forest
KV
Lemmon
Manufacturing Chemists
M.M. Mast
O'Neal, Jones & Feldman
Pharm Basics
Private Formulations
Reid-Provident
Rexar
Vitarine/Phoenix
Zenith

PHENERGAN

SEE Promethazine

PHENERGAN WITH CODEINE

SEE Promethazine/Codeine

PHENERGAN WITH DEXTROMETHORPHAN

SEE Promethazine/Dextromethorphan

PHENERGAN SYRUP PLAIN

SEE Promethazine Syrup

PHENERGAN VC

SEE Promethazine/Phenylephrine

PHENERGAN VC WITH CODEINE

SEE Promethazine/Codeine/Phenylephrine

PHENOBARBITAL

BRAND NAME:
Barbita (Vortech)
Luminal Ovoids (Winthrop)
Solfoton (Poythress)
DOSAGE FORM:
Tablet 15 mg (¼ grain)
Tablet 30 mg (½ grain)
Tablet 60 mg (1 grain)
Elixir 20 mg/5 ml

USE:

As a sedative; as an anticonvulsant in epilepsy.

AVOID USE:

If there is a history of impairment of porphyrin metabolism; in certain liver problems; with various breathing difficulties; in individuals predisposed toward addiction to similar type drugs; if allergic to phenobarbital or to any other barbiturate.

SIDE EFFECTS:

Sedation; excitement; breathing difficulties; various skin reactions and other allergic responses; hangover; nausea; vomiting; diarrhea; headache; dizziness; liver dysfunction (jaundice, hepatitis); various blood abnormalities; joint and muscle pain.

$ BRAND OR GENERIC?

Since this is a pre-1938 drug, it is not subject to the FDA's bioequivalency approval process. Its use as a sedative makes precise dosage control less critical than when employed to control epileptic seizures. Not all brands are marketed in all strengths.

Tablet 15 mg (¼ grain)   In this category, Solfoton, manufactured by Poythress, emerges as the most expensive choice. Among the other brand-name products a savings approaching 30% can be realized with the use of Luminal Ovoids, manufactured by Winthrop. The other brand name, Barbita, can save up to 36%.

In the generic category savings of up to 43% are possible. Lilly's product, with savings of up to 38%, is an excellent generic choice, yielding a substantial savings while at the same time having a reputation for excellence.

Tablet 30 mg (½ grain)   The field starts to narrow in this tablet strength, with two of the previously mentioned brand-name products, Solfoton and Barbita, dropping out. Luminal Ovoids emerges as the most expensive brand. Generics can yield savings of up to 38%. Here again Lilly's product, with a 27% discount, would be considered the most intelligent choice, offering a substantial savings together with a reputation for quality.

Tablet 60 mg (1 grain)   This strength tablet has even fewer competitors than the previous categories, with Luminal Ovoids dropping out. This leaves the various generics, including Lilly's, which now qualifies as the most expensive. Generics show up to a 27% discount over Lilly. But this is an inexpensive drug so dollar savings may not be great.

Elixir 20 mg/5 ml   There are no brand names in this dosage form; Lilly's product would be considered the most expensive among the various manufacturers, but the drug is inexpensive. When prescription prices are calculated the difference between Lilly and the other generics works out to a maximum of only 16%, with many offering less of a discount than that.

FDA-APPROVED BIOEQUIVALENT MANUFACTURERS:

This is a pre-1938 drug and is exempt from the FDA's bioequivalency approval process.

PHENTERMINE

BRAND NAME:
Fastin (Beecham)

DOSAGE FORM:
Capsule 30 mg

USE:
As a short-term aid for weight reduction.

AVOID USE:
Advanced circulatory disease; certain heart ailments; moderate to severe high blood pressure; overactive thyroid; glaucoma; preexisting agitation; within 14 days of taking a monoamine oxidase inhibitor drug; patients with history of drug abuse; children under 12 years old; if allergic to this drug or to any related compound.

SIDE EFFECTS:
Elevated blood pressure; palpitations or fast heartbeat; insomnia; headache; dizziness; restlessness; dry mouth; skin itching; changes in sex drive; unpleasant taste; diarrhea; constipation; impotence.

$ BRAND OR GENERIC?
By the brand-name manufacturer's own admission, this drug is of questionable value, so use of generics will not be any less effective than the brand-name product. In otherwise healthy individuals side effects should be minimal, with generic use having little bearing on adverse reactions. A major price savings of 70% over the brand makes generics the best choice by far.

FDA-APPROVED BIOEQUIVALENT MANUFACTURERS:
*Beecham
Camall
Chelsea
Drummer/Phoenix
Ferndale
Lannett
Lemmon
M. M. Mast
Pharm Basics
Rexar
Vitarine/Phoenix
Zenith

PHENYLBUTAZONE

BRAND NAME:
Azolid (USV)
Butazolidan (Geigy/Ciba-Geigy)

DOSAGE FORM:
Tablet 100 mg.
Capsule 100 mg.

USE:
As an antiinflammatory drug to relieve various arthritic conditions and gout.

AVOID USE:
Children 14 years of age or younger; heart disease; blood abnormalities; bone marrow disease; inflammation of the pancreas; inflammation of the parotid glands; mouth irritation; large artery inflammatory disease; senility; in presence of disease of or impaired function of kidneys, heart, thyroid, liver; if there is a history of gastrointestinal ulceration or inflammation; as initial drug therapy; if prescribed for mild or trivial complaints; if allergic to this drug or to oxyphenbutazone; any drug allergy (consult your doctor).

SIDE EFFECTS:
Nausea; upset stomach; heartburn; indigestion; abdominal discomfort; vomiting; stomach bloating and gas; constipation; diarrhea; irritation of the esophagus; enlargement of the salivary glands; irritation or ulceration of the mouth; ulceration and perforation of the intestinal tract; gastrointestinal bleeding that can show up as bloody vomiting or blood in the stool; anemia due to gastrointestinal bleeding; liver dysfunction (jaundice or hepatitis); various blood abnormalities; bone marrow depression; various skin reactions and numerous allergic responses; fluid retention and swelling; congestive heart failure; high blood pressure; various kidney dysfunctions including decreased urine output; headache; drowsiness; agitation; confusion; numbness; weakness; tremors; eye damage or visual impairment; high blood sugar; ringing in the ears and hearing loss.

$ BRAND OR GENERIC?
This is a very potent, potentially toxic, and unpredictable drug. Whenever possible, it is used on a short-term basis. Although some generic products are considered bioequivalent to the brand and moderate savings are possible, therapy is usually limited to one week. Because there are many hazards with this medication and it is used short-term, stick to the brand-name product. Azolid can save you up to 8% in tablet form but offers no savings in capsule form when compared to Butazolidan. Generic products can offer savings of up to 55% in tablet and as much as 38% in capsule form over the brand-name products.

FDA-APPROVED BIOEQUIVALENT MANUFACTURERS:

Tablet 100 mg

Chelsea	*Geigy/Ciba-Geigy
Cord	*USV
Danbury	

Capsule 100 mg

Chelsea	*USV
Cord	Zenith
*Geigy/Ciba-Geigy	

PHENYLPROPANOLAMINE/CHLORPHENIRAMINE

BRAND NAME:

Ornade (SK & F)

DOSAGE FORM:

Capsule—Time-Release

USE:

As a decongestant and an antihistamine to relieve symptoms of allergies and the common cold.

AVOID USE:

If taking a monoamine oxidase inhibitor drug; severe high blood pressure; bronchial asthma; certain heart disease; peptic ulcer; certain gastrointestinal and bladder obstructions; during an asthma attack; if a nursing mother; newborn or premature infants; if allergic to any ingredient in this product or to any related drug.

SIDE EFFECTS:

Dry mouth, nose, and throat; headache; weakness; drowsiness; various blood abnormalities; skin rash; anginal chest pain; heart palpitations; high or low blood pressure; insomnia; nervousness; dizziness; lack of coordination; tremor; convulsions; visual problems; nausea; vomiting; stomach upset; diarrhea; loss of appetite; constipation; difficult or painful urination.

$ BRAND OR GENERIC?

The generic is not recognized as bioequivalent to the brand. This is a time-release drug and as such is not easily duplicated. If used short-term, stick to the brand. But on a long-term basis tremendous savings of up to 60% can be had with generic use. Consult your doctor.

FDA-APPROVED BIOEQUIVALENT MANUFACTURERS:

None

This is a time-release product and is not considered bioequivalent in generic form by the FDA.

PHENYLPROPANOLAMINE/PHENYLEPHRINE/ PHENYLTOLOXAMINE/CHLORPHENIRAMINE

BRAND NAME:

Naldecon (Bristol)

DOSAGE FORM:

Tablet—Time-Release
Syrup
Pediatric Syrup

USE:

As a decongestant and an antihistamine to relieve symptoms of colds, upper respiratory infection, sinus inflammation, hay fever, or various allergies.

AVOID USE:

Severe high blood pressure; overactive thyroid; certain heart disease; severe diabetes; if taking a monoamine oxidase inhibitor drug; narrow angle glaucoma; difficulty in urinating; peptic ulcer; during an asthma attack; if allergic to any ingredient in this product or to any related drug.

SIDE EFFECTS:

Palpitations and fast heartbeat; headache; dizziness; nausea; vomiting; sedation; restlessness; tremor; weakness; breathing difficulties; painful or excessive urination; insomnia; convulsions; hallucinations; low blood pressure; dry mouth; loss of appetite; blurred vision; skin rash.

$ **BRAND OR GENERIC?**

Syrup and pediatric syrup   A savings of up to 46% is possible with generic use. Syrups present few formulation problems, so performance should be on par with the brand product even though the FDA has not published bioequivalency evaluations.

Tablet   This is a time-release formulation and as such is not considered bioequivalent in generic form. There is a staggering difference of up to 70% in price between brand and generic. This drug is not usually used in serious situations and the side effects, while potentially many, are not common. Even if the generic does not perform as well as the brand, the tremendous savings make generic use an alternative worth discussing with your doctor.

FDA-APPROVED BIOEQUIVALENT MANUFACTURERS:

None

PHENYTOIN

BRAND NAME:

Dilantin (Parke-Davis/W-L)

DOSAGE FORM:

Capsule 100 mg (Prompt)
Capsule 100 mg (Extended)

USE:

To control certain epilepsies.

AVOID USE:

If a nursing mother; if allergic to this or to any related drug.

SIDE EFFECTS:

Rapid movements of the eyeball, usually from side to side (nystagmus); loss of coordination; slurred speech; mental confusion; dizziness; insomnia; headache;

nervousness (usually temporary); nausea; vomiting; constipation; various skin reactions; various blood abnormalities; lymphatic system dysfunction; enlargement of the lips and other coarsening of facial features; overgrowth of gums; unusual hair growth; fibrous thickening in the penis called Peyronie's disease; liver dysfunction (hepatitis) and damage; bone marrow depression.

$ BRAND OR GENERIC?

There is a major distinction to be made between the two types of phenytoin capsules available: Those labeled *prompt* are suitable for multiple daily dosing, while *extended* capsules can be taken once a day. The *prompt* capsule is only available generically, but it is not considered bioequivalent and interchangeable. For this reason it is best to have your dosage stabilized on one manufacturer's product and stick with it, if possible, for all prescription refills.

The brand-name product, Dilantin, is the extended-dosage form, and switching to a generic is only advisable if it is one of those approved as bioequivalent by the FDA.

Generic use yields savings approaching 55%, but check your pharmacy's price first. Many stores have specials on Dilantin, making generic use less attractive. Discuss any generic alternative with your doctor first.

FDA-APPROVED BIOEQUIVALENT MANUFACTURERS:

Capsule 100 mg (Prompt)

None

Capsule 100 mg (Extended)

Bolar
*Parke-Davis/W-L

PIPERAZINE

BRAND NAME:
Antepar (Burroughs Wellcome)

DOSAGE FORM:
Tablet 500 mg
Syrup 500 mg/5 ml

USE:
To treat roundworm and pinworm infections.

AVOID USE:
Impaired kidney or liver function; convulsive disorders; if allergic to this drug or to any related drug.

SIDE EFFECTS:

Nausea; vomiting; stomach cramps; diarrhea; headache; loss of coordination; tremors; muscle weakness; burning sensations of the skin; blurred vision; convulsions; various skin reactions and allergic responses.

$ BRAND OR GENERIC?

This drug is used to treat pinworm and roundworm infections, both very uncomfortable conditions. Treatment with this drug can have notoriously unpleasant side effects, making it a medicine you do not want to have to take more than once.

For roundworm infections the treatment lasts only two days. A small quantity of drug is required, making savings practically nonexistent with a generic substitute.

Pinworm infections require a seven-day therapy, necessitating a larger supply of the drug. Savings for the generic syrup can approach 30%, while tablet savings hover at around 24%. There are no tablets considered to be bioequivalent by the FDA in generic form.

Since this drug is inexpensive, dollar savings will not really amount to much. When balanced against the potential unpleasant side effects, the scale tips in favor of paying the extra dollar or so to avoid having to take this drug a second time.

FDA-APPROVED BIOEQUIVALENT MANUFACTURERS:

Tablet 500 mg

None

Syrup 500 mg/5 ml

Bluline	National/Barre
*Burroughs Wellcome	Reid-Provident
Lannett	Winthrop/Sterling
Natcon Chemical	

PLEGINE

SEE Phendimetrazine

POLARAMINE

SEE Dexchlorpheniramine

POLYCILLIN

SEE Ampicillin

POLYMOX

SEE Amoxicillin

POTASSIUM

BRAND NAME:

Liquids

Kaochlor (Adria)   Klor-10% (Upsher-Smith)
Kay Ciel (Berlex)   Klorvess 10% (Dorsey)

Powder (Packets)

Kato (Syntex)   K-Lor (Abbott)
Kay Ciel (Berlex)   Klor-Con (Upsher-Smith)

Effervescent Tablets

Kaochlor-Eff (Adria)   K-Lyte (Mead-Johnson)
Klorvess (Dorsey)   K-Lyte/Cl (Mead-Johnson)

DOSAGE FORM:

Liquid 10% (20 meq/15 ml)
Powder (Packets) 20 meq
Powder (Packets) 25 meq
Effervescent Tablets 20 meq
Effervescent Tablets 25 meq

USE:

To treat potassium deficiency.

AVOID USE:

Severely impaired kidney function; if there is already a high blood potassium level; if already receiving a potassium-sparing diuretic such as spirinolactone or triamterene; if there is low blood potassium combined with metabolic acidosis; if allergic to any form of this drug.

SIDE EFFECTS:

Vomiting; nausea; stomach upset; potassium intoxication; diarrhea; skin rash.

$ BRAND OR GENERIC?

There is no reason to use a brand-name product. All forms of this drug are easy to manufacture and work well. When using the powder form, a good alternative is

Klor-Con, which is very palatable and can match the 70% savings offered by generics over other brands. In elixir form savings of up to 65% are possible with generic use.

One note of caution: in most normal uses of potassium as a replacement for low levels caused by diuretic drug therapy, any form of the product suffices. But some special situations exist in which complicating factors can make the salt form of the drug (such as chloride, gluconate, citrate, bicarbonate) critical to the patient's response. Make sure that generic substitution is done with the same salt of potassium if this is a factor in the doctor's therapeutic goals. Discuss this with your physician.

FDA-APPROVED BIOEQUIVALENT MANUFACTURERS:
None

This product is presently in bureaucratic limbo. Its status awaits completion of administrative proceedings, but at this time it is considered low priority.

PREDNISOLONE

BRAND NAME:
Delta-Cortef (Upjohn)
Sterane (Pfipharmecs/Pfizer)

DOSAGE FORM:
Tablet 5 mg

USE:
As an antiinflammatory drug having a wide range of uses, including treatment of various endocrine disorders; certain arthritic and rheumatoid disorders; various allergic conditions; many eye disorders; skin problems; breathing difficulties; some blood disorders; certain cancers; and several intestinal diseases.

AVOID USE:
Widespread fungal infections of the blood; during use of live virus vaccines; if already receiving large amounts of this or a similar drug; if allergic to this or to other related steroid drugs.

SIDE EFFECTS:
Fluid retention and swelling; congestive heart failure (in certain predisposed patients); high blood pressure; potassium loss; muscle weakness; bone decomposition; loss of muscle mass; peptic ulcer with perforation or bleeding; inflammation of the pancreas; inflammation or ulceration of the esophagus; delayed wound healing; various skin reactions; increased sweating; convulsions; increased skull pressure; headache; vertigo; menstrual irregularities; growth suppression in children; Cushing's syndrome; loss of diabetic control; various eye disorders including glaucoma; increased appetite; decreased resistance to infection; various mental disturbances.

$ BRAND OR GENERIC?

The FDA has placed prednisolone in a special category because of many documented problems with bioequivalence. The USP/NF, the organization that develops standards by which drugs are evaluated by the FDA, is in the process of formalizing meaningful in vitro tests (those performed outside the human body on laboratory equipment). Until this process is completed, the FDA considers all prednisolones to be inequivalent to each other.

If your doctor prescribes a brand-name product, stick to it. If the prescription is written generically, that is, by the name "prednisolone," any manufacturer's product can be used, but it would be prudent to stay with the same manufacturer each time the prescription is refilled. Switching among generics may cause a significant fluctuation in the dose. This can result in unpleasant or even dangerous side effects.

The most expensive alternative is the brand name Delta-Cortef. The other brand, Sterane, is only marginally cheaper. Various generics can offer from 30% to almost 60% savings, depending on the number of tablets purchased, with the maximum discount obtained on quantities of 100.

FDA-APPROVED BIOEQUIVALENT MANUFACTURERS:
None

The FDA considers all brands of this drug to have unresolved bioequivalency problems at this time.

PREDNISONE

BRAND NAME:
Deltasone (Upjohn)
Meticorten (Schering)
SK-Prednisone (SK & F)

DOSAGE FORM:
Tablet 5 mg
Tablet 10 mg
Tablet 20 mg

USE:
As an antiinflammatory drug having a wide range of uses, including treatment of various endocrine disorders; certain arthritic and rheumatoid disorders; various allergic conditions; many eye disorders; skin problems; breathing difficulties; some blood disorders; certain cancers; and several intestinal diseases.

AVOID USE:
Widespread fungal infections of the blood; during use of live virus vaccines; if already receiving large amounts of this or a similar drug; if allergic to this or to other related steroid drugs.

SIDE EFFECTS:

Fluid retention and swelling; congestive heart failure (in certain predisposed patients); high blood pressure; potassium loss; muscle weakness; bone decomposition; loss of muscle mass; peptic ulcer with perforation or bleeding; inflammation of the pancreas; inflammation or ulceration of the esophagus; delayed wound healing; various skin reactions; increased sweating; convulsions; increased skull pressure; headache; vertigo; menstrual irregularities; growth suppression in children; Cushing's syndrome; loss of diabetic control; various eye disorders including glaucoma; increased appetite; decreased resistance to infection; various mental disturbances.

$ BRAND OR GENERIC?

The FDA has placed prednisone in a special category because of many documented problems with bioequivalence. The USP/NF, the organization that develops standards by which drugs are evaluated by the FDA, is in the process of formalizing meaningful in vitro tests (those performed outside the human body on laboratory equipment). Until this process is completed, the FDA considers all prednisones to be inequivalent to each other.

If your doctor prescribes a brand-name product, stick to it. If the prescription is written generically, that is, by the name "prednisone," any manufacturer's product can be used, but it would be prudent to stay with the same manufacturer each time the prescription is refilled. Switching among generics may cause a significant fluctuation in the dose. This can result in unpleasant or even dangerous side effects.

In the 5-mg tablet, the most expensive brand is Meticorten. The other brand-name products offer the following savings; Deltasone—up to 32%; SK-Prednisone—up to 61%. Various generics can offer up to a 66% discount. The SK-Prednisone, while offering almost as big a savings as the generics, also has the advantage of brand-name assurance.

For the 10-mg and 20-mg strengths, the only brand name marketed is Deltasone. Generics can save about 30% in both strengths.

FDA-APPROVED BIOEQUIVALENT MANUFACTURERS:

None

The FDA considers all brands of this drug to have unresolved bioequivalency problems at this time.

PREMARIN

SEE Estrogens, Conjugated

PRIMIDONE

BRAND NAME:

Mysoline (Ayerst/AMHO)

DOSAGE FORM:

Tablet 250 mg

USE:

To control seizures associated with epilepsy.

AVOID USE:

Porphyrin metabolism disturbances; if allergic to this drug or to phenobarbital or to any related drug.

SIDE EFFECTS:

Loss of coordination; vertigo; nausea, vomiting; loss of appetite; fatigue; various skin reactions; impotence; emotional disturbances.

$ BRAND OR GENERIC?

Several generic products are considered bioequivalent to the brand by the FDA and offer good savings. The drug is readily absorbed into the body when taken orally, making tablet formulation straightforward. The generic is a good choice, offering savings as high as 40%.

FDA-APPROVED BIOEQUIVALENT MANUFACTURERS:

*Ayerst/AMHO
Bolar
Danbury
Lannett

PRINCIPEN

SEE Ampicillin

PRO-BANTHINE

SEE Propantheline

PROBENECID

BRAND NAME:

Benemid (MSD/Merck)

DOSAGE FORM:

Tablet 500 mg

USE:

To lower uric acid levels associated with gout; to increase blood levels of penicillin and other similar antibiotics.

AVOID USE:

Children under 2 years; certain blood abnormalities; in presence of uric acid kidney stones; if currently experiencing an acute gout attack; if allergic to this drug or to any related drug.

SIDE EFFECTS:

Headache; loss of appetite; nausea; vomiting; frequent urination; various allergic responses and skin reactions; painful gums; dizziness; anemia; kidney dysfunction; liver damage.

$ **BRAND OR GENERIC?**

Generally recognized as bioequivalent, the generic product offers a very big price break. Since it is used long-term, the savings should be major, with up to a 47% discount possible.

FDA-APPROVED BIOEQUIVALENT MANUFACTURERS:

Chelsea
Danbury
Lannett
Lederle Labs
*MSD/Merck
Mylan
Zenith

PROCAINAMIDE

BRAND NAME:

Procan SR (Parke-Davis/W-L)
Pronestyl (E. R. Squibb)
Pronestyl-SR (E. R. Squibb)

DOSAGE FORM:

Capsule and Tablet 250 mg
Capsule and Tablet 375 mg
Capsule and Tablet 500 mg
Tablet (Sustained Release) 250 mg
Tablet (Sustained Release) 500 mg
Tablet (Sustained Release) 750 mg

USE:

As an antiarrhythmic to restore normal heart rhythm.

AVOID USE:

Myasthenia gravis; certain heart block conditions; if allergic to this drug or to any related drug.

SIDE EFFECTS:

Drop in blood pressure (rare with capsule formulation); lupus erythematosus-like symptoms (arthritic pains, skin lesions, fibrous deposits in the sac surrounding the heart, fever); various skin reactions and other allergic responses; nausea; vomiting; diarrhea; abdominal pain; bitter taste; weakness; mental depression; giddiness; hallucinations; certain anemia; lowered white blood cell counts; liver enlargement.

$ BRAND OR GENERIC?

Three different formulations are available. The plain tablet and capsule offer an excellent savings over the brand name Pronestyl, approaching 70% in all three strengths. With many FDA-approved bioequivalent products, the generic capsules are an excellent alternative. Tablets are not considered generically bioequivalent.

The sustained-release tablet also comes in three strengths, but not all brand-name products are available for each. The 250-mg tablet has only one brand name, Procan SR. Generics offer about a 35% savings. Procan SR and Pronestyl-SR are both formulated in the 500-mg tablet form and sell for about the same price. Generics save up to 40%. The 750-mg tablet has only one brand name, Procan SR; generics save up to 40%. Since few sustained-release tablets are FDA-approved as bioequivalent, savings may only be worthwhile provided an approved manufacturer's product can be used. Consult your doctor.

FDA-APPROVED BIOEQUIVALENT MANUFACTURERS:

Capsule 250 mg and 500 mg

Ascot	Panray/Ormont (250-mg strength only)
Bolar	Roxane
Chelsea	*E. R. Squibb
Danbury	Vangard Labs/MWM
Lannett	Zenith
Lederle Labs	

Capsule 375 mg

Ascot	Lederle Labs
Chelsea	*Parke-Davis/W-L
Danbury	Zenith

Tablet 250 mg, 375 mg, 500 mg

None

Tablet (sustained release) 250 mg, 500 mg, 750 mg

Bolar
Copley (500 mg only)
*Parke-Davis/W-L

PROCAN SR

SEE Procainamide

PROCHLORPERAZINE

BRAND NAME:
Compazine (SK & F)

DOSAGE FORM:
Tablet 5 mg
Tablet 10 mg
Tablet 25 mg

USE:
To control nausea and vomiting; to manage certain psychotic disorders, anxiety, tension, and agitation.

AVOID USE:
If comatose; bone marrow depression; children under 2 years or under 20 pounds; in presence of extreme central nervous system depression; if allergic to this drug or to any related phenothiazine drugs.

SIDE EFFECTS:
Drowsiness; dizziness; loss of menstruation; blurred vision; various skin reactions and other allergic responses; liver dysfunction (jaundice, hepatitis); nasal congestion; difficult urination; constipation; bone marrow depression; parkinson-like reactions; dystonias (muscle spasms of the neck, back, face, and extremities; difficulty in swallowing; protrusion of the tongue; grimacing; arching of the back; cramping of the hands and feet); various blood abnormalities; a sometimes irreversible condition known as tardive dyskinesia.

$ BRAND OR GENERIC?
Very few generic products are FDA-approved as bioequivalent to the brand, pending the results of ongoing tests. Used short-term, in small quantities, savings with generic use should average about 40% for the 5-mg tablet, 50% for the 10-mg tablet, and up to 53% for the 25-mg strength. Larger quantities, such as 100 tablets, should yield generic savings in excess of 50% for all three strengths.

FDA-APPROVED BIOEQUIVALENT MANUFACTURERS:

Tablet 5 mg, 10 mg, 25 mg

Bolar
*SK & F

PROCHLORPERAZINE WITH ISOPROPAMIDE

BRAND NAME:
Combid (SK & F)

DOSAGE FORM:
Capsule—Time-Release

USE:

To treat peptic ulcer; irritable bowel syndrome; nausea and vomiting; certain diarrheas.

AVOID USE:

Drug-induced central nervous system depression; children under 12 years; glaucoma; certain stomach obstructions; enlarged prostate; bladder obstruction; certain intestinal disease or growths; bone marrow depression; some liver disease; blood abnormalities; myasthenia gravis; certain heart conditions; certain intestinal paralysis in elderly or debilitated people; if allergic to either component of this product or to any related drug.

SIDE EFFECTS:

Dry mouth; difficult urination; palpitations or fast heartbeat; blurred vision and other eye problems; constipation; nausea; fever; nasal congestion; drowsiness; headache; loss of taste; insomnia; vomiting; impotence; various skin reactions and other allergic responses; mental confusion or excitement; decreased sweating; liver dysfunction (jaundice, hepatitis); bone marrow depression; parkinsonlike reactions; dystonias (muscle spasms of the neck, face, back, and extremities; difficulty in swallowing; protrusion of the tongue; grimacing; arching of the back; cramping of the hands and feet); a sometimes irreversible condition known as tardive dyskinesia.

$ BRAND OR GENERIC?

This is a time-release dosage form and, as such, generic products are not considered bioequivalent to the brand. There is a big potential savings with generic use, but unless used long-term, in which case savings can be in excess of 65%, stick to the brand. Due to administrative procedures having nothing to do with bioequivalency, the FDA has not published its findings on generic bioequivalency.

FDA-APPROVED BIOEQUIVALENT MANUFACTURERS:

None

The FDA currently lists this product as ineffective. Bioequivalency ratings await completion of administrative proceedings.

PROLOPRIM

SEE Trimethoprim

PROMETHAZINE

BRAND NAME:

Phenergan (Wyeth/AMHO)

DOSAGE FORM:

Tablet 12.5 mg

Tablet 25 mg

USE:

An an antihistamine to treat various allergies; to control nausea, vomiting, and motion sickness; used with certain painkillers to enhance their effectiveness; as a general sedative.

AVOID USE:

Glaucoma; newborn infants; if allergic to this or to any related drug.

SIDE EFFECTS:

Dry mouth; blurred vision; dizziness; possible sensitivity to sunlight; slight increase or decrease in blood pressure; excitability or nightmares (in children).

$ BRAND OR GENERIC?

This drug has a wide range of uses and generally causes few side effects. The tablet form of this medication has no FDA-approved bioequivalent generics.

In normal quantities of about 30 tablets, the 12.5-mg strength should save about 33% generically, while the 25-mg dosage form can yield savings in excess of 50%.

If used long-term in quantities of 100 tablets, generic savings become truly impressive, with over a 70% discount possible for the 12.5-mg tablet and a potential 80% savings for the 25-mg strength.

FDA-APPROVED BIOEQUIVALENT MANUFACTURERS:

Tablet 12.5 mg and 25 mg

None

The FDA considers all brands of this product to have unresolved bioequivalency problems at this time.

PROMETHAZINE/CODEINE

BRAND NAME:

Phenergan with Codeine (Wyeth/AMHO)

DOSAGE FORM:

Syrup

USE:

To control coughs and upper respiratory symptoms due to colds and allergies.

AVOID USE:

If asthmatic or suffering from lower respiratory tract symptoms; children under 2 years of age; if allergic to any component of this product or to any related drug.

SIDE EFFECTS:

Sedation; blurred vision; dry mouth; dizziness; difficulty in breathing; euphoria; headache; hallucinations (temporary); convulsions; increased or decreased blood pressure; palpitations; fast or slow heartbeat; dizziness upon standing; fainting; skin rash or sensitivity to sunlight; various skin reactions and allergic responses; blood abnormalities; constipation; nausea; vomiting; difficult urination; flushing of the face; sweating; weakness.

$ BRAND OR GENERIC?

This product is a syrup which presents few formulation problems. Due to administrative proceedings, the FDA is only now beginning to certify various generic products as bioequivalent. While generics can save up to 20%, the product is inexpensive, making dollar savings unimpressive. Unless used in large quantities on a long-term basis, which is not usual, stick to the brand-name product.

FDA-APPROVED BIOEQUIVALENT MANUFACTURERS:
Bay
National/Barre
*Wyeth/AMHO

PROMETHAZINE/CODEINE/PHENYLEPHRINE

BRAND NAME:

Phenergan VC with Codeine (Wyeth/AMHO)

DOSAGE FORM:

Syrup

USE:

To control coughs, upper respiratory symptoms, and nasal congestion due to colds and allergies.

AVOID USE:

High blood pressure or poor circulation to the extremities; if taking a monoamine oxidase inhibitor drug; if asthmatic or suffering from lower respiratory tract symptoms; children under 2 years of age; if allergic to any component of this product or to any related drug.

SIDE EFFECTS:

Sedation; blurred vision; dry mouth; dizziness; difficulty in breathing; euphoria; headache; hallucinations (temporary); convulsions; anxiety; increased or decreased blood pressure; palpitations; fast or slow heartbeat; dizziness upon standing; fainting; skin rash or sensitivity to sunlight; various skin reactions and allergic responses; blood abnormalities; constipation; nausea; vomiting; difficult urination; flushing of the face; sweating; weakness; chest pain; tremor.

$ BRAND OR GENERIC?

This product is a syrup which presents few formulation problems. Due to administrative proceedings, the FDA is only now beginning to certify various generic products as bioequivalent. While generics can save up to 20%, the product is inexpensive, making dollar savings unimpressive. Unless used in large quantities on a long-term basis, which is not usual, stick to the brand-name product.

FDA-APPROVED BIOEQUIVALENT MANUFACTURERS:
Bay
National/Barre
*Wyeth/AMHO

PROMETHAZINE/DEXTROMETHORPHAN

BRAND NAME:
Phenergan with Dextromethorphan (Wyeth/AMHO)

DOSAGE FORM:
Syrup

USE:
To control coughs and upper respiratory symptoms due to colds and allergies.

AVOID USE:
If taking a monoamine oxidase inhibitor drug; if asthmatic or suffering from lower respiratory tract symptoms; children under 2 years of age; if allergic to any component of this product or to any related drug.

SIDE EFFECTS:
Sedation; blurred vision; dizziness; stomach upset; increased or decreased blood pressure; skin rash or sensitivity to sunlight; blood abnormalities; nausea; vomiting.

$ BRAND OR GENERIC?
This product is a syrup which presents few formulation problems. Due to administrative proceedings, the FDA is only now beginning to certify various generic products as bioequivalent. While generics can save up to 20%, the product is inexpensive, making dollar savings unimpressive. Unless used in large quantities on a long-term basis, which is not usual, stick to the brand-name product.

FDA-APPROVED BIOEQUIVALENT MANUFACTURERS:
Bay
National/Barre
*Wyeth/AMHO

PROMETHAZINE/PHENYLEPHRINE

BRAND NAME:
Phenergan VC (Wyeth/AMHO)

DOSAGE FORM:

Syrup

USE:

To control upper respiratory symptoms and nasal congestion due to colds and allergies.

AVOID USE:

High blood pressure or poor circulation to the extremities; if taking a mono-amine oxidase inhibitor drug; if asthmatic or suffering from lower respiratory tract symptoms; children under 2 years of age; if allergic to any component of this product or to any related drug.

SIDE EFFECTS:

Sedation; anxiety; blurred vision; dry mouth; dizziness; increased or decreased blood pressure; skin rash or sensitivity to sunlight; blood abnormalities; nausea; vomiting; tremor; weakness; chest pain; breathing difficulties.

$ **BRAND OR GENERIC?**

This product is a syrup which presents few formulation problems. Due to administrative proceedings, the FDA is only now beginning to certify various generic products as bioequivalent. While generics can save up to 20%, the product is inexpensive, making dollar savings unimpressive. Unless used in large quantities on a long-term basis, which is not usual, stick to the brand-name product.

FDA-APPROVED BIOEQUIVALENT MANUFACTURERS:

Bay
National/Barre
*Wyeth/AMHO

PROMETHAZINE SYRUP

BRAND NAME:

Phenergan Syrup Plain (Wyeth/AMHO)

DOSAGE FORM:

Syrup 6.25 mg/5 ml

USE:

As an antihistamine to treat allergic symptoms; to control nausea; as a sedative.

AVOID USE:

If asthmatic or suffering from lower respiratory tract symptoms; children under 2 years of age; if allergic to this drug or to any related drug.

SIDE EFFECTS:

Sedation; blurred vision; dry mouth; dizziness; increased or decreased blood pressure; skin rash or sensitivity to sunlight; blood abnormalities; nausea; vomiting.

$ BRAND OR GENERIC?

This product is a syrup which presents few formulation problems. Due to administrative proceedings, the FDA is only now beginning to certify various generic products as bioequivalent. While generics can save up to 20%, the product is inexpensive, making dollar savings unimpressive. Unless used in large quantities on a long-term basis, which is not usual, stick to the brand-name product.

FDA-APPROVED BIOEQUIVALENT MANUFACTURERS:
Bay
KV
National/Barre
Pharms Assoc/Beach
Towne Paulsen
*Wyeth/AMHO

PRONESTYL

SEE Procainamide

PRONESTYL-SR

SEE Procainamide

PROPANTHELINE

BRAND NAME:
Pro-Banthine (Searle)

DOSAGE FORM:
Tablet 7.5 mg
Tablet 15 mg

USE:
To treat peptic ulcer.

AVOID USE:
Glaucoma; gastrointestinal tract obstruction; urinary tract obstruction; elderly or infirmed patients with impaired intestinal movement; ulcerative colitis; hiatis hernia; certain heart problems; myasthenia gravis; if allergic to this or to any related drug.

SIDE EFFECTS:
Dry mouth; decreased sweating; blurred vision and other eye problems; difficulty in urinating; palpitations and fast heartbeat; loss of taste; headache; ner-

vousness; drowsiness; confusion; insomnia; weakness; dizziness; nausea; vomiting; constipation; impotence; various skin reactions and allergic responses.

$ BRAND OR GENERIC?

This is one drug with truly major savings possible with generic use. Although there are few FDA-approved generics in the 7.5-mg strength, the higher 15-mg tablet has many certified generic products. Savings in excess of 75% are possible when used generically.

FDA-APPROVED BIOEQUIVALENT MANUFACTURERS:

Tablet 7.5 mg

Roxane
* Searle

Tablet 15 mg

Ascot	Par
Bolar	Private Formulations
Cord	Richlyn
Danbury	Roxane
Heather	* Searle
Mylan	Tablicaps

PROPOXYPHENE HYDROCHLORIDE

BRAND NAME:
Darvon (Eli Lilly)
Dolene (Lederle Labs)

DOSAGE FORM:
Capsule 65 mg

USE:
To relieve pain.

AVOID USE:
Children under 12 years of age; if allergic to this or to any related drug.

SIDE EFFECTS:
Dizziness; drowsiness; nausea; vomiting; constipation; abdominal pain; headache; weakness; euphoria; lightheadedness; visual disturbances; skin rash; liver dysfunction (hepatitis, jaundice); insomnia.

$ BRAND OR GENERIC?

Many generic products are FDA-approved as bioequivalent to the brand. Since this drug is well absorbed by the body when taken by mouth, formulation is rather straightforward. Offering over a 40% savings, the generic emerges as the best choice.

FDA-APPROVED BIOEQUIVALENT MANUFACTURERS:
Anabolic
Barr
Chelsea
Cord
Danbury
Drummer/Phoenix
Halsey
ICN
*Lederle Labs
Lemmon
*Eli Lilly
MK
Mylan
Private Formulations
Purepac/Kalipharma
Richlyn
Roxane
SK & F
Towne Paulsen
West-Ward
Zenith

PROPOXYPHENE NAPSYLATE/ACETAMINOPHEN

BRAND NAME:
Darvocet-N (Eli Lilly)

DOSAGE FORM:
Tablet (50 mg propoxyphene napsylate/325 mg acetaminophen)
Tablet (100 mg propoxyphene napsylate/650 mg acetaminophen)

USE:
To relieve pain.

AVOID USE:
Children under 12 years of age; if allergic to this or to any related drug.

SIDE EFFECTS:
Dizziness; drowsiness; nausea; vomiting; constipation; abdominal pain; headache; weakness; euphoria; lightheadedness; visual disturbances; skin rash; liver dysfunction (hepatitis, jaundice); insomnia.

$ **BRAND OR GENERIC?**
Since generic versions of this drug have only recently become available, the FDA has not yet listed on any products a bioequivalent.

The 50-mg strength shows generic savings of about 16% over the brand while better than 20% can be saved generically with the 100-mg version. As more generic competitors enter the market, savings with substitution should increase.

FDA-APPROVED BIOEQUIVALENT MANUFACTURERS:

Tablet 50 mg/325 mg

Barr
*Eli Lilly

Tablet 100 mg/650 mg

Barr
Lemmon
*Eli Lilly
Mylan

PROPOXYPHENE/ACETAMINOPHEN

BRAND NAME:
Dolene AP-65 (Lederle Labs)
Wygesic (Wyeth/AMHO)

DOSAGE FORM:
Tablet

USE:
To relieve pain.

AVOID USE:
Children under 12 years of age; if allergic to propoxyphene or acetaminophen or to any related drug.

SIDE EFFECTS:
Dizziness; drowsiness; nausea; vomiting; constipation; abdominal pain; headache; weakness; euphoria; lightheadedness; visual disturbances; skin rash; liver dysfunction (hepatitis, jaundice); insomnia.

$ BRAND OR GENERIC?
Despite bad publicity attributed to one ingredient in this product, propxyphene, this is still a widely used drug. It is mostly free of side effects when taken according to the doctor's directions.

Wygesic is the most expensive product, with Lederle's Dolene AP-65 offering up to a 28% savings. FDA-approved bioequivalent generic products can offer savings of up to 44%. Consult your doctor.

FDA-APPROVED BIOEQUIVALENT MANUFACTURERS:
*Lederle Labs
Mylan
*Wyeth/AMHO

PROPOXYPHENE/ASPIRIN/CAFFEINE

BRAND NAME:
Darvon Compound-65 (Eli Lilly)

DOSAGE FORM:
Capsule

USE:
To relieve pain.

AVOID USE:
Children under 12 years of age; if allergic to any ingredient in this product or to any related drug.

SIDE EFFECTS:
Dizziness; drowsiness; nausea; vomiting; constipation; abdominal pain; headache; weakness; euphoria; lightheadedness; visual disturbances; skin rash; liver dysfunction (hepatitis, jaundice); insomnia.

$ BRAND OR GENERIC?
The FDA recognizes several generics as bioequivalent to the brand. Use of these products can save 45% to 50% off the brand-name price. Other generics, which are not approved as bioequivalent by the FDA, are not any cheaper, so there is really no incentive for their use.

FDA-APPROVED BIOEQUIVALENT MANUFACTURERS:
Chelsea
Drummer/Phoenix
*Eli Lilly
Lemmon
SK & F
Zenith

PROPRANOLOL

BRAND NAME:
Inderal (Ayerst)

DOSAGE FORM:
Tablet 10 mg
Tablet 20 mg
Tablet 40 mg
Tablet 80 mg

USE:
To treat anginal heart pain; to treat high blood pressure; as an antiarrhythmic; to prevent migraine headaches.

AVOID USE:

In bronchial asthma; if experiencing seasonal hay fever; in presence of cardiogenic shock; if suffering from certain heart block or slowed heartbeat; in presence of overt congestive heart failure; if taking or have taken within the last two weeks any monoamine oxidase inhibitor drug; if allergic to this or to any related drug.

SIDE EFFECTS:

Slowed heartbeat; lowered blood pressure; burning or tingling sensation of the hands; lightheadedness; mental depression; insomnia; weakness; fatigue; visual disturbances; hallucinations; short-term amnesia; disorientation; confusion; nausea; vomiting; diarrhea; constipation; congestive heart failure; worsening of certain heart block; various allergic responses; skin reactions including rash; increased risk of asthma; various blood abnormalities; reversible hair loss.

$ BRAND OR GENERIC?

Since this drug is mostly used long-term in large quantities, it is a prime candidate for meaningful generic savings. Although only a few generics were officially listed by the FDA and rated for bioequivalence to the brand at the time of this writing, pricing information indicates potential generic savings in the 30% range for all strengths. It should attract many more competitors and drive generic prices even lower in the future.

FDA-APPROVED BIOEQUIVALENT MANUFACTURERS:

Tablet 10 mg, 20 mg, 40 mg, 80 mg

* Ayerst
Chelsea
Lederle Labs

PROSTAPHLIN

SEE Oxacillin

PROTOSTAT

SEE Metronidazole

PROVERA

SEE Medroxyprogesterone

PURODIGIN

SEE Digitoxin

PYRIDIUM

SEE Phenazopyridine

QUAALUDE

SEE Methaqualone

QUIBRON T/SR

SEE Theophylline

QUINAGLUTE DURA-TAB

SEE Quinidine Gluconate

QUINIDINE GLUCONATE

BRAND NAME:
Quinaglute Dura-Tab (Berlex)
DOSAGE FORM:
Tablet—Time-Release 324 mg
USE:
To treat various heart rhythm irregularities.
AVOID USE:
Certain heart conditions that may preclude use of this drug; use of digitalis preparations under certain conditions; myasthenia gravis; if allergic to quinidine or to any related drug.
SIDE EFFECTS:
Cinchonism (ringing in the ears, headache, nausea, visual disturbances); vomiting; diarrhea; various heart rhythm irregularities; lowered blood pressure; various blood abnormalities; headache; fever; excitement; fainting; blurred vision and many other visual abnormalities; various skin reactions including sensitivity to sunlight; various allergic responses; liver dysfunction (hepatitis); bone marrow depression.

$ BRAND OR GENERIC?

The amount of drug needed to be effective varies widely from person to person. For this reason careful adjustment of the dosage schedule must be accomplished by the doctor. Once the optimum drug regimen has been achieved, it is very important that variables be kept to a minimum. This includes switching from one manufacturer of the drug to another. Although any FDA-approved bioequivalent generic should be interchangeable, it would be prudent to use the same manufacturer's product if possible with each prescription refill.

Since this is a time-release tablet, duplication is difficult and the FDA seldom considers products as interchangeable. Manufacturers rarely approach this formulation in exactly the same way. Those products listed below and considered bioequivalent by the FDA have had to be backed up by detailed bioequivalency studies from their manufacturers. Make sure any generic you use appears on the following list.

Savings in excess of 40% are possible with generic use. Since this is an expensive drug that is used long-term in large quantities, generic savings can be truly impressive and well worth talking to your doctor about.

FDA-APPROVED BIOEQUIVALENT MANUFACTURERS:

Ascot
*Berlex
Bolar
Chelsea
Danbury
Roxane

QUINIDINE SULFATE

BRAND NAME:

Cin-Quin (Rowell)
Quinidine Sulfate (Eli Lilly)
Quinora (Key)

DOSAGE FORM:

Tablet 200 mg

USE:

To treat certain heart rhythm irregularities.

AVOID USE:

Certain heart conditions that may rule out use of this drug; use of digitalis preparations under certain conditions; myasthenia gravis; if allergic to quinidine or to any related drug.

SIDE EFFECTS:

Cinchonism (ringing in the ears, headache, nausea, visual disturbances); vomiting; diarrhea; various heart rhythm irregularities; lowered blood pressure; various blood abnormalities; headache; fever; excitement; fainting; blurred vision and many other visual abnormalities; various skin reactions including sensitivity to sunlight; various allergic responses; liver dysfunction (hepatitis); bone marrow depression.

$ BRAND OR GENERIC?

Unlike quinidine gluconate tablets, which are manufactured as a time-release formulation, quinidine sulfate is available as a straightforward tablet. Since the drug is very efficiently used by the body when taken orally, there are few problems in tablet manufacture. For this reason, once the correct dosing schedule has been achieved by the doctor, switching among FDA-approved bioequivalent generics should present no compromise to this drug's effectiveness.

There are many generics considered bioequivalent by the FDA, assuring wide availability of acceptable substitutes. Of the three brand-name products, Lilly's is the most expensive, with Quinora offering over a 50% discount. Cin-Quin has intermediate savings approaching 40%, while generics can yield up to a 60% discount.

FDA-APPROVED BIOEQUIVALENT MANUFACTURERS:
Barr
Beecham
Bell
Chelsea
Cord
Danbury
First Texas/Scherer
Halsey
ICN
*Key
KV
Lannett
Lederle Labs
*Eli Lilly
Parke-Davis/W-L
Pharmavite Pharms
Pharm Basics
Phoenix
Private Formulations
Purepac/Kalipharma
Quantum
Richlyn
Roxane
Stanlabs/Simpak
Superpharm
Towne Paulsen
Vangard Labs/MWM
Vitarine/Phoenix
West-Ward
Zenith

QUINORA

SEE Quinidine Sulfate

RAUDIXIN

SEE Rauwolfia Serpentina

RAUWOLFIA SERPENTINA

BRAND NAME:
Raudixin (E. R. Squibb)

DOSAGE FORM:
Tablet 50 mg
Tablet 100 mg

USE:
To control high blood pressure; to treat certain psychotic states accompanied by agitation.

AVOID USE:
Mental depression; peptic ulcer; ulcerative colitis; during electroconvulsive therapy; if allergic to this drug or to any related drug.

SIDE EFFECTS:
Nausea; vomiting; loss of appetite; diarrhea; excessive gastrointestinal secretions; drowsiness; mental depression; nightmares; anxiety; hearing and eye problems; anginal chest pains; heart rhythm irregularities; nasal congestion; skin itch and rash; dry mouth; headache; dizziness; difficult breathing; decreased sex drive or impotence; weight gain.

$ BRAND OR GENERIC?
Bioequivalence of generic products is still an unresolved issue with this drug. Generic use, however, offers a major savings over the brand. Since there are no FDA-approved bioequivalent generics, savings from substitution are only worthwhile provided the same manufacturer's product can be used with each prescription refill. Discuss this alternative with your doctor before making any decision.

The 50-mg tablet can save you over 50% generically, while savings of up to 70% are possible in the 100-mg strength.

FDA-APPROVED BIOEQUIVALENT MANUFACTURERS:
None
The FDA considers all brands of this product to have unresolved bioequivalency problems at this time.

REGLAN

SEE Metoclopramide

RELA

SEE Carisoprodol

RESERPINE

BRAND NAME:
Reserpoid (Upjohn)
Sandril (Eli Lilly)
Serpasil (Ciba/Ciba-Geigy)

DOSAGE FORM:
Tablet 0.1 mg
Tablet 0.25 mg

USE:
To control high blood pressure.

AVOID USE:
Mental depression; peptic ulcer; ulcerative colitis; when receiving electroconvulsive therapy; if allergic to this or to any related drug.

SIDE EFFECTS:
Nausea; vomiting; loss of appetite; increased secretion of the gastrointestinal tract; diarrhea; various heart rhythm irregularities; sedation; mental depression; anxiety; nightmares; nasal congestion; various hearing and vision problems; skin rash; itching; dry mouth; dizziness; headache; difficult breathing; fainting; nosebleed; various blood abnormalities; decreased sex drive or impotence; difficulty in urinating; muscle pain; increase in weight; breast fullness, secretion, or enlargement (in men); fluid retention and swelling.

$ BRAND OR GENERIC?
Generic bioequivalence has not been demonstrated at this time. With many side effects and a very low milligram dose, tablet variation is difficult to control. There is hardly any difference in price between brand and generic, so stick to the brand product.

FDA-APPROVED BIOEQUIVALENT MANUFACTURERS:
None
The FDA considers all brands of this product to have unresolved bioequivalency problems at this time.

RESERPOID

SEE Reserpine

RITALIN

SEE Methylphenidate

ROBAMOX

SEE Amoxicillin

ROBAXIN

SEE Methocarbamol

ROBAXISAL

SEE Methocarbamol/Aspirin

ROBICILLIN VK

SEE Penicillin VK

ROBINUL

SEE Glycopyrrolate

ROBINUL FORTE

SEE Glycopyrrolate

ROBITET

SEE Tetracycline

ROBITUSSIN A-C

SEE Guaifenesin/Codeine

ROBITUSSIN-DAC

SEE Guaifenesin/Pseudoephedrine/Codeine

RUFEN

SEE Ibuprofen

SALURON

SEE Hydroflumethiazide

SALUTENSIN

SEE Hydroflumethiazide/Reserpine

SANDRIL

SEE Reserpine

SCABENE

SEE Lindane

SECOBARBITAL

BRAND NAME:
  Seconal (Eli Lilly)
DOSAGE FORM:
  Capsule 50 mg
  Capsule 100 mg
USE:
  As a sedative and sleeping aid.

AVOID USE:

Liver function impairment; problems with porphyrin metabolism; certain respiratory disease; in the presence of chronic or acute pain; if allergic to this drug or to any barbiturate.

SIDE EFFECTS:

Drowsiness; sluggishness; breathing difficulties; various skin reactions and allergic responses; nausea; vomiting; diarrhea; headache; dizziness; hangover; liver dysfunction (jaundice, hepatitis); anemia.

$ BRAND OR GENERIC?

Even though this drug is placed in a highly restricted prescription category (Schedule II), its danger does not come from ordinary, doctor-supervised use. The hazard is in its misuse or overuse. Taken at normal prescriptive doses, side effects are minimal. This allows for some variation among manufacturers without seriously compromising the product's effectiveness.

With numerous FDA-approved bioequivalent generics, savings of up to 25% for the 50-mg capsule and nearly 40% with the 100-mg strength make their use worthwhile.

FDA-APPROVED BIOEQUIVALENT MANUFACTURERS:

Capsule 50 mg

Lannett
*Eli Lilly

Capsule 100 mg

Anabolic	*Eli Lilly
Barr	Parke-Davis/W-L
Bell	Purepac/Kalipharma
Chelsea	Stanlabs/Simpak
Drummer/Phoenix	Towne Paulsen
Halsey	Vitarine/Phoenix
ICN	West-Ward
KV	Wyeth/AMHO
Lannett	Zenith

SECONAL

SEE Secobarbital

SELENIUM SULFIDE

BRAND NAME:

Exsel (Herbert/Allergan)
Selsun (Abbott)

DOSAGE FORM:
Lotion/Shampoo 2.5%

USE:
To control dandruff and to treat certain other scalp conditions.

AVOID USE:
If allergic to selenium sulfide or to any related drug.

SIDE EFFECTS:
Skin irritation; hair loss; hair discoloration; oily or dry hair and scalp.

$ BRAND OR GENERIC?
Few side effects are associated with this preparation. In fact, it is available over-the-counter, without prescription, in a weaker strength in products such as Selsun Blue.

This is an excellent candidate for generic use. The FDA has approved many products as bioequivalent, with savings of over 50% possible.

FDA-APPROVED BIOEQUIVALENT MANUFACTURERS:
* Abbott
  Bay
* Herbert/Allergan
  National/Barre
  Syosset
  Thames

SELSUN

SEE Selenium Sulfide

SEPTRA

SEE Sulfamethoxazole/Trimethoprim

SEPTRA DS

SEE Sulfamethoxazole/Trimethoprim

SERAPES

SEE Hydrochlorothiazide/Reserpine/Hydralazine

SEROPHENE

SEE Clomiphene

SERPASIL

SEE Reserpine

SINEQUAN

SEE Doxepin

SK-PREDNISONE

SEE Prednisone

SOLFOTON

SEE Phenobarbital

SOMA

SEE Carisoprodol

SORBITRATE

SEE Isosorbide Dinitrate

SPIRINOLACTONE

BRAND NAME:
Aldactone (Searle)
DOSAGE FORM:
Tablet 25 mg
USE:
Alone or in combination to treat high blood pressure, water retention, various adrenal gland problems, and low blood potassium levels.
AVOID USE:
Kidney problems; lack of urine output; high blood potassium levels; if a nursing mother; if allergic to this or to any related drug.

SIDE EFFECTS:

Enlargement of male breasts; stomach upset; nausea; diarrhea; vomiting; drowsiness; headache; various skin reactions and allergic responses; confusion; loss of coordination; loss of erection; menstrual irregularities; unusual hair growth and deepening of the female voice; stomach ulcer.

$ BRAND OR GENERIC?

Generic use yields big savings. This drug is well absorbed in the body when taken by mouth, making tablet manufacture straightforward. Many generic products are FDA-certified as bioequivalent to the brand. Savings in excess of 50% make generic use an excellent choice.

FDA-APPROVED BIOEQUIVALENT MANUFACTURERS:

Ascot
Barr
Bolar
Chelsea
Cord
Lederle Labs
Mylan
Parke-Davis/W-L
Purepac/Kalipharma
*Searle
Upsher-Smith
Vangard Labs/MWM
Zenith

SPIRINOLACTONE/HYDROCHLOROTHIAZIDE

BRAND NAME:

Aldactazide (Searle)

DOSAGE FORM:

Tablet 25 mg spirinolactone/25 mg hydrochlorothiazide

USE:

To control high blood pressure; to treat water retention.

AVOID USE:

Various kidney problems; lack of urine output; high blood potassium levels; if a nursing mother; severe liver failure; if allergic to either ingredient in this product, to any sulfa drug, or to any other related drug.

SIDE EFFECTS:

Enlargement of male breasts; nausea; vomiting; diarrhea; stomach upset; loss of appetite; drowsiness; dizziness; headache; various skin reactions and allergic responses; confusion; loss of coordination; loss of erection; menstrual irregularities; unusual hair growth and deepening of the female voice; burning sensations of the skin; inflammation of the pancreas; various blood abnormalities; dizziness upon standing; muscle spasm and weakness.

$ BRAND OR GENERIC?

Very large savings are possible with generic use. Although this tablet contains two active ingredients, the FDA has rated many generics as bioequivalent to the brand. This is a real money saver and a good choice in generic form, with savings of up to 56% possible.

FDA-APPROVED BIOEQUIVALENT MANUFACTURERS:
Ascot
Barr
Bolar
Chelsea
Cord
Danbury
Lederle Labs
Mylan
Parke-Davis/W-L
Pharm Basics
Purepac/Kalipharma
*Searle
Upsher-Smith
Vangard Labs/MWM
Zenith

STELAZINE

SEE Trifluoperazine

STERANE

SEE Prednisolone

SULFABENZAMIDE/SULFACETAMIDE/ SULFATHIAZOLE

BRAND NAME:
Sultrin (Ortho)

DOSAGE FORM:
Vaginal cream
Vaginal tablet

USE:

To treat Hemophilus vaginalis infection.

AVOID USE:

Kidney disease; if allergic to any component of this product or to any related drug.

SIDE EFFECTS:

Local irritation; itching; rash; inflammation of the vulva.

$ BRAND OR GENERIC?

The cream form of this product poses fewer formulation problems than the tablet for the manufacturer and would be more likely to perform as well as the brand. With generics offering discounts of over 60%, substitution is worthwhile.

The vaginal tablet is a more complex dosage form to manufacture and has only recently become available as an FDA-approved bioequivalent generic. Savings should approach 65%, making substitution worth consulting your doctor about.

FDA-APPROVED BIOEQUIVALENT MANUFACTURERS:

Vaginal cream

Byk-Gulden   *Ortho
Clay-Park   Pharmaderm
NMC

Vaginal tablets

Fougera
*Ortho
Pharmaderm

SULFAMETHOXAZOLE

BRAND NAME:

Gantanol (Hoffmann-La Roche)

DOSAGE FORM:

Tablet 500 mg

USE:

As an antiinfective to treat various infections.

AVOID USE:

Infants under 2 months old; near the end of pregnancy; if a nursing mother; if allergic to this or to other sulfa drugs.

SIDE EFFECTS:

Various blood abnormalities; numerous skin reactions and allergic responses; nausea; vomiting; abdominal pain; diarrhea; loss of appetite; liver damage and dysfunction (hepatitis); inflammation of the pancreas; mouth irritation; headache; numbness and tingling of the extremities; mental depression; loss of coordination; hallucinations; convulsions; ringing in the ears; insomnia; kidney damage; little or no urine output; fever; chills; bone marrow depression.

$ BRAND OR GENERIC?

The FDA rates several generic products as bioequivalent to the brand. Although not as many generic manufacturers make the list as with this drug's closely related cousin Sulfisoxazole (brand name Gantrisin), there are still enough makers to assure wide availability of acceptable substitutes. With generic savings of up to 60%, it is an alternative worth discussing with your doctor.

FDA-APPROVED BIOEQUIVALENT MANUFACTURERS:
Ascot
Barr
Bolar
Cord
Heather
*Hoffmann-La Roche
Shionogi USA

SULFAMETHOXAZOLE/TRIMETHOPRIM

BRAND NAME:
Bactrim (Hoffmann-La Roche)
Bactrim DS (Hoffmann-La Roche)
Septra (Burroughs Wellcome)
Septra DS (Burroughs Wellcome)

DOSAGE FORM:
Tablet (Regular Strength)
Tablet (Double Strength)
Suspension

USE:
As an antiinfective to treat urinary tract infections; to treat certain infections of the ear, chest, and intestinal tract.

AVOID USE:
Certain anemias; the latter part of pregnancy; if a nursing mother; infants under 2 months old; if allergic to either ingredient in this product, to any sulfa drug, or to another related drug.

SIDE EFFECTS:
Various blood abnormalities; numerous skin reactions and allergic responses; irritation of the mouth and tongue; nausea; vomiting; abdominal pain; liver damage and dysfunction (hepatitis); diarrhea; inflammation of the pancreas; headache; numbness and tingling of the extremities; mental depression; loss of

coordination; hallucinations; convulsions; ringing in the ears; insomnia; muscle weakness and fatigue; fever; chills; little or no urine output.

$ BRAND OR GENERIC?

This two-component product has many generics considered bioequivalent by the FDA. Although it is mostly taken on a short-term basis, savings can still amount to enough to warrant generic use. In average prescription quantities, the following savings can be expected.

Tablet (Regular Strength)   The two brand-name products sell for the same price, so either brand-name product is of comparable value. The generic, however, can yield savings of up to 35% and is worth considering.

Tablet (Double Strength)   Here, too, both brand-name products are comparably priced. Up to a 40% savings is possible with generic use, making it a good alternative.

Suspension   The two brand-name competitors again retail at an equal price. But the generic can save up to 27% over the brand, making it an alternative worth discussing with your doctor.

FDA-APPROVED BIOEQUIVALENT MANUFACTURERS:

Tablet (Regular Strength and Double Strength)

Barr	Heather
Biocraft	*Hoffmann-La Roche
*Burroughs Wellcome	Lemmon
Chelsea	Par
Danbury	Superpharm
Drummer/Phoenix	

Suspension

Biocraft	*Hoffmann-La Roche
*Burroughs Wellcome	National/Barre

SULFANILAMIDE/AMINACRINE/ALLANTOIN

BRAND NAME:

AVC (Merrell Dow)

Vagitrol (Lemmon)

DOSAGE FORM:

Vaginal suppository

Vaginal cream

USE:

To treat various vaginal infections when isolation of a specific causative agent cannot be accomplished.

AVOID USE:

If allergic to any ingredient in this product, to any sulfa drug, or to any other related drug.

SIDE EFFECTS:
Vaginal discomfort or burning sensation possible but not usual.

$ BRAND OR GENERIC?
At present the FDA does not publish bioequivalency data on this product. It is being reclassified as to its effectiveness, but until a final determination is made, bioequivalency ratings will be withheld. Many states have listed acceptable generic manufacturers, and it is prudent to consult these listings in your state for guidance.

Used generically, the cream can yield savings of up to 64% over AVC, while a discount approaching 60% is possible for the vaginal suppositories. The other brand-name product, Vagitrol, shows a 24% savings over AVC in cream form, and up to 30% in the suppository. This product offers intermediate savings together with a brand name.

FDA-APPROVED BIOEQUIVALENT MANUFACTURERS:
None

The FDA is awaiting revised labeling and additional information on this product's effectiveness.

SULFASALAZINE

BRAND NAME:
Azulfadine (Pharmacia)
Azulfadine EN-tabs (Pharmacia)

DOSAGE FORM:
Tablet 500 mg
Tablet—Enteric Coated 500 mg

USE:
As an antiinfective to treat ulcerative colitis.

AVOID USE:
Infants under 2 years of age; if intestinal or urinary obstruction exists; if any porphyrin metabolism abnormalities exist; if allergic to this drug, to any other sulfa drugs, or to aspirinlike drugs.

SIDE EFFECTS:
Loss of appetite; nausea; vomiting; upset stomach; abdominal pain; diarrhea with or without blood; irritation of the mouth; inflammation of the pancreas; liver dysfunction (hepatitis); various blood abnormalities; numerous skin reactions including sensitivity to sunlight; many allergic responses; hair loss; headache; ringing in the ears and hearing loss; numbness and tingling of the extremities; loss of coordination; convulsions; mental depression; hallucinations; insomnia; sedation; little or no urine output; kidney damage or dysfunction.

$ BRAND OR GENERIC?

Because this drug is used regularly by chronic colitis sufferers, it is a prime candidate for large savings through generic use. There are two types of tablets available: a regular one and an enteric-coated formulation, called EN-tab in the case of the brand-name product. Only the regular tablet has FDA-approved generic versions. The EN-tab, because of its delayed-action tablet coating, is difficult to duplicate.

Generic use of the plain tablet can save an impressive 50% over the brand. Since this is an expensive product, savings make generic use well worthwhile.

Use of a generic substitute for the enteric-coated tablet will save over 30%, but since savings are not nearly as great as with the plain tablet, and generics, although available, are not FDA-approved as bioequivalent, the prudent choice would be to stick to the brand-name product.

FDA-APPROVED BIOEQUIVALENT MANUFACTURERS:

Tablet 500 mg

Bolar
Chelsea
Danbury
Drummer/Phoenix

Lederle Labs
*Pharmacia
Rowell

Tablet—Enteric Coated 500 mg

*Pharmacia

SULFINPYRAZONE

BRAND NAME:
Anturane (Ciba/Ciba-Geigy)

DOSAGE FORM:
Tablet 100 mg
Capsule 200 mg

USE:
To treat gouty arthritis.

AVOID USE:
Active stomach or intestinal ulcer; certain blood disorders; if allergic to phenylbutazone, or similar drugs, or to this drug.

SIDE EFFECTS:
Stomach pain; nausea; vomiting; diarrhea; various blood abnormalities; skin rash; bone marrow depression; stomach bleeding; intestinal bleeding.

$ BRAND OR GENERIC?
The principle danger when using this product is the possibility of developing certain blood abnormalities. Because of this, periodic blood tests are highly rec-

ommended. In light of this potential hazard, FDA guidelines for bioequivalent generic products are very important.

Use of the generic 100-mg tablet will yield impressive savings of up to 44%, while generics in the 200-mg capsule should show savings of up to 35%.

FDA-APPROVED BIOEQUIVALENT MANUFACTURERS:

Tablet 100 mg

Barr	Danbury
*Ciba/Ciba-Geigy	Zenith

Capsule 200 mg

Barr	Vangard Labs
*Ciba/Ciba-Geigy	Zenith

SULFISOXAZOLE

BRAND NAME:

Gantrisin (Hoffmann-La Roche)

DOSAGE FORM:

Tablet 500 mg

USE:

As an antiinfective to treat various infections.

AVOID USE:

Infants under 2 months old; near the end of pregnancy; if a nursing mother; if allergic to this or to other sulfa drugs.

SIDE EFFECTS:

Various blood abnormalities; numerous skin reactions and allergic responses; nausea; vomiting; abdominal pain; diarrhea; loss of appetite; liver damage and dysfunction (hepatitis); inflammation of the pancreas; mouth irritation; headache; numbness and tingling of the extremities; mental depression; loss of coordination; hallucinations; convulsions; ringing in the ears; insomnia; kidney damage; little or no urine output; fever; chills; bone marrow depression.

$ BRAND OR GENERIC?

The FDA has certified many generic products as bioequivalent to the brand. Savings approaching 50% are possible with generic use. Consult your doctor.

FDA-APPROVED BIOEQUIVALENT MANUFACTURERS:

Barr
Cord
Heather
*Hoffmann-La Roche
ICN

Lannett
Lederle Labs
MK
Parke-Davis/W-L
Purepac/Kalipharma
Reid-Provident
Richlyn
Roxane
SK & F
West-Ward
Zenith

SULTRIN

SEE Sulfabenzamide/Sulfacetamide/Sulfathiazole

SUMYCIN

SEE Tetracycline

SUSTAIRE

SEE Theophylline

SYNACORT

SEE Hydrocortisone

SYNALAR

SEE Flucinolone

SYNALOGOS-DC

SEE Dihydrocodeine/Aspirin/Caffeine

SYNTHROID

SEE L-Thyroxine

TEGOPEN

SEE Cloxacillin

TENUATE

SEE Diethylpropion

TEPANIL

SEE Diethylpropion

TERRAMYCIN

SEE Oxytetracycline

TETRACYCLINE

BRAND NAME:
Achromycin V (Lederle Labs)
Bristacycline (Bristol)
Cyclopar (Parke-Davis/W-L)
Panmycin (Upjohn)
Robitet (A. H. Robins)
Sumycin (E. R. Squibb)
Tetracyn (Pfipharmecs/Pfizer)

DOSAGE FORM:
Capsule 250 mg
Capsule 500 mg
Syrup 125 mg/5 ml

USE:
As an antibiotic to treat various infections.

AVOID USE:

During pregnancy; if a nursing mother; if allergic to tetracycline or to any related drug.

SIDE EFFECTS:

Loss of appetite; nausea; vomiting; diarrhea; irritation of the tongue; black tongue; superinfection due to yeast overgrowth affecting the mouth, intestinal tract, rectum, and vagina; various skin reactions including sensitivity to sunlight; kidney dysfunction; various allergic responses; various blood abnormalities; tooth discoloration or malformation in children under 9 years of age (including infants and unborn).

$ BRAND OR GENERIC?

Capsule 250 mg and 500 mg Many generic products are considered bioequivalent to the brand, but since the brand product sells almost as cheaply as the generic, for the same price, you can get the quality assurance of a brand-name manufacturer.

Syrup There is a major difference in price between the brand and generic product. Generic bioequivalence is approved by the FDA for many products and offers reliable performance. The best choice, however, is the brand Sumycin, which sells almost as cheaply as the generic alternatives yet carries the quality assurance of a brand-name product. The generic can save up to 68% off the price of Achromycin V, while Sumycin can yield savings of up to 58%.

FDA-APPROVED BIOEQUIVALENT MANUFACTURERS:

Capsule 250 mg

Barr	*Pfipharmecs/Pfizer
Boots	Purepac/Kalipharma
*Bristol	Quantum
Chelsea	Rachelle
Danbury	Reid-Provident
Halsey	Richlyn
Heather	*A. H. Robins
ICN	*E. R. Squibb
*Lederle Labs	Superpharm
MK	*Upjohn
M. M. Mast	West-Ward
Mylan	Wyeth/AMHO
*Parke-Davis/W-L	Zenith

Capsule 500 mg

Barr	*Parke-Davis/W-L
Boots	*Pfipharmecs/Pfizer
Chelsea	Purepac/Kalipharma
Danbury	Rachelle
Halsey	Reid-Provident
Heather	Richlyn
ICN	*A. H. Robins
*Lederle Labs	Roxane
Mylan	*E. R. Squibb

Superpharm Wyeth/AMHO
West-Ward Zenith

Syrup 125 mg/5 ml

*Lederle Labs Purepac/Kalipharma
MK *E. R. Squibb
National/Barre Zenith
*Pfipharmecs/Pfizer

TETRACYN

SEE Tetracycline

THEO-DUR

SEE Theophylline

THEOLAIR-SR

SEE Theophylline

THEOPHYLLINE

BRAND NAME:

Elixir

Elixophyllin (Berlex)

Tablet—Time-Release

Constant-T (Geigy) Sustaire (Roerig)
Duraphyl (McNeil) Theo-Dur (Key)
Quibron T/SR (Mead Johnson) Theolair-SR (Riker)

DOSAGE FORM:

Elixir 80 mg/15 ml
Tablet—Time-Release 100 mg
Tablet—Time-Release 200 mg
Tablet—Time-Release 300 mg

USE:

As a bronchodilator to relieve symptoms of bronchial asthma, bronchitis, and emphysema.

AVOID USE:

Peptic ulcer; if allergic to this or to any related drug.

SIDE EFFECTS:

Stomach upset; nausea; vomiting; headache; nervousness; rapid breathing; insomnia; rapid heartbeat; skin rash; diarrhea; flushing; low blood pressure.

$ BRAND OR GENERIC?

In the elixir form, many generics are FDA-certified as bioequivalent. Up to 40% savings are possible, making generic use an excellent option. Consult your doctor.

Different brands of the time-release tablet are almost never considered bioequivalent and interchangeable by the FDA but there are generics available. All three strengths show generic savings in excess of 40%. Consult your doctor before allowing subsitution.

FDA-APPROVED BIOEQUIVALENT MANUFACTURERS:

Elixir

Bay	Life
Bell	National/Barre
*Berlex	Panray/Ormont
H. R. Cenci	Pharms Assoc/Beach
Halsey	*Riker/3M
Lannett	Roxane

Tablet—Time-Release 100 mg and 200 mg

None

Tablet—Time-Release 300 mg

*Key
Forest

THIORIDAZINE

BRAND NAME:

Mellaril (Sandoz)

DOSAGE FORM:
Tablet 10 mg
Tablet 25 mg
Tablet 50 mg
Tablet 100 mg

USE:
As a tranquilizer to treat psychotic disorders, including depression accompanied by anxiety, agitation, and certain insomnias; to control hyperactivity and excessive aggression in children.

AVOID USE:
Certain heart disease; children under 2 years of age; severe central nervous system depression or coma; if allergic to this and to other phenothiazine drugs.

SIDE EFFECTS:
Drowsiness; dry mouth; blurred vision; nasal congestion; nausea; vomiting; diarrhea; constipation; loss of appetite; production of breast milk; breast engorgement; menstrual irregularities; inability to ejaculate; various skin reactions; various blood abnormalities; swelling of the salivary glands; liver dysfunction (hepatitis, jaundice); bone marrow depression; convulsions; parkinsonlike symptoms (fixed masklike facial expression; trembling hands, legs, and arms; stiff arm and leg movements).

$ BRAND OR GENERIC?
There are numerous FDA-approved generics available for this drug. When used on a long-term basis in quantities of 100 tablets, savings with generics can really add up. For the 10-mg, 25-mg, 50-mg, and 100-mg tablet strengths, savings with generic use should equal or exceed 50%.

FDA-APPROVED BIOEQUIVALENT MANUFACTURERS:

Tablet 10 mg

Barr	Par
Biocraft	Roxane
Bolar	*Sandoz
Chelsea	Superpharm
Cord	West-Ward
Danbury	Zenith
Mylan	

Tablet 25 mg and 50 mg

Barr	Par
Bolar	Roxane
Chelsea	*Sandoz
Cord	Superpharm
Danbury	West-Ward
Mylan	Zenith

Tablet 100 mg

Barr	Bolar
Biocraft	Chelsea

Cord	Roxane
Danbury	*Sandoz
Mylan	Zenith
Par	

THORAZINE

SEE Chlorpromazine

THYROID, DESSICATED

BRAND NAME:
Armour Thyroid (USV)

DOSAGE FORM;
Tablet 16 mg (¼ grain)
Tablet 32 mg (½ grain)
Tablet 65 mg (1 grain)

USE:
As replacement therapy for decreased or absent thyroid gland function.

AVOID USE:
Overactive thyroid; certain heart disease; certain adrenal gland insufficiency; if allergic to this or to any related drug.

SIDE EFFECTS:
Side effects would result from overdosage, since the proper dose would restore the body to its normal level of thyroid hormone. Signs of overdosage include rapid or irregular heartbeat; weight loss; tremors; headache; diarrhea; insomnia; sweating; heat and fever intolerance; anginal pain.

$ BRAND OR GENERIC?
This is a pre-1938 drug and is exempt from the FDA's bioequivalency approval process. This is an inexpensive drug no matter which manufacturer is selected. Since dosage control is vital when using this product, and the potential generic savings of up to 25% don't add up to much in dollars, there seems little point to using anything except the brand-name drug.

FDA-APPROVED BIOEQUIVALENT MANUFACTURERS:
This is a pre-1938 drug and is exempt from the FDA's bioequivalency approval process.

TOFRANIL

SEE Imipramine

TOLAZAMIDE

BRAND NAME:
Tolinase (Upjohn)

DOSAGE FORM:
Tablet 100 mg
Tablet 250 mg
Tablet 500 mg

USE:
As an antidiabetic to lower blood sugar.

AVOID USE:
In the presence of infection; severe trauma; if undergoing surgery; if there is a history of impaired liver function; in cases of juvenile onset diabetes; if prone to ketosis, acidosis, or coma; if pregnant or about to become pregnant; brittle diabetes; kidney disease; endocrine disease; if allergic to this or to any related drug.

SIDE EFFECTS:
Nausea; vomiting; indigestion; diarrhea; blood abnormalities; low blood sugar (usually due to too large a dose or inadequate food intake); liver dysfunction (hepatitis, jaundice); various skin reactions and allergic responses; weakness; fatigue; dizziness; headache; bone marrow depression.

$ BRAND OR GENERIC?
Since tolazamide was developed to treat those individuals not responsive to first-line oral antidiabetic agents such as chlorpropamide (Diabinese) or tolbutamide (Orinase), its market is not that big. For this reason it is unlikely that the brand-name drug, Tolinase, would be as widely discounted as its first-line competitors. While chlorpropamide and tolbutamide may not yield as large a generic discount because of this, it is probably not the case with tolazamide.

Expect to see generic savings for all three strengths at about 35% to 40%. However, as many manufacturers scramble to market this relatively new generic, the discounts may increase.

FDA-APPROVED BIOEQUIVALENT MANUFACTURERS:

Tablet 100 mg, 250 mg, 500 mg

*Upjohn
Zenith

TOLBUTAMIDE

BRAND NAME:
Orinase (Upjohn)

DOSAGE FORM:

Tablet 500 mg

USE:

As an antidiabetic to lower blood sugar.

AVOID USE:

In presence of infection; severe trauma; if undergoing surgery; severe kidney dysfunction; in cases of juvenile onset diabetes; in brittle diabetes; if prone to ketosis, acidosis, or coma; if pregnant or about to become pregnant; if allergic to this or to any related drug.

SIDE EFFECTS:

Nausea; indigestion; heartburn; diarrhea; headache; low blood sugar (usually due to too large a dose or inadequate food intake); various skin reactions and allergic responses; liver dysfunction (jaundice, hepatitis); bone marrow depression; various blood abnormalities; weakness; fatigue.

$ BRAND OR GENERIC?

Since this drug is used long-term, savings with generic use can be great. With many products considered bioequivalent by the FDA, competition among manufacturers is intense, assuring low prices. Watch for specials on the brand product, as some pharmacies price it low. If the brand is sold at normal prescription price, generic savings can approach 70%.

FDA-APPROVED BIOEQUIVALENT MANUFACTURERS:

Ascot
Barr
Chelsea
Cord
Danbury
Drummer/Phoenix
Lederle Labs
Mylan
Parke-Davis/W-L
Purepac/Kalipharma
SK & F
Superpharm
*Upjohn
Vangard Labs/MWM
Zenith

TOLINASE

SEE Tolazamide

TOTACILLIN

SEE Ampicillin

TRANCOPAL

SEE Chlormezanone

TREMIN

SEE Trihexyphenidyl

TRIAMCINOLONE

BRAND NAME:
Aristocort (Lederle Labs)
Kenacort (E. R. Squibb)

DOSAGE FORM:
Tablet 4 mg

USE:
As an antiinflammatory to treat allergies, various arthritic diseases, endocrine disorders, respiratory conditions, and gastrointestinal problems.

AVOID USE:
Fungal infections of the blood; if allergic to this or to any related drug.

SIDE EFFECTS:
Fluid retention and swelling; congestive heart failure (in predisposed individuals); high blood pressure; electrolyte imbalances; muscle weakness; loss of muscle mass; decomposition of bones; peptic ulcer; inflammation of the pancreas; ulceration of the esophagus; delayed wound healing; increased sweating; skin rash; facial flushing; headache; convulsions; dizziness; insomnia; menstrual irregularities; growth suppression in children; Cushing's syndrome; decreased diabetic control; various eye problems including cataracts and glaucoma; emotional disturbances.

$ BRAND OR GENERIC?
The FDA does not consider any generics to be bioequivalent. While it is best to be assured of strict quality control and tablet consistency, the difference in price between brand and generic can be over 80%. Bioequivalence data for generic products is still pending, but if used in any non-life-threatening situation, the incredible savings warrant consulting your doctor about generic use.

FDA-APPROVED BIOEQUIVALENT MANUFACTURERS:
None
The FDA considers all brands of this product to have unresolved bioequivalency problems at this time.

TRIAMCINOLONE ACETONIDE

BRAND NAME:
Aristocort (Lederle Labs)
Kenalog (E. R. Squibb)

DOSAGE FORM:
Cream and Ointment 0.025%
Cream and Ointment 0.1%
Cream and Ointment 0.5%

USE:
To relieve skin inflammation or itching.

AVOID USE:
Viral skin disease; ophthalmic use; tuberculosis of the skin; herpes simplex; if allergic to this or to any related drug.

SIDE EFFECTS:
Burning sensation of the skin; itching; skin irritation; dryness of the skin.

$ BRAND OR GENERIC?
The FDA has certified many generics as bioequivalent. The two brand-name manufacturers market their respective products in a somewhat different manner. They do not use the same size tubes, making price comparisons difficult for the uninitiated. For purposes of accurate comparison, savings quoted here are figured on an equal weight basis, regardless of which size tube is marketed by various manufacturers. A small tube is considered to be 15 gm (½ ounce) and the large is calculated on the basis of 60 gm (2 ounces).

Cream and ointment 0.025%   For the 15-gm size, both brand names sell for the same price. Generics, however, can offer savings of up to 30%.

For the large size (60 gm), Kenalog is about 5% cheaper than Aristocort, while generics can save an impressive 63%.

Cream and ointment 0.1%   In the 15-gm size, the brand Aristocort offers only about a 5% savings over the other brand, Kenalog. Generics are a more attractive alternative with possible savings approaching 54%.

The 60-gm tube shows the two brand-name products even. The real bargain here is the generic, offering savings approaching 70%.

Cream and ointment 0.5%   Generally dispensed only in a small-size tube (about ½ ounce), the two brand-name products are priced closely, with a 7% advantage going to Kenalog. Generics can offer an impressive 67% discount, making them the best choice.

FDA-APPROVED BIOEQUIVALENT MANUFACTURERS:

Cream 0.025%

Ambix/Organics	*Lederle Labs
Bay	Lemmon
Byk-Gulden	NMC
Clay-Park	Pharmaderm/Byk-Gulden

Pharmafair   Syosset
Savage Labs/Byk-Gulden Thames
*E. R. Squibb

Ointment 0.025%

Bay   Pharmaderm/Byk-Gulden
Byk-Gulden Savage Labs/Byk-Gulden
Clay-Park   *E. R. Squibb

Cream 0.1%

Bay   Pharmaderm/Byk-Gulden
Byk-Gulden   Pharmafair
Clay-Park   Rowell
Del-Ray   Savage Labs/Byk-Gulden
*Lederle Labs *E. R. Squibb
Lemmon   Syosset
NMC   Thames

Ointment 0.1%

Bay   Pharmaderm/Byk-Gulden
Byk-Gulden   Savage Labs/Byk-Gulden
Clay-Park   *E. R. Squibb
*Lederle Labs Thames
NMC

Cream 0.5%

Bay   Pharmafair
Byk-Gulden   Savage Labs/Byk-Gulden
Clay-Park   *E. R. Squibb
*Lederle Labs   Syosset
Lemmon   Thames
Pharmaderm/Byk-Gulden

Ointment 0.5%

Bay   *Lederle Labs
Byk-Gulden *E. R. Squibb
Clay-Park

TRICHLORMETHIAZIDE

BRAND NAME:
Metahydrin (Merrell Dow)
Naqua (Schering)

DOSAGE FORM:
Tablet 2 mg
Tablet 4 mg

USE:

As an antihypertensive and diuretic.

AVOID USE:

Lack of urine output; if pregnant; if breast-feeding an infant; if allergic to this drug, to any sulfa drug, or to any other related drug.

SIDE EFFECTS:

Loss of appetite; stomach upset; nausea; diarrhea; constipation; vomiting; cramps; inflammation of the pancreas; liver dysfunction (jaundice); dizziness; burning sensations of the skin; headache; various blood abnormalities; various skin reactions including sensitivity to sunlight; dizziness upon standing; high blood sugar and uric acid levels; muscle spasm and weakness.

$ BRAND OR GENERIC?

Although the FDA does not recognize any generics as bioequivalent, a substantial savings is nevertheless possible with them. Expect up to a 50% discount for the 2-mg strength, while the 4-mg tablet should offer savings in excess of 60%. Consult your doctor.

FDA-APPROVED BIOEQUIVALENT MANUFACTURERS:

None

The FDA has found all brands of this drug to have potential bioequivalence problems.

TRIDIHEXETHYL/MEPROBAMATE

BRAND NAME:

Pathibamate (Lederle)

DOSAGE FORM:

Tablet (25 mg tridihexethyl/200 mg meprobamate)
Tablet (25 mg tridihexethyl/400 mg meprobamate)

USE:

To relieve symptoms of peptic ulcer and irritable bowel syndrome.

AVOID USE:

Glaucoma; urinary tract or gastrointestinal obstruction; lack of intestinal movement in the elderly or debilitated; certain heart disease; ulcerative colitis; myasthenia gravis; severe disturbance of porphyrin metabolism; during first three months of pregnancy; children under 12 years of age; allergy to either ingredient in this product or to any related drug.

SIDE EFFECTS:

Dry mouth; difficulty in urinating; fast or irregular heartbeat; blurred vision and other visual difficulties; fainting; euphoria; loss of taste; headache; nervousness; drowsiness; loss of coordination; slurred speech; weakness; burning sensation of the skin; nausea; vomiting; diarrhea; impotence; constipation; various allergic reactions including skin rash and itching; decreased sweating; mental excitement or confusion; various blood abnormalities; bone marrow depression; swelling.

$ BRAND OR GENERIC?

With usual prescription quantities of 100 tablets, generic savings could approach 70%. Due to current reclassification of this product's status by the FDA, bioavailability evaluations are not yet available to judge the value of current marketed generics.

FDA-APPROVED BIOEQUIVALENT MANUFACTURERS:
None

The FDA currently lists all brands of this product as ineffective. Bioequivalency ratings await completion of administrative proceedings.

TRIFLUOPERAZINE

BRAND NAME:
Stelazine (SK & F)

DOSAGE FORM:
Tablet 1 mg
Tablet 2 mg
Tablet 5 mg
Tablet 10 mg

USE:
As a tranquilizer.

AVOID USE:
Coma; severe central nervous system depression; certain blood abnormalities; bone marrow depression; certain liver problems; if allergic to this or to other phenothiazine drugs.

SIDE EFFECTS:
Drowsiness; dry mouth; constipation; dizziness; various skin reactions; insomnia; muscle spasms; loss of menstruation; production of breast milk; parkinsonlike symptoms; a dangerous condition called tardive dyskinesia; weakness; fatigue.

$ BRAND OR GENERIC?

Until recently the FDA did not recognize any generic products as bioequivalent to the brand-name drug. Even now only a few are accepted as interchangeable. Since approved generics may not have wide enough distribution to be available in all parts of the country, the only alternative may in some cases be the brand.

Expect savings with generic use to be as much as 59% for the 1-mg tablet, 57% for the 2-mg strength, 60% with the 5-mg tablet, and 66% for the 10-mg strength.

FDA-APPROVED BIOEQUIVALENT MANUFACTURERS:

Tablet 1 mg, 2 mg, 5 mg, 10 mg

Cord	*SK & F
Duramed	Zenith

TRIHEXYPHENIDYL

BRAND NAME:
Artane (Lederle Labs)
Tremin (Schering)

DOSAGE FORM:
Tablet 2 mg
Tablet 5 mg

USE:
To control symptoms of Parkinson's disease; to treat side effects of some drugs acting on the central nervous system.

AVOID USE:
If allergic to this or to any related drug.

SIDE EFFECTS:
Dry mouth; blurred vision; dizziness; nausea; constipation; difficult urination; nervousness; inflammation of the salivary glands; skin rash; fast heartbeat; headache; weakness.

$ BRAND OR GENERIC?
Bioequivalence for many generics has been approved by the FDA. There is a tremendous savings possible with generic use, especially in the higher (5-mg) tablet strength. The 2-mg tablet can offer generic savings of over 50%, while up to a 73% discount is possible in the 5-mg strength.

FDA-APPROVED BIOEQUIVALENT MANUFACTURERS:

Tablet 2 mg

Bolar	*Schering
Danbury	Vangard Labs/MWM
*Lederle Labs	

Tablet 5 mg

Bolar	*Schering
Danbury	Tablicaps
*Lederle Labs	

TRIMETHOPRIM

BRAND NAME:
Proloprim (Burroughs Wellcome)
Trimpex (Hoffmann-La Roche)

DOSAGE FORM:
Tablet 100 mg

USE:
As an antiinfective to treat certain urinary tract infections.

AVOID USE:
Certain anemias; if allergic to trimethoprim or to any related drug.

SIDE EFFECTS:
Various skin reactions; stomach upset; nausea; vomiting; inflammation of the tongue; various blood abnormalities.

$ BRAND OR GENERIC?
The two brand-name products sell for the same price. The FDA recognizes few generics as bioequivalent, but use of these should yield a savings of up to 33%, making it the best choice.

FDA-APPROVED BIOEQUIVALENT MANUFACTURERS:
Biocraft
*Burroughs Wellcome
Danbury
*Hoffmann-La Roche

TRIMOX

SEE Amoxicillin

TRIMPEX

SEE Trimethoprim

TRIPELENNAMINE

BRAND NAME:
PBZ (Geigy/Ciba-Geigy)

DOSAGE FORM:
Tablet 50 mg
Elixir 25 mg/5 ml

USE:

As an antihistamine to relieve symptoms of various allergies.

AVOID USE:

Newborn or premature infants; asthmatics; if taking a monoamine oxidase inhibitor drug; certain glaucomas; if a nursing mother; certain peptic ulcers; enlarged prostate gland; certain bladder obstructions; certain intestinal obstructions; if allergic to this or to any related drug.

SIDE EFFECTS:

Drowsiness; sedation; dry mouth, nose, and throat; thickened bronchial mucus; dizziness; impaired coordination; stomach upset; mental confusion; chills; irritability; euphoria; loss of appetite; nausea; vomiting; diarrhea; constipation; low blood pressure; blurred vision and other visual disturbances; ringing in the ears; headache; convulsions; nasal congestion; frequent or difficult urination; various blood abnormalities; various skin reactions including sensitivity to sunlight.

$ BRAND OR GENERIC?

This is a widely used, long-established antihistamine that has been well tested over time. The range of recommended dosage varies greatly, allowing for some differences in bioavailability among manufacturers without seriously compromising the product's effectiveness.

With many generics approved as being bioequivalent by the FDA, savings in tablet form (50 mg) should approach 75% when purchased in quantities of 100.

In elixir form the average quantity prescribed is usually smaller. Children's doses are usually lower than those prescribed for adults. A 4-ounce bottle, a common size, should save about 30% generically. Generic elixirs on the market, however, are not FDA-approved as being bioequivalent to the brand. Consult your doctor.

FDA-APPROVED BIOEQUIVALENT MANUFACTURERS:

Tablet 50 mg

Anabolic	*Geigy/Ciba-Geigy
Barr	Heather
Bolar	Lannett
Chelsea	Richlyn
Danbury	Tablicaps

Elixir 25 mg/5 ml

None

TRIPOLIDINE

BRAND NAME:

Actidil (Burroughs Wellcome)

DOSAGE FORM:
Tablet 2.5 mg
Syrup 1.25 mg/5 ml

USE:
As an antihistamine to relieve some symptoms of hay fever and to relieve allergic reactions such as skin itching, hives, and rash.

AVOID USE:
Newborn infants; if a nursing mother; if asthmatic; if taking a monoamine oxidase inhibitor drug; if allergic to this drug or to any related drug.

SIDE EFFECTS:
Sedation; dizziness; impaired coordination; stomach upset; thickening of bronchial secretions; dry mouth, nose, and throat; difficult urination; skin rash; excitation; insomnia.

$ BRAND OR GENERIC?
The FDA has approved several generics as being bioequivalent to the brand. Savings should be in excess of 40% for the generic tablet, while the syrup offers only a marginal 10% discount in generic form.

FDA-APPROVED BIOEQUIVALENT MANUFACTURERS:

Tablet

Bolar	Danbury
*Burroughs Wellcome	Drummer/Phoenix

Syrup

Bay	National/Barre
*Burroughs Wellcome	Pharms Assoc/Beach
Halsey	

TRIPOLIDINE/PSEUDOEPHEDRINE

BRAND NAME:
Actifed (Burroughs Wellcome)

DOSAGE FORM:
Tablet
Syrup

USE:
As an antihistamine and a decongestant to relieve symptoms of allergies and colds.

AVOID USE:
Severe high blood pressure; certain heart disease; to treat lower respiratory symptoms or asthma; glaucoma; if taking a monoamine oxidase inhibitor drug;

newborn or premature infants; if a nursing mother; if allergic to either ingredient in this product to or any related drug.

SIDE EFFECTS:

Dry mouth, nose, and throat; various skin reactions including sensitivity to sunlight; itching; increased sweating; chills; various blood abnormalities; drowsiness; dizziness; impaired coordination; excitation; euphoria; blurred vision and other eye problems; insomnia; burning sensations of the skin; ringing in the ears; nerve inflammation; convulsions; hallucinations; difficult or frequent urination; menstrual irregularities; stomach upset; loss of appetite, vomiting; diarrhea; constipation; thickening of the bronchial mucus; wheezing; nasal congestion.

$ BRAND OR GENERIC?

The brand-name product, Actifed, is now sold over-the-counter without prescription. Most generics, however, are still classified as prescription only. This has created a situation in which the brand is almost as cheap as prescription generics.

Even with its over-the-counter status, Actifed is still about 7% more expensive in tablet form and 9% more expensive in syrup form than prescription generic equivalents.

If an insurance company reimburses you for prescription medication only, this could be a deciding factor in using a generic still considered a prescription product. If this situation does not apply, stick to the brand, since the generic savings in dollars are not significant.

FDA-APPROVED BIOEQUIVALENT MANUFACTURERS:

Since the brand-name product has been switched to over-the-counter status, Burroughs Wellcome, the maker of Actifed, does not appear on this list. This list applies to prescription drug products only.

Tablet

Bolar	Lemmon
Chelsea	Newtron
Cord	Private Formulations
Drummer/Phoenix	Superpharm
Halsey	Zenith

Syrup

H. R. Cenci	Newtron
Halsey	Pharmafair
Life	

TUSS-ORNADE

SEE Caramiphen/Phenylpropanolamine

TYLENOL WITH CODEINE

SEE Acetaminophen/Codeine

URECHOLINE

SEE Bethanechol

UTICILLIN VK

SEE Penicillin VK

UTIMOX

SEE Amoxicillin

VAGITROL

SEE Sulfanilamide/Aminacrine/
Allantoin

VALISONE

SEE Betamethasone Valerate

VALIUM

SEE Diazepam

VASODILAN

SEE Isoxsuprine

V-CILLIN K

SEE Penicillin VK

VEETIDS

SEE Penicillin VK

VIBRAMYCIN

SEE Doxycycline

VICODIN

SEE Hydrocodone/Acetaminophen

VIOFORM HC

SEE Iodochlorhydroxyquin/Hydrocortisone

VISTARIL

SEE Hydroxyzine Pamoate

WARFARIN

BRAND NAME:
Coumadin (DuPont)
Panwarfin (Abbott)

DOSAGE FORM:
Tablet 2 mg
Tablet 2.5 mg
Tablet 5 mg
Tablet 7.5 mg
Tablet 10 mg

USE:
As an anticoagulant to restore normal blood clotting function; to prevent clot formation in various heart and circulatory disorders.

AVOID USE:
Any hemorrhagic condition; if you have recently had or will soon have any surgery (ask your doctor); certain bleeding tendencies; during pregnancy; active peptic ulcer; if there are no adequate laboratory facilities available; ulcerative colitis; if allergic to this or to any related drug.

SIDE EFFECTS:

Certain bleeding and several less frequent problems such as rash; hair loss; nausea; vomiting and diarrhea; bruising.

$ BRAND OR GENERIC?

Precise dosage control is critical to successful use and avoidance of dangerous side effects. Exact blood levels of this drug are so important that your doctor must monitor it through frequent blood tests. There are few generics considered bioequivalent to the brand. Savings are not even that good for the generic products available. Of the two brand-name products, Panwarfin saves about 11%. Do not under any circumstances use anything but the brand-name drug without consulting your doctor; it could threaten your life.

FDA-APPROVED BIOEQUIVALENT MANUFACTURERS:

Tablet 2 mg and 5 mg

Colmed
*DuPont

Tablet 2.5 mg, 7.5 mg and 10 mg

None

WYAMICIN E

SEE Erythromycin Ethylsuccinate

WYAMYCIN S

SEE Erythromycin Stearate

WYGESIC

SEE Propoxyphene/Acetaminophen

WYMOX

SEE Amoxicillin

ZYLOPRIM

SEE Allopurinol

GENERIC DRUG LAWS FOR EACH STATE

No aspect of generic drug substitution is as important yet as poorly understood as the differing state laws governing substituting a generic for a brand-name product. Often the patient is not even aware that the pharmacist has made a substitution, although he or she has done nothing more than carry out either the letter or spirit of the law. All the good intentions of your physician in prescribing you the best drug for the least money can be confounded at the prescription counter by the intricacies and nuances of these statutes.

Kentucky became the first state to adopt a generic drug substitution law in 1972. The Federal Trade Commission encouraged other states to enact these laws by drawing up a model for them to use as a basis for their own. With Indiana joining the ranks by passing its law in 1984, all fifty states now have these statutes.

HOW TO INTERPRET THE STATE LISTINGS THAT FOLLOW

Generic Drug List in Use

In order for your pharmacist to choose a generic drug for substitution, states have adopted a variety of formulary systems. Some states use lists of manufacturers that are judged acceptable (a positive formulary) and some take the opposite approach and list the manufacturers to avoid (a negative formulary). Some states use no formulary, leaving the choice entirely to the pharmacist's discretion.

The Food and Drug Administration has also done its part by establishing a guide many states can refer to when deciding which drugs they will allow to be freely interchanged. This listing of bioequivalent products is published under the title *Approved Prescription Drug Products with Therapeutic Equivalence Evaluations* and is periodically updated by FDA supplements.

Those states using a positive formulary system publish a list of manu-facturers that produce a drug considered bioequivalent and suitable for in-terchange with the brand-name drug. Most states using this method take the FDA's list of *Approved Prescription Drug Products* as a basis, making additions or deletions based on their own evaluations. A pharmacist must make his or her selection from the manufacturers listed under each drug in this formulary.

In states using a negative formulary, drug product selection is based on avoiding those generic products that appear on this list. It is possible for a company to make this list for one product, meaning it is unacceptable, while having other drugs considered bioequivalent and suitable to dispense. This leaves a fairly wide variety of drug products for the pharmacist to se-lect from while still protecting the consumer from substandard generics. The drawback to this system is that a new manufacturer may market a ge-neric drug before it can be properly evaluated by the state board of phar-macy. It would not be prohibited from being dispensed, even though it might eventually be found to be bioinequivalent. If your state uses a nega-tive formulary, it pays to double-check whichever generic manufacturer's product you receive with those listed in THE GUIDE TO GENERIC DRUGS under FDA-Approved Bioequivalent Manufacturers for each pre-scription drug.

Some states have no listing of acceptable or unacceptable generic drugs. This means that drug product selection is not limited to only ap-proved manufacturers' products; neither are any generic drugs, regardless of their approval status, prohibited from use. Under this system a drug not certified as bioequivalent to its brand-name counterpart by the FDA could still, under certain conditions, be dispensed by a pharmacist. This lack of guidelines leaves product selection totally to the discretion of the pharma-cist. When all the facts about a product are available, pharmacists are uniquely qualified to make a choice. But in reality, it is sometimes difficult to gather all the necessary information to make a knowledgeable decision. Again, as with states on the negative formulary system, the most prudent course of action is to check whichever generic manufacturer's product you receive against those listed in THE GUIDE TO GENERIC DRUGS under FDA-Approved Bioequivalent Manufacturers.

Prescription Form Requirements

One of the most visible changes to emerge from the massive reform of state generic laws in the 1980s has been on the prescription form itself. More than half the states now either require or make optional the use of prescription blanks bearing two signature lines. Signing the line saying "DIS-PENSE AS WRITTEN" or words to that effect means the brand-name drug must be provided by the pharmacist. Signing the line saying "SUBSTITUTION PERMISSIBLE" or a similar expression indicates that generic interchange is permitted.

Your physician is, in most states, the one who ultimately decides what drug you take, that is, brand or generic. Although it would appear that physicians have free choice in this matter, they are really influenced in many subtle ways.

In those states using a double-line prescription form, the doctor is being prompted to prescribe a brand-name drug, since forbidding substitution is so easily accomplished by signing the line marked "DISPENSE AS WRITTEN." A further refinement in this strategy concerns which phrase appears on the lower right- or left-hand side of the Rx blank. The natural instinct is to sign on the lower right, as we are conditioned to do on checks or letters. Whichever phrase appears in this spot receives the advantage of our natural bias.

Recognizing the ease with which a physician can prevent substitution on a double-line form, many states have prohibited their use, making it much more difficult for the prescriber to insist on a brand-name product. Often the physician must print in her or his own handwriting words such as "Dispense as written," "No substitution," "Do not substitute, brand necessary," "Medically necessary," or "No drug product substitution/NDPS." These phrases vary from state to state but the intent is clear: to encourage generic substitution by making more demands on the doctor's limited time should he or she wish to prescribe a brand-name drug.

Some states include a box on the prescription form that the physician can check or initial to prohibit generic interchange. This method would seem to represent a fair compromise, since it does not exert an undue bias in either direction.

In a recent National Substitution Audit conducted by Market Measures Inc., data showed a substitution rate on new prescriptions of 3.9% in states using a two-line Rx form. In states without this requirement the rate was higher, at 5.5%. Interpreting these results in another way, the study reveals that prescribers in double-line states prohibit substitution 60% to 70% of the time, while other states experience only a 3% to 5% prohibition.

The audit went on to explain that in states using the two-line form, when a doctor signs on the line permitting interchange, pharmacists tend to comply at a higher rate since they interpret this as explicit permission, while in states without this type of Rx blank, the approval is only felt to be tacit.

Substitution: Optional or Mandatory?

Your pharmacist is frequently the member of the health care team who really determines when and how generic substitution takes place. In states where interchange is mandatory if so indicated by the physician, there is obviously little choice. But most states have adopted a permissive attitude; if the doctor indicates generic substitution by whatever means used in that state, the pharmacist is not obligated to effect interchange but can still dispense the brand-name drug.

Record-Keeping Requirements

Most states require the pharmacist to keep a record of which generic manufacturer's product was dispensed. This is a valuable law, since it assures that you will know if you are receiving the same supplier's product each time you refill your prescription. Although some have touted all generics as being equal in their performance, this is, sadly, not always the case. Should you opt for or be forced to use a generic drug, your best assurance of therapeutic continuity is to at least use the same maker's product each time.

Consumer Notification

Depending on where you live, you may or may not have much to say about the prescription drug product you receive from your pharmacist. If your state's law has made provision for consumer consultation before substitution can take place, your input may be significant. Some states, although mandating that you be informed, do not allow you the option of choosing between a brand and a generic drug. Still other states do not require your being consulted at all.

In states that either don't give you the choice or make it impractical to express your wishes (such as the pharmacist having to contact the doctor to convince him or her to change his or her mind, which may not always be realistic due to time restraints on both the pharmacist and the physician), the time to make your preference known is at the doctor's office. If you live in a state where the pharmacist is not required to make a generic substitution even if the physician indicates it, discuss the choice with your pharmacist. In any case, do not hesitate to express your preference to your doctor or your pharmacist.

Generic Savings Pass-Along

If it has been determined that you will be receiving a generic drug substitute, how do you know if the savings you realize truly reflects the full difference in price possible between it and its brand-name counterpart? In a practical sense, you don't.

Although store-to-store variation in prices and differences in cost from the many manufacturers producing the same generic drug make specific savings almost impossible to agree on, some states make provisions for a savings pass-along to the consumer. This may range from all the savings realized by the pharmacist over the cost of the corresponding brand-name product, to a percentage of the discount, to no pass-along at all. There is really no way to enforce these provisions, since too many variables can influence the pricing structure of prescription drugs and, in fact, there has never been a successful action brought against any pharmacist for violation of the pass-along regulation in any state having this requirement.

Regardless of the laws of your state, the only way to get the maximum benefit of generic savings is to be well-informed in advance. Consult THE GUIDE TO GENERIC DRUGS.

The following summary of each state's generic drug laws concentrates on aspects of these statutes that affect the vast majority of prescription drug users and allows you to take full advantage of your state's regulations most of the time. Details applying to rare situations have been omitted. While some of the terms used on your state's prescription blanks may differ slightly from what you read here, the law's intent is clear and these variations do not affect its spirit.

When reading about your state's regulations, keep in mind that laws are dynamic, constantly changing and adapting to the times. What was valid at the time of this book's printing may have been amended by the time you see this. Consult your pharmacist, doctor, or state board of pharmacy if in doubt about the latest interpretations.

ALABAMA

Year Generic Drug Law Passed: 1979
Generic Drug List in Use: None
Prescription Form Requirements: Two-line form is required
Substitution: Optional or Mandatory? Optional
Record-Keeping Requirements? Yes
Consumer Notification for Generic Substitution? No
Generic Savings Pass-Along Requirement? No

ALASKA

Year Generic Drug Law Passed: 1976

Generic Drug List in Use: None

Prescription Form Requirements: A two-line prescription form is optional. If the two-line form is not used, the prescriber must indicate whether or not substitution is desired. If there is no such indication on the prescription, substitution may not take place and the brand-name drug must be dispensed.

Substitution: Optional or Mandatory?   Optional

Record-Keeping Requirements?   No

Consumer Notification for Generic Substitution?   Yes

Generic Savings Pass-Along Requirement?   Yes

ARIZONA

Year Generic Drug Law Passed: 1978; amended to its current version in 1979

Generic Drug List in Use: None. Arizona stipulates that substitution is limited to drugs manufactured by those companies having the capability to effect recalls and returns in the event a product is deemed unsafe or defective. They must file a statement to this effect with the State Board of Pharmacy.

Prescription Form Requirements: Two-line form is required

Substitution: Optional or Mandatory?   Optional

Record-Keeping Requirements?   Yes

Consumer Notification for Generic Substitution?   Yes

Generic Savings Pass-Along Requirement?   Yes

ARKANSAS

Year Generic Drug Law Passed: 1975; amended to its current version in 1981

Generic Drug List in Use: Negative formulary

Prescription Form Requirements: Two-line form is not required

Substitution: Optional or Mandatory?   Optional

Record-Keeping Requirements?   No

Consumer Notification for Generic Substitution?   Yes

Generic Savings Pass-Along Requirement?   Yes

CALIFORNIA

Year Generic Drug Law Passed: 1975; amended to its current version in 1980

Generic Drug List in Use: Negative formulary

Prescription Form Requirements: Two-line form is not required. To prohibit substitution, the doctor must indicate the term "Dispense As Written" or hand-initial a preprinted box marked "Dispense As Written."

Substitution: Optional or Mandatory?   Optional

Record-Keeping Requirements?   No

Consumer Notification for Generic Substitution?   Yes

Generic Savings Pass-Along Requirement?   No

COLORADO

Year Generic Drug Law Passed: 1976

Generic Drug List in Use: None

Prescription Form Requirements: Two-line form is not required. To prohibit substitution, the doctor must indicate on the prescription, in his or her own handwriting, "Dispense As Written," or hand-initial a preprinted box marked "Dispense As Written."

Substitution: Optional or Mandatory?   Optional

Record-Keeping Requirements?   No

Consumer Notification for Generic Substitution?   Yes

Generic Savings Pass-Along Requirement?   Yes

CONNECTICUT

Year Generic Drug Law Passed: 1976

Generic Drug List in Use: None

Prescription Form Requirements: Two-line form is not required. To prohibit substitution, the doctor must specifically indicate on the prescription the term "No Substitution" in his or her own handwriting.

Substitution: Optional or Mandatory?   Optional

Record-Keeping Requirements? Yes

Consumer Notification for Generic Substitution? Yes

Generic Savings Pass-Along Requirement? Yes

DELAWARE

Year Generic Drug Law Passed: 1976; amended to its current version in 1981

Generic Drug List in Use: Positive Formulary: Delaware does not publish its own drug list but relies on the FDA's product evaluations.

Prescription Form Requirements: Two-line form is required

Substitution: Optional or Mandatory? Optional

Record-Keeping Requirements? Yes

Consumer Notification for Generic Substitution? Yes

Generic Savings Pass-Along Requirement? Yes

DISTRICT OF COLUMBIA

Year Generic Drug Law Passed: 1976

Generic Drug List in Use: Positive formulary

Prescription Form Requirements: Two-line form is not required. To prohibit substitution, the doctor must indicate on the prescription the term "Brand Necessary" or "BN" in his or her own handwriting.

Substitution: Optional or Mandatory? Optional

Record-Keeping Requirements? Yes

Consumer Notification for Generic Substitution? No

Generic Savings Pass-Along Requirement? No

FLORIDA

Year Generic Drug Law Passed: 1974; amended to its current version in 1976

Generic Drug List in Use: Negative formulary. In addition, Florida requires each pharmacy to draw up a list of brand-name drugs with acceptable generic equivalent products that they stock. This list must be made available to the public.

Prescription Form Requirements: Two-line form is not required. To prohibit substitution, the doctor must write "Medically Necessary" on the prescription in his or her own handwriting.

Substitution: Optional or Mandatory?   Mandatory unless requested otherwise by the purchaser and in the absence of the the prescriber's designation "Medically Necessary"

Record-Keeping Requirements?   Yes

Consumer Notification for Generic Substitution?   Yes

Generic Savings Pass-Along Requirement?   Yes

GEORGIA

Year Generic Drug Law Passed: 1977

Generic Drug List in Use: None

Prescription Form Requirements: Two-line form is required

Substitution: Optional or Mandatory?   Optional

Record-Keeping Requirements?   Yes

Consumer Notification for Generic Substitution?   No

Generic Savings Pass-Along Requirement?   No

HAWAII

Year Generic Drug Law Passed: 1980; amended to its current version in 1982

Generic Drug List in Use: Positive formulary

Prescription Form Requirements: Two-line form is not required

Substitution: Optional or Mandatory?   Mandatory

Record-Keeping Requirements?   Yes

Consumer Notification for Generic Substitution?   Yes

Generic Savings Pass-Along Requirement?   Yes

IDAHO

Year Generic Drug Law Passed: 1978
Generic Drug List in Use: None
Prescription Form Requirements: Two-line form is required
Substitution: Optional or Mandatory?   Optional
Record-Keeping Requirements?   Yes
Consumer Notification for Generic Substitution?   Yes
Generic Savings Pass-Along Requirement?   Yes

ILLINOIS

Year Generic Drug Law Passed: 1977; amended to its current version in 1981
Generic Drug List in Use: Positive formulary
Prescription Form Requirements: Two-line form is not required
Substitution: Optional or Mandatory?   Optional
Record-Keeping Requirements?   Yes
Consumer Notification for Generic Substitution?   No
Generic Savings Pass-Along Requirement?   No

INDIANA

Year Generic Drug Law Passed: 1984
Generic Drug List in Use: None. Indiana requires that any drug considered suitable for interchange must meet the same USP (United States Pharmacopeia) standards applied to the brand-name product. Substitution is prohibited for any drug listed by the FDA "as having actual or potential bioequivalence problems."
Prescription Form Requirements: Two-line form is required
Substitution: Optional or Mandatory?   Optional
Record-Keeping Requirements?   Yes
Consumer Notification for Generic Substitution?   Yes
Generic Savings Pass-Along Requirement?   No

IOWA

Year Generic Drug Law Passed: 1976

Generic Drug List in Use: Positive. The Iowa Board of Pharmacy is empowered to develop a nonequivalent (negative) drug formulary but has not yet done so. In the interim a positive formulary published by the FDA is being used.

Prescription Form Requirements: Two-line form is not required

Substitution: Optional or Mandatory?   Optional

Record-Keeping Requirements?   No

Consumer Notification for Generic Substitution?   Yes

Generic Savings Pass-Along Requirement?   Yes

KANSAS

Year Generic Drug Law Passed: 1978

Generic Drug List in Use: None

Prescription Form Requirements: Two-line form is optional. If the two-line form is not used, the doctor must write "Dispense As Written" in his or her own handwriting to prevent substitution.

Substitution: Optional or Mandatory?   Optional

Record-Keeping Requirements?   No

Consumer Notification for Generic Substitution?   No

Generic Savings Pass-Along Requirement?   No

KENTUCKY

Year Generic Drug Law Passed: 1972; amended to its current version in 1982. Kentucky was the first state to adopt a generic substitution law.

Generic Drug List in Use: Negative. Based on the FDA's evaluations of drugs with known bioequivalence problems.

Prescription Form Requirements: Two-line form is not required. To prevent substitution, the doctor must indicate on the prescription "Do Not Substitute."

Substitution: Optional or Mandatory?   Mandatory

Record-Keeping Requirements?   Yes

Consumer Notification for Generic Substitution?   No

Generic Savings Pass-Along Requirement?   No

LOUISIANA

Year Generic Drug Law Passed: 1980

Generic Drug List in Use: None. Although Louisiana does not publish a drug formulary, the law stipulates that only those drug products rated as pharmaceutically or therapeutically interchangeable or equivalent by the FDA are suitable for dispensing when substitution takes place.

Prescription Form Requirements: Two-line form is not required. To prevent substitution, the doctor may indicate this preference in any way desired.

Substitution: Optional or Mandatory?   Optional

Record-Keeping Requirements?   Yes

Consumer Notification for Generic Substitution?   Yes

Generic Savings Pass-Along Requirement?   Yes

MAINE

Year Generic Drug Law Passed: 1975; amended to its current version in 1978

Generic Drug List in Use: Positive formulary. Maine does not publish its own formulary but relies on one put out by the FDA.

Prescription Form Requirements: Two-line form is not required. The doctor must check a preprinted box on the prescription form to prevent generic substitution.

Substitution: Optional or Mandatory?   Optional

Record-Keeping Requirements?   No

Consumer Notification for Generic Substitution?   Yes

Generic Savings Pass-Along Requirement?   No

MARYLAND

Year Generic Drug Law Passed: 1977; amended to its current version in 1979

Generic Drug List in Use: Positive formulary. Maryland does not publish its own formulary but relies on one put out by the FDA.

Prescription Form Requirements: Two-line prescription form is not required

Substitution: Optional or Mandatory?   Optional

Record-Keeping Requirements?   Yes

Consumer Notification for Generic Substitution?   No
Generic Savings Pass-Along Requirement?   Yes

MASSACHUSETTS

Year Generic Drug Law Passed: 1976; amended to its current version in 1977
Generic Drug List in Use: Positive formulary
Prescription Form Requirements: Two-line form is required
Substitution: Optional or Mandatory?   Mandatory
Record-Keeping Requirements?   No
Consumer Notification for Generic Substitution?   No
Generic Savings Pass-Along Requirement?   No

MICHIGAN

Year Generic Drug Law Passed: 1975; amended to its current version in 1976
Generic Drug List in Use: None
Prescription Form Requirements: Two-line form is not required. To prohibit substitution, the doctor must indicate, in his or her own handwriting, "Dispense As Written" or write "DAW" next to a preprinted statement to that effect.
Substitution: Optional or Mandatory?   Optional
Record-Keeping Requirements?   No
Consumer Notification for Generic Substitution?   No
Generic Savings Pass-Along Requirement?   Yes

MINNESOTA

Year Generic Drug Law Passed: 1976
Generic Drug List in Use: None
Prescription Form Requirements: Two-line form is not required. To prohibit substitution, the doctor must indicate, in his or her own handwriting, the term "Dispense As Written" or "DAW."

Substitution: Optional or Mandatory? Optional

Record-Keeping Requirements? No

Consumer Notification for Generic Substitution? Yes

Generic Savings Pass-Along Requirement? Yes

MISSISSIPPI

Year Generic Drug Law Passed: 1979

Generic Drug List in Use: None

Prescription Form Requirements: Two-line form is optional. If the two-line form is not used, the doctor must write "Dispense As Written" in his or her own handwriting to prevent substitution.

Substitution: Optional or Mandatory? Optional

Record-Keeping Requirements? No

Consumer Notification for Generic Substitution? No

Generic Savings Pass-Along Requirement? Yes

MISSOURI

Year Generic Drug Law Passed: 1979

Generic Drug List in Use: Negative formulary

Prescription Form Requirements: Two-line form is required

Substitution: Optional or Mandatory? Optional

Record-Keeping Requirements? No

Consumer Notification for Generic Substitution? No

Generic Savings Pass-Along Requirement? Yes

MONTANA

Year Generic Drug Law Passed: 1977

Generic Drug List in Use: None

Prescription Form Requirements: Two-line form is not required. To prohibit generic substitution, the doctor must indicate on prescription the term "Medically Necessary," either written by hand or preprinted on the prescription blank.

Substitution: Optional or Mandatory? Optional

Record-Keeping Requirements? No

Consumer Notification for Generic Substitution? Yes

Generic Savings Pass-Along Requirement? Yes

NEBRASKA

Year Generic Drug Law Passed: 1977; amended to its current version in 1983

Generic Drug List in Use: Negative formulary

Prescription Form Requirements: Two-line prescription form is not required. To prohibit generic substitution, the doctor must indicate the term "No Drug Product Selection" or "NDPS" either in his or her own handwriting or preprinted on the prescription blank.

Substitution: Optional or Mandatory? Optional

Record-Keeping Requirements? No

Consumer Notification for Generic Substitution? Yes

Generic Savings Pass-Along Requirement? Yes

NEVADA

Year Generic Drug Law Passed: 1979; amended to its current version in 1981

Generic Drug List in Use: None. The only time substitution may not take place is when the drug's brand name appears on a list of products that have no acceptable bioequivalent substitutes.

Prescription Form Requirements: Two-line form is required

Substitution: Optional or Mandatory? Optional

Record-Keeping Requirements? Yes

Consumer Notification for Generic Substitution? Yes

Generic Savings Pass-Along Requirement? Yes

NEW HAMPSHIRE

Year Generic Drug Law Passed: 1981

Generic Drug List in Use: Positive formulary. New Hampshire does not publish its own formulary but relies on one put out by the FDA.

Prescription Form Requirements: Two-line form is not required. To indicate substitution, the doctor must add, in his or her own handwriting after the drug's brand name, the phrase "or its generic equivalent drug listed in the New Hampshire Drug Formulary."

Substitution: Optional or Mandatory?   Optional

Record-Keeping Requirements?   Yes

Consumer Notification for Generic Substitution?   Yes

Generic Savings Pass-Along Requirement?   Yes

NEW JERSEY

Year Generic Drug Law Passed: 1977

Generic Drug List in Use: Positive formulary

Prescription Form Requirements: Two-line form is required

Substitution: Optional or Mandatory?   Mandatory

Record-Keeping Requirements?   No

Consumer Notification for Generic Substitution?   Yes

Generic Savings Pass-Along Requirement?   Yes

NEW MEXICO

Year Generic Drug Law Passed: 1976; amended to its current version in 1982

Generic Drug List in Use: Positive formulary. New Mexico does not publish its own formulary but relies on one put out by the FDA.

Prescription Form Requirements: Two-line form is not required. To prevent substitution, the doctor must indicate the term "No Substitution" or "No Sub" in his or her own handwriting.

Substitution: Optional or Mandatory?   Optional

Record-Keeping Requirements?   No

Consumer Notification for Generic Substitution? No
Generic Savings Pass-Along Requirement? No

NEW YORK

Year Generic Drug Law Passed: 1977
Generic Drug List in Use: Positive formulary
Prescription Form Requirements: Two-line form is required
Substitution: Optional or Mandatory? Mandatory
Record-Keeping Requirements? Yes
Consumer Notification for Generic Substitution? Yes. The prescriber must inform the patient of substitution.
Generic Savings Pass-Along Requirement? No

NORTH CAROLINA

Year Generic Drug Law Passed: 1979
Generic Drug List in Use: None
Prescription Form Requirements: Two-line form is optional. If the two-line form is not used, the doctor must indicate "Dispense As Written" in his or her own handwriting to prevent substitution.
Substitution: Optional or Mandatory? Optional
Record-Keeping Requirements? Yes
Consumer Notification for Generic Substitution? No
Generic Savings Pass-Along Requirement? Yes

NORTH DAKOTA

Year Generic Drug Law Passed: 1979
Generic Drug List in Use: None
Prescription Form Requirements: Two-line form is required. For title XIX prescriptions, the prescriber must add the term "Brand Necessary" in his or her own

handwriting in addition to signing the line "Dispense As Written" to prohibit substitution.

Substitution: Optional or Mandatory? Optional

Record-Keeping Requirements? Yes

Consumer Notification for Generic Substitution? Yes

Generic Savings Pass-Along Requirement? Yes

OHIO

Year Generic Drug Law Passed: 1977; amended to its current version in 1981

Generic Drug List in Use: Positive formulary. Each pharmacy is required to draw up a list of brand-name prescription drugs with acceptable generic equivalents that they keep in stock. These products must be selected from those rated as bioequivalent and interchangeable by the FDA.

Prescription Form Requirements: Two-line form is not required. To prevent substitution, the doctor must indicate the term "Dispense As Written" or "DAW" in his or her own handwriting.

Substitution: Optional or Mandatory? Optional

Record-Keeping Requirements? Yes

Consumer Notification for Generic Substitution? Yes

Generic Savings Pass-Along Requirement? Yes

OKLAHOMA

Year Generic Drug Law Passed: 1976

Generic Drug List in Use: None

Prescription Form Requirements: Two-line form is not required. To prevent substitution, the doctor can indicate, in his or her own handwriting, the term "Dispense As Written" or "DAW."

Substitution: Optional or Mandatory? Optional. A 1976 Oklahoma Attorney General's opinion states: "A pharmacist may make a generic substitution either with the consent of the prescriber *or* the purchaser."

Record-Keeping Requirements? No

Consumer Notification for Generic Substitution?   Need consent of either the consumer *or* the prescriber

Generic Savings Pass-Along Requirement?   Yes

OREGON

Year Generic Drug Law Passed: 1975

Generic Drug List in Use: None

Prescription Form Requirements: Two-line form is not required. To prevent substitution, the doctor must indicate "No Substitution" or "NS" in his or her own handwriting.

Substitution: Optional or Mandatory?   Optional

Record-Keeping Requirements?   Yes

Consumer Notification for Generic Substitution?   Yes

Generic Savings Pass-Along Requirement?   No

PENNSYLVANIA

Year Generic Drug Law Passed: 1976

Generic Drug List in Use: Positive formulary

Prescription Form Requirements: Two-line form is required

Substitution: Optional or Mandatory?   Mandatory

Record-Keeping Requirements?   Yes

Consumer Notification for Generic Substitution?   Yes

Generic Savings Pass-Along Requirement?   Yes

PUERTO RICO

Year Generic Drug Law Passed: 1976; amended to its current version in 1980

Generic Drug List in Use: Positive formulary

Prescription Form Requirements: Two-line form is not required
Substitution: Optional or Mandatory? Optional
Record-Keeping Requirements? Yes
Consumer Notification for Generic Substitution? Yes
Generic Savings Pass-Along Requirement? Yes

RHODE ISLAND

Year Generic Drug Law Passed: 1976; amended to its current version in 1981
Generic Drug List in Use: None. Rhode Island's Board of Pharmacy is empowered to develop a negative drug formulary. To date, no products have been included on this list.
Prescription Form Requirements: Two-line form is required
Substitution: Optional or Mandatory? Mandatory
Record-Keeping Requirements? Yes
Consumer Notification for Generic Substitution? No
Generic Savings Pass-Along Requirement? Yes

SOUTH CAROLINA

Year Generic Drug Law Passed: 1978
Generic Drug List in Use: None
Prescription Form Requirements: Two-line form is required
Substitution: Optional or Mandatory? Optional
Record-Keeping Requirements? Yes
Consumer Notification for Generic Substitution? Yes
Generic Savings Pass-Along Requirement? No

SOUTH DAKOTA

Year Generic Drug Law Passed: 1978
Generic Drug List in Use: None

Prescription Form Requirements: Two-line form is required
Substitution: Optional or Mandatory?   Optional
Record-Keeping Requirements?   No
Consumer Notification for Generic Substitution?   No
Generic Savings Pass-Along Requirement?   No

TENNESSEE

Year Generic Drug Law Passed: 1977
Generic Drug List in Use: Positive formulary
Prescription Form Requirements: Two-line form is required
Substitution: Optional or Mandatory?   Optional
Record-Keeping Requirements?   Yes
Consumer Notification for Generic Substitution?   No
Generic Savings Pass-Along Requirement?   Yes

TEXAS

Year Generic Drug Law Passed: 1981
Generic Drug List in Use: None
Prescription Form Requirements: Two-line form is required
Substitution: Optional or Mandatory?   Optional
Record-Keeping Requirements?   Yes
Consumer Notification for Generic Substitution?   Yes
Generic Savings Pass-Along Requirement?   No

UTAH

Year Generic Drug Law Passed: 1977
Generic Drug List in Use: Negative formulary

Prescription Form Requirements: Two-line form is not required. To prohibit substitution, the doctor must indicate the term "Dispense As Written" in his or her own handwriting or initial a preprinted box with the same phrase.

Substitution: Optional or Mandatory?   Optional

Record-Keeping Requirements?   Yes

Consumer Notification for Generic Substitution?   Yes

Generic Savings Pass-Along Requirement?   Yes

VERMONT

Year Generic Drug Law Passed: 1978

Generic Drug List in Use: Positive formulary

Prescription Form Requirements: Two-line form is not required. To prohibit substitution, the doctor must indicate the term "No Substitution" or "Brand Necessary" in his or her own handwriting.

Substitution: Optional or Mandatory?   Mandatory

Record-Keeping Requirements?   No

Consumer Notification for Generic Substitution?   Yes

Generic Savings Pass-Along Requirement?   No

VIRGINIA

Year Generic Drug Law Passed: 1977; amended to its current version in 1978

Generic Drug List in Use: Positive formulary

Prescription Form Requirements: Two-line form is required

Substitution: Optional or Mandatory?   Optional

Record-Keeping Requirements?   Yes

Consumer Notification for Generic Substitution?   Yes

Generic Savings Pass-Along Requirement?   No

WASHINGTON

Year Generic Drug Law Passed: 1977; amended to its current version in 1979

Generic Drug List in Use: None. Either a negative or positive drug formulary can be used, although the Board of Pharmacy is not required to adopt either.

Prescription Form Requirements: Two-line form is required

Substitution: Optional or Mandatory?   Mandatory

Record-Keeping Requirements?   Yes

Consumer Notification for Generic Substitution?   Yes

Generic Savings Pass-Along Requirement?   Yes. At least 60% of any savings to the pharmacist on the cost of a generic drug over that of its brand-name counterpart must be passed on to the consumer.

WEST VIRGINIA

Year Generic Drug Law Passed: 1978

Generic Drug List in Use: Negative formulary

Prescription Form Requirements: Two-line form is optional. If the two-line form is not used, the doctor must indicate the term "Dispense As Written" in his or her own handwriting to prevent substitution.

Substitution: Optional or Mandatory?   Optional

Record-Keeping Requirements?   Yes

Consumer Notification for Generic Substitution?   Yes

Generic Savings Pass-Along Requirement?   Yes

WISCONSIN

Year Generic Drug Law Passed: 1976; amended to its current version in 1984

Generic Drug List in Use: Positive formulary. Wisconsin does not publish its own formulary but relies on one put out by the FDA.

Prescription Form Requirements: Two-line form is not required

Substitution: Optional or Mandatory?   Optional

Record-Keeping Requirements?   No

Consumer Notification for Generic Substitution?   Yes

Generic Savings Pass-Along Requirement?   Yes

WYOMING

Year Generic Drug Law Passed: 1979

Generic Drug List in Use: None

Prescription Form Requirements: Two-line form is required

Substitution: Optional or Mandatory?   Optional

Record-Keeping Requirements?   Yes

Consumer Notification for Generic Substitution?   No

Generic Savings Pass-Along Requirement?   Yes

APPENDIX B

SCHEDULE OF DRUG PATENT EXPIRATIONS

DRUGS WHOSE PATENTS HAVE ALREADY EXPIRED AND WHICH
WILL SOON BE AVAILABLE GENERICALLY UNDER THE NEW
DRUG PRICE COMPETITION AND PATENT TERM RESTORATION ACT OF 1984

BRAND NAME AND MANUFACTURER	GENERIC NAME	DRUG USE
Aldoril (MSD/Merck)	Methyldopa w/hydro-chlorothiazide	Antihypertensive
Atromid-S (Ayerst/AMHO)	Clofibrate	Cholesterol-lowering agent
Dalmane (Hoffmann-La Roche)	Flurazepam HCL	Hypnotic
Danocrine (Winthrop)	Danazol	Pituitary inhibitor
Depakene (Abbott)	Valproic acid	Antiepileptic
Desyrel (Mead Johnson)	Trazodone HCL	Antidepressant
Dyazide (SK&F)	Triamterine w/hydrochlorothiazide	Antihypertensive
Dymelor (Eli Lilly)	Acetohexamide	Antidiabetic
Intal (Fisons)	Cromolyn sodium	Antiasthmatic
Lidex (Syntex)	Flucinonide	Anti-inflammatory
Ludiomil (Ciba/Ciba-Geigy)	Maprotiline HCL	Antidepressant
Meclomen (Parke-Davis/W-L)	Meclofenamate sodium	Antiarthritic
Megace (Mead John-son/B-M)	Megestrol acetate	Anticancer
Minocin (Lederle Labs)	Minocycline HCL	Antibiotic
Navane (Roerig)	Thiothixene	Tranquilizer Antipsychotic
Nubain (Endo)	Nalbuphine HCL	Analgesic
Oncovin (Eli Lilly)	Vincristine sulfate	Anticancer
Restoril (Sandoz)	Temazepam	Hypnotic
Serax (Wyeth/AMHO)	Oxazepam	Tranquilizer
Tegretol (Ciba/Ciba-Geigy)	Carbamazepine	Anticonvulsant Analgesic
Triavil (MSD/Merck)	Amitriptyline HCL w/perphenazine	Antidepressant Tranquilizer
Yutopar (Astra)	Ritodrine HCL	Inhibits preterm labor
Zaroxolyn (Pennwalt)	Metolazone	Diuretic Antihypertensive

BRAND NAME AND MANUFACTURER	GENERIC NAME	DRUG USE
Patent Expires 1986		
Adapin (Pennwalt)	Doxepin HCL	Antidepressant Antipsychotic
Alupent (Boehringer Ingelheim)	Metaproterenol sulfate	Broncholdilator
Bretylol (American Critical Care)	Bretylium tosylate	Antiarrhythmic
Carafate (Marion)	Sucralfate	Antiulcer
Catapres (Boehringer Ingelheim)	Clonidine HCL	Antihypertensive
Cephulac (Merrell Dow)	Lactulose	Laxative
Haldol (McNeil)	Haloperidol	Antipsychotic
Sinequan (Roerig)	Doxepin HCL	Antidepressant Antipsychotic
Velosef (E. R. Squibb)	Cephradine	Antibiotic
Patent Expires 1987		
Ancef (SK&F)	Cefazolin sodium	Antibiotic
Cleocin (Upjohn)	Clindamycin HCL	Antibiotic
Duricef (Mead Johnson/B-M)	Cefadroxil	Antibiotic
Loxitane (Lederle Labs)	Loxapine succinate	Antipsychotic
Minipress (Pfizer)	Prazosin HCL	Antihypertensive
Tranxene (Abbott)	Clorazepate dipotassium	Tranquilizer
Unipen (Wyeth/AMHO)	Nafcillin sodium	Antibiotic
Patent Expires 1988		
Adriamycin (Adria)	Doxorubicin HCL	Anticancer
Feldene (Pfizer)	Piroxicam	Antiarthritic
Lopressor (Ciba/Ciba-Geigy)	Metoprolol tartrate	Antihypertensive
Nalfon (Eli Lilly)	Fenoprofen calcium	Antiarthritic
NegGram (Winthrop)	Nalidixic acid	Antiinfective
Pavulon (Organon)	Pancuronium Br	Muscle relaxant
Timoptic (MSD/Merck)	Timolol maleate	Antiglaucoma
Patent Expires 1989		
Ascendin (Lederle Labs)	Amoxapine	Antidepressant
Blenoxane (Bristol)	Bleomycin sulfate	Anticancer
Clinoril (MSD/Merck)	Sulindac	Antiarthritic
Keflex (Eli Lilly)	Cephalexin	Antibiotic
Lotrimin (Schering)	Clotrimazole	Antifungal
Mutamycin (Bristol)	Mitomycin	Anticancer
Naprosyn (Syntex)	Naproxen	Antiarthritic
Proventil (Schering)	Albuterol sulfate	Bronchodilator
Patent Expires 1990		
Amikin (Bristol)	Amikacin sulfate	Antibiotic
Dolobid (MSD/Merck)	Diflunisal	Antiarthritic
Imodium (Janssen)	Loperamide HCL	Antidiarrheal

BRAND NAME AND MANUFACTURER	GENERIC NAME	DRUG USE
Parlodel (Sandoz)	Bromocriptine mesylate	Antiamenorrheic Prevents lactation
Retin-A (Ortho)	Tretinoin	Antiacne
Tolectin (McNeil)	Tolmetin sodium	Antiarthritic
Zomax (McNeil)	Zomepirac sodium	Antiarthritic

REFERENCES

Books

Bevan, John A. (ed.) *Essentials of Pharmacology*. New York: Harper & Row, 1976.

Burack, Richard, & Fox, Fred J. *The New Handbook of Prescription Drugs*. New York: Ballantine, 1981.

Chodos, Dale J. "Generic substitution: A form of pharmaceutical Russian roulette?" In L. Lasagna (ed.), *Controversies in Therapeutics*. Philadelphia: W. B. Saunders, 1980, 72–81.

Chodos, D. J., & DiSanto, A. R. *Basics of Bioavailability and Description of Upjohn Single-dose Study Design*. Kalamazoo, MI: The Upjohn Company, 1974.

DiSanto, A. R. "Bioavailability and bioequivalency testing." In J. L. Hoover (ed.), *Remington's Pharmaceutical Sciences*, 16th ed. Easton, PA: Mack, 1980.

Dittert, Lewis W. (ed.) *Sprowl's American Pharmacy*. Philadelphia: Lippincott, 1974.

Egan, John W. *Economics of the Pharmaceutical Industry*. New York: Praeger, 1982.

Florey, K. (ed.) *Analytical Profiles of Drug Substances*, Vol. 5. New York: Academic Press, 1976, 345–73.

Goth, A. *Medical Pharmacology: Principles and Concepts*. St. Louis: Mosby, 1976.

Grabowsky, Henry G. *Drug Regulation and Innovation*. Washington, DC: American Enterprise Institute for Public Policy Research, 1976.

Hansen, Ronald W. "The pharmaceutical development process: Estimates of development costs and times and the effects of proposed regulatory changes." In R. I. Chien (ed.), *Issues in Pharmaceutical Economics*. Lexington, MA: Lexington Books, Heath, 1979.

Hansten, Philip D. *Drug Interactions*, 4th ed. Philadelphia: Lea & Febiger, 1979.

Helms, Robert B. (ed.) *Drug Development and Marketing*. Washington, DC: American Enterprises Institute for Public Policy Research, 1975.

Hoover, John E. (ed.) *Dispensing of Medication*. Easton, PA: Mack, 1976.

Hoover, John E. (ed.) *Remington's Pharmaceutical Sciences*, 16th ed. Easton, PA: Mack, 1980.

Johnson, George. *The Pill Conspiracy*. Los Angeles: Sherbourne Press, 1967.

Kastrup, E. K., & Schwach, Gene M. (eds.) *Facts and Comparisons*. St. Louis: Facts and Comparisons, 1984.

Long, James W. *The Essential Guide to Prescription Drugs*, 4th ed. New York: Harper & Row, 1985.

Mintz, Morton. *By Prescription Only*. Boston: Houghton Mifflin, 1967.

Pharmaceutical Manufacturers Association. *Brands, Generics, Prices and Quality: The Prescribing Debate After a Decade.* Washington, DC: P.M.A., 1971.

Physicians' Desk Reference. Oradell, NJ: Medical Economics, 1984.

Silverman, Milton Morris. *Pills and the Public Purse: The Routes to National Drug Insurance.* Berkeley: University of California Press, 1981.

Temin, Peter. *Taking Your Medicine: Drug Regulation in the U.S.* Cambridge, MA: Harvard University Press, 1980.

U.S. Department of Health and Human Services. *Approved Prescription Drug Products with Therapeutic Equivalence Evaluations,* 5th ed. Rockville, MD: U.S. Government Printing Office, 1984.

U.S. Department of Health and Human Services. *Guide to Prescription Drug Costs.* Rockville, MD: U.S. Government Printing Office, April 1980.

U.S. Department of Health, Education and Welfare. *Task Force Prescription Drugs: Drug Maker and Drug Distributor.* Washington, DC: U.S. Government Printing Office, 1968.

Wiener, Harry. *Generic Drugs: Safety and Effectiveness.* New York: Pfizer, Inc., 1973.

Articles

American Pharmacy. "Compromise readies bill for ANDA/Patent term restoration." Sept. 1984, *NS24* (9), p. 10.

Apharmacy Weekly. "For practicing pharmacists: latest drug recalls." *American Pharmaceutical Association, 22* (1-48).

Azarnoff, David L., & Huffman, David H. "Therapeutic implications of bioavailability." *Annual Review of Pharmacology and Toxicology,* 1976, *16,* 53–66.

Bergen, John V. "Drug product equivalence—are specifications necessary?" *Journal of the American Pharmaceutical Association,* 1972, *12,* 21.

Blanchard, James. "Gastrointestinal absorption II. Formulation factors affecting drug bioavailability." *American Journal of Pharmacy,* Sept.–Oct. 1978, *150* (5), 132–50.

Chain Drug Review. "Rapidly increasing Rx prices fuel the controversy in generic drugs." Jan. 30, 1984, *6* (10), 22, 27.

Chain Drug Review. "Some branded Rxs weather intrusion of generic products." Jan. 31, 1983, *5* (10), 11, 18.

Chain Drug Review. "States support substitution." Jan. 31, 1983, *5* (10), 14, 17.

Check, William A. "New drugs and drug delivery systems in the year 2000." *American Pharmacy,* Sept. 1984, *NS24* (9), 44–56.

Cooper, Jack, & Rees, John E. "Tableting research and technology." *Journal of Pharmaceutical Science,* Oct. 1972, *61,* 1511.

Dickenson, James G. "Substitution after a decade: Oh what a tangled web!" *Drug Topics,* March 15, 1982, *126* (6), 45–50.

DiSanto, A. R., Chodos, D. J., DeSante, K. A., et al. "Clinical bioavailability of nitrofurantoin—a case of bioequivalence." *International Journal of Clinical Pharmacology, Therapy, and Toxicology,* 1976, *13* (3), 220–27.

Drug Information Bulletin, 1969, *3,* 59.

Drug Information Bulletin, 1969, *3*, 72.

Drug Topics. "FDA urged to require listing inactive drug ingredients." Feb. 20, 1984, *128* (4), 12.

Glasser, Martha. "Generic drug plan saves money for all." *Drug Topics*, Feb. 20, 1984, 9.

Jinks, Martin J. "Psychotropic drugs in the elderly." *Pharmacy Times*, Aug. 1984, 86–97.

Kirshner, Howard. "Phenytoin toxicity when tablets substituted for capsules." *The New England Journal of Medicine*, 1983, *308*, 1106.

Koch-Weser, Jan. "Drug therapy: bioavailability of drugs." *New England Journal of Medicine*, August 1 & Sept. 5, 1974, *291*, 233–37, 503–6.

Kolata, G. B. "Large drug firms fight generic substitution." *Science*, Nov. 30, 1979, 1054–56.

Kulp, Stan. "No pale imitations: generic drugs enjoy vigorous growth." *Barron's*, May 10, 1982, *LXII* (19), 13, 18–19.

Martin, B. K., Uihlen, M., Ings, R. M., Stevens, L. A., & McEven, J. "Comparative bioavailability of two furosemide formulations in humans." *Journal of Pharmaceutical Science*, April 1984, *73* (4), 437–41.

The Medical Letter on Drugs and Therapeutics. "Dilantin vs. generic phenytoin sodium." June 1980, *22* (12), 49–50.

Medical World News. "The battle over bioequivalence." Nov. 8, 1974, 71–83.

Meyer, M. C., Slywka, G. W. A., Whyatt, P. L., et al. "Inequivalency of nitrofurantoin products." *Journal of the American Medical Association*, 1975, *232* (10), 1009.

Mindel, Joel S. "Bioavailability and generic prescribing." *Survey of Ophthalmology*, Nov.–Dec. 1976, 262–75.

Morgan, J. P., Schwartz, Leroy, & Sherman, Frederick T. "A survey of generic drug legislation and geriatric pharmacotherapy." *Journal of the American Geriatric Society*, Sept. 1983, 535–39.

Murphy, Dana. "Nonprescription drug labels to list all ingredients." *American Pharmacy*, July 1984/403, *NS24* (7), 10, 11.

The National Pharmaceutical Council. Proceedings of a Symposium and Workshop: "The Effectiveness of Medicines in Containing Health Care Costs: Impact of Innovation, Regulation and Quality." *National Pharmaceutical Council*, Washington, DC, 1982.

Pflag, Solomon C. "Rational drug procurement or caveat emptor?" *Military Medicine*, July 1972, *137* (8), 321–22.

Rosenberg, H. A., & Bates, T. R. "The influence of food on nitrofurantoin bioavailability." *Clinical Pharmacology and Therapeutics*, 1976, *20*, 227–32.

Rutgers College of Pharmacy. "Therapeutic Equivalency." Excerpts from 32nd Annual Rutgers Pharmaceutical Conference. New Brunswick, NJ, 1983.

Schild, Irving. "Generics gain on brand-name products in R.Ph. preferences." *American Druggist*, Oct. 1983, *188* (4), 15, 72.

Shacknai, Jonah C., & Squadron, William. "Liability for substitution of generic for brand-name drugs." *U.S. Pharmacist*, April 1983, 8–11.

Slywka, G. W. A., Ryan, M. R., Melikian, A. P., et al. "Relationship of price to bioavailability for four multiple source drug products." *Journal of the American Pharmaceutical Association*, 1977, *NS17*, 30–32.

Smith, T. "The drug industry: the goose that lays the golden drugs." *British Medical Journal*, Nov. 1980, 1255–57.

Stetler, C. Joseph. "FDA funding for fiscal year 1985 vs. 1984." *Pharmacy Times*, April 1984, 19.

Tindula, R. J. "Generic phenytoin versus Dilantin for once-a-day dosing." *American Journal of Hospital Pharmacy*, Aug. 1981, 1114, 1116.

Varley, A. B. "The generic inequivalence of drugs." *Journal of the American Medical Association*, 1968, *206*, 1745.

Von Grebner, K. "Competition in a structurally changing pharmaceutical market." *Social Sciences Medicine (Medical Economics)*, June 1981, 77–86.

Wagner, John G. "Drug bioavailability studies." *Hospital Practice*, Jan. 1977, *12* (1), 119–27.

WCBS-TV "Channel Two News." Broadcast excerpt. Special report on generic drugs. Feb. 22, 1984 (6 P.M.), New York.

WCBS-TV "60 Minutes." "Oraflex." Transcript of broadcast aired from New York, Sept. 11, 1983, and April 17, 1983.

Annual Reports

Bristol-Myers Annual Report, 1983, New York.

Eli Lilly and Company Annual Report, 1983, Indianapolis, IN.

Pfizer Annual Report, 1983, New York.

Smith Kline Beckman Corporation Annual Report, 1983, Philadelphia, PA.